British Air Power

Also available from Bloomsbury

Air Warfare: History, Theory and Practice, by Peter Gray
The Leadership, Direction and Legitimacy of the RAF Bomber Offensive from Inception to 1945, by Peter Gray
The RAF's French Foreign Legion: De Gaulle, the British and the Re-emergence of French Airpower 1940-45, by G. H. Bennett

British Air Power

The Doctrinal Path to Jointery

Viktoriya Fedorchak

BLOOMSBURY ACADEMIC
LONDON • NEW YORK • OXFORD • NEW DELHI • SYDNEY

BLOOMSBURY ACADEMIC
Bloomsbury Publishing Plc
50 Bedford Square, London, WC1B 3DP, UK
1385 Broadway, New York, NY 10018, USA

BLOOMSBURY, BLOOMSBURY ACADEMIC and the Diana logo
are trademarks of Bloomsbury Publishing Plc

First published in Great Britain 2019
Paperback edition first published 2020

Copyright © Viktoriya Fedorchak, 2019

Viktoriya Fedorchak has asserted her right under the Copyright,
Designs and Patents Act, 1988, to be identified as Author of this work.

For legal purposes the Acknowledgements on p.xi constitute
an extension of this copyright page.

Cover image: A Royal Air Force Tornado GR4 during low fly training in
North Wales. (© Andrew Chittock/Stocktrek Images/Getty Images)

All rights reserved. No part of this publication may be reproduced or
transmitted in any form or by any means, electronic or mechanical,
including photocopying, recording, or any information storage or retrieval
system, without prior permission in writing from the publishers.

Bloomsbury Publishing Plc does not have any control over, or responsibility for,
any third-party websites referred to or in this book. All internet addresses given
in this book were correct at the time of going to press. The author and publisher
regret any inconvenience caused if addresses have changed or sites have
ceased to exist, but can accept no responsibility for any such changes.

A catalogue record for this book is available from the British Library.

A catalog record for this book is available from the Library of Congress.

ISBN: HB: 978-1-3500-4399-2
PB: 978-1-3501-5525-1
ePDF: 978-1-3500-4405-0
eBook: 978-1-3500-4406-7

Typeset by Integra Software Services Pvt. Ltd.

To find out more about our authors and books visit
www.bloomsbury.com and sign up for our newsletters.

For Olga Semenivna, Olga Pavlivna and Tony Mason

Contents

Foreword	ix
Acknowledgements	xi
Abbreviations	xii
Introduction	1

1	Theory	7
	The definition of doctrine	7
	The purposes of doctrine	9
	Relationship between policy, strategy and doctrine	16
	Relationship between doctrine, technology and policy	18
	Doctrine hierarchy	20
	Debates on doctrine	25
	A wider perspective of doctrinal functionality	34
	Conclusion	36

2	The Historical Context	37
	Preconditions of the first RAF doctrine	37
	The first RAF doctrine	40
	Air Publication (AP) 1300	47
	AP 1300, second edition (February 1940)	51
	AP 1300, third edition (January 1950)	55
	A nuclear aspect and the fourth edition of AP 1300 (March 1957)	58
	Doctrinal vacuum in the 1970s–1980s	60
	A new chapter in the history of RAF doctrine	65
	AP 3000, second edition, 1993	69
	The lessons of history	72

3	Case Study of the Third Edition of AP 3000 (Part I)	77
	Factors of the external environment	78
	Domestic politics	90

4	Case Study of the Third Edition of AP 3000 (Part II)	105
	Networks (academics)	105
	Doctrine authors and personalities	114
	Conclusion	120
5	Case Study of the Fourth Edition of AP 3000	125
	The context: The absence of doctrine	126
	Lessons of previous operations	130
	The internal environment	137
	The role of academics	145
	The role of authors	147
	Conclusion	149
6	Case Study of JDP 0–30	153
	The external environment/operational experience of Libya	155
	Internal factors	162
	The role of academics	172
	The role of authors	175
	Conclusion	178
7	Air Power Today and the Future	183
	Doctrine today	183
	A conceptual component, public perception and organizational transformation	187
	Thinking to Win	197
	Instead of conclusion	201

Conclusion	203
Notes	209
Bibliography	239
Index	257

Foreword

'National safety would be endangered by an air force whose doctrines and techniques are tied solely to the equipment and processes of the moment. Present equipment is but a step in progress and any air force which does not keep its doctrines ahead of its equipment and its vision far into the future, can only delude the nation into a false sense of security.' General H H Arnold, Commanding General of the US Army Air Forces, to the Secretary of War, 12th November 1945. That is arguably the most unequivocal assertion of the importance of doctrine since air forces began their contribution to warfare a century ago.

Since Hap Arnold's trenchant assertion many excellent books have been written on the evolution of air power. Several have covered theories and concepts as well as operations. For the first time, in this study Viktoriya Fedorchak objectively and comprehensively examines the evolution of Royal Air Force doctrine from its origins in the First World War up to its assimilation within the Joint Service Development, Concepts and Doctrine Centre (DCDC) in 2013. She traces critically the considerable influence of Trenchard and his emphasis on the offensive in the inter war years, which carried over into and beyond the Second World War. She identifies the stagnation of RAF doctrine in the shadow of nuclear deterrence until the then CAS, Sir Neil Cameron, in 1976 personally stimulated the re-emergence of thinking about air power within the Service and beyond.

Dr Fedorchak then sharpens her focus on the subsequent periodic formulation and revisions of RAF Doctrine from 1990 onwards. In these chapters, she enriches her sound primary and secondary sources by drawing heavily and productively on interviews with individuals closely associated with the process. She identifies the factors which came to complicate the formulation and application of a single service doctrine, including differing operational environments, periodic defence reviews, rapidly advancing technology, financial constraints, inter-service rivalry and an increasing emphasis on Joint Service and allied operations. Underlying such influences, permanent doctrinal issues remained: How to avoid doctrine lapsing into obsolescence or worse, into dogma? How to ensure that the doctrine would be heard and applied within the Service and understood beyond it?

Dr Fedorchak emphasizes the importance of highly visible and personal association of the CAS with the formulation and promulgation of Doctrine. Finally, she traces the absorption into the DCDC of the hitherto doctrinal partnership function of the CAS and his Director of Defence Studies. She identifies the transfer of responsibility from personalities to institution but refrains from judgement on possible implications.

The recent emphasis by successive CAS on 'the conceptual component' and 'thinking to win' amply reinforces the permanent importance of Dr Fedorchak's study and the contemporary relevance of Hap Arnold's stern warning. It is in fact essential that the Royal Air Force retains the ability to think clearly, objectively, flexibly and persuasively about its future, especially now within a Joint Service environment.

Air Vice Marshal Tony Mason
17 December 2017

Acknowledgements

The completion of this book would not have been possible without people who supported me at each stage of this unforgettable journey. This book could not have happened without people who taught me about air power. I am incredibly grateful to Tony Mason for widening my view on air power and creative thinking. He inspired me through all these years. His trust and support kept me going. Many thanks to Peter Gray for opening my eyes on the practical aspects of the chosen topic; Andrew Vallance for bringing me to the roots of air power doctrine; Chris Finn for finding the missing parts of the puzzle and the great excursion at RAF College Cranwell. Many thanks to Alistair Byford who found time to share his insight into the recent trends in doctrine writing. I am grateful to Philip Sabin for his timely advice and encouragement. I am much obliged to the Chief Librarian at the Defence Academy at Shrivenham, Chris Hobson, who arranged my visit to the Academy and supported my historical requests. I would also like to thank Philip Meilinger and Benjamin Lambeth for widening the scope of my inquiry and their helpful suggestions. Special thanks to John Olsen for sharing his experience in writing Norwegian doctrine. Finally, I would like to thank my mother, Fedorchak Olha Semenivna, who has always supported and believed in me, and my tutor, Ivanytska Olha Pavlivna, who inspired my interest in defence studies. I dedicate this book to them.

1 February 2018   Viktoriya Fedorchak

Abbreviations

AAP-47 (A)	Allied Administrative Publication (Allied Joint Doctrine Development)
ABCA	American, British, Canadian, Australian and New Zealand Armies programme
ADP	Army Doctrinal Publication Operations
AEW	Airborne Early Warning
AFDC	Air Force Doctrine Center Commanders (US)
AFM	Army Field Manual
AJOD	Allied Joint Operations Doctrine
AJP - 01 (D)	Allied Joint Doctrine (Allied Joint Operations)
AHB	Air Historical Branch
ALARM	Air Launched Anti-Radiation Missile
AP 1300	Air Publication 1300 (Royal Air Force War Manual)
AP 3000	Air Publication 3000 (British Air Power Doctrine)
AP 3001	Air Publication 3001 (Air Power Essentials)
AP 3002	Air Publication 3002 (Air Operations)
AP 3003	Air Publication 3003 (A Brief History of the Royal Air Force)
ASM	Air Staff Manuals
BAI	Battlefield Air Interdiction
BBD	British Defence Doctrine
BMDG	British Military Doctrine Group
BR 1806	British Maritime Doctrine
C4I	Command, Control, Communications, Computers And Intelligence
C2W	Command and Control Warfare
CAOC	Combined Air Operation Centre

CAS	Close Air Support
CAS	Chief of the Air Staff
CD 22	Confidential Document 22 (Operations Manual, Royal Air Force)
CDS	Chief of the Defence Staff
CENTAF	United States Central Command Air Forces
CJCSI 5120.02C	Chairman of the Joint Chiefs of Staff Instruction (Joint Doctrine Development System)
CJCSM 5120.01	Chairman of the Joint Chiefs of Staff Manual (Joint Doctrine Development Process)
COIN	Counterinsurgency
DCS	Defensive Counter-Space Operations
DCDC	Development, Concepts and Doctrine Centre
DDefS	Director of Defence Studies for the RAF
DfiD	Department of International Development
DTI	Department of Trade
FCO	Foreign and Commonwealth Office
GWOT	Global War on Terror
HCDC	House of Commons Defence Committee
HMSO	Her Majesty's Stationery Office
HQ	Headquarters
IED	Improvised Explosive Device
IFOR	Implementation Force
IR	International Relations
ISAF	International Security Assistance Force
ISR	Intelligence, Surveillance and Reconnaissance
ISTAR	Intelligence, Surveillance, Target Acquisition and Reconnaissance
JDC	Joint Defence Centre
JDCB	Joint Doctrine and Concept Board
JDCC	Joint Doctrine and Concepts Centre
JDN	Joint Doctrine Note

JDP	Joint Doctrinal Publication
JDSC	Joint Doctrine Steering Committee
JFACC	Joint Force Air Component Commander
JIPTL	Joint Integrated Prioritised Target List
JSCSC	Joint Services Command and Staff College
JWP	Joint Warfare Publication
JTCB	Joint Targeting Coordination Board
MBT	Main Battle Tanks
MOD	Ministry of Defence
NATO	North Atlantic Treaty Organisation
NCC	Network-Centric Capability
NEC	Network Enabling Capability
NGO	Non-Governmental Organisation
NSA	NATO Standardized Agency
NSO	NATO Standardized Office
OCA	Offensive Counter-Air Operations
OCS	Offensive Counter-Space Operations
OPLAN	Operational Plan
PGM	Precision-Guided Munition
PSO	Peace Support Operations
RAF	Royal Air Force
RAND	Research And Development Corporation
RFC	Royal Flying Corps
RMA	Revolution in Military Affairs
RN	Royal Navy
RNAS	Royal Naval Air Service
ROE	Rules of Engagement
RUSI	Royal United Services Institute for Defence Studies
SDR	Strategic Defence Review
SDSR	Strategic Defence and Security Review
SEAD	Suppression Of Enemy Air Defences

SO1	Staff Officer Grade 1
SOF	Special Operations Forces
SOP	Standard Operating Procedures
TRADOC	US Army Training and Doctrine Command
UAS	University Air Squadron
UAV	Unmanned Air Vehicle
UCAV	Unmanned Combat Air Vehicle
UK	United Kingdom
UN	United Nations
UNPROFOR	United Nations Protection Force
UOR	Urgent Operational Requirements
USAF	United States Air Force
USMC	United States Marine Corps
WMD	Weapons of Mass Destruction
WOT	War on Terror
WPK	Wider Peacekeeping
2C	Command and Control

Introduction

The date 1 April 2018 is a big date in the history of air power. It is the centenary of the first air force in the world – the Royal Air Force (RAF). This century was rich in events: world wars, conflicts, humanitarian disasters and peace-building processes. Air power had something to contribute in every situation. No matter what attitude one might have towards air power, it has undeniably become an integral part of contemporary warfare. Given a relatively long history of the RAF and air power itself, it is to be expected that much has been written on its history, its organizational culture, the evolution of air power and its operational analysis. In fact, while there is an abundance of works exploring diverse aspects of RAF history and the development of air power, one aspect remains relatively underexplored. That aspect is a conceptual component – the thought process of establishing the principles and concepts for using air power in diverse operational settings. The conceptual component consists of the principles of war, doctrine and conceptual innovation. Air power doctrine is often underexplored in the contemporary time frame.

The first RAF air power doctrine dates back to 1922, when Confidential Document (CD) 22 was published, establishing Trenchard's concept of strategic bombing. Subsequent editions in 1928, 1940, 1950 and 1957 illustrated the complex role of doctrine in domestic politics and interservice relations, and its ambiguous status within the service. During the doctrinal vacuum of the 1970s–1980s, doctrine became associated with dogma. The post–Cold War decades saw the revival of doctrine in the national military practice and the establishment of Air Publication (AP) 3000 series. The establishment of jointery in national military discourse, following the Strategic Defence Review (SDR) 1998, made significant contributions to the ways that air power was articulated and how environmental doctrines were written. Different stages in the institutionalization of jointery had different degrees of influence on doctrine writing and the positioning of air power in the joint discourse.

There are many ways of presenting history. The majority of books follow a chronological approach. Thus, an equal attention is paid to focal points and crucial events. History textbooks are written that way to help readership grasp the essence of historical epochs and cause–effect relationship of events. Another way to explain history is by in-depth analysis of a specific theme across years or a single event in its interdisciplinary depth. For instance, many military histories explore single battles or assess performance of the national armed forces. This approach provides an insight into multiple factors influencing decision-making and actions that led to the known outcome. Both approaches serve its purpose. However, there is another way of presenting history. First, the chronological outline of the further decades sets a scene in order to explore the main subject in depth. Second, the main theme is explored through the factors influencing decision-making in each situation. These situations are categorized as case studies in order to provide in-depth analysis and changes of influences. The last approach includes the benefits of the first two. Moreover, this approach is beneficial in concentrating attention on the actual research time frame, while a more remote history serves as a context for understanding contemporary events.

This book is not a chronological history of the RAF or British air power. Nor is it aimed to be an exhaustive source on the history of RAF doctrine from 1922 until 1999. Many excellent books cover in depth the establishment of the RAF as an independent service. Much has been written on the evolution of British air power and its use in various operational settings across decades. Certain insights into the early features of RAF doctrine development are also available. This book has none of the aforementioned intentions. The primary purpose of this monograph is to explain the contemporary trend of RAF doctrine development in the post–Cold War era within the process of jointery. Jointery was introduced as a means of post–Cold War reforming the British Armed Forces in 1998 SDR. As a result, the time frame of the original research is 1999–2013, when the first doctrine and the last air power doctrines were published within the process of jointery. Nevertheless, a chapter on the history of RAF air power doctrine provides an insight into reasons of doctrinal vacuum and the complexity of doctrinal revival in the RAF after the end of the Cold War. However, once again, this chapter is not on history of the RAF *per se*, but rather the doctrinal reflection of its thought process. This author is convinced that without knowing a historical context of organizational thinking, it is impossible to understand contemporary trends.

The originality of this monograph is precisely in covering underexplored contemporary time frame of doctrine development and establishment of RAF's conceptual component. The relatively new nature of the subject and lack of formal or academic works covering this time frame required an alternative approach to methodology of this research. Thus, the contextual history is explored through the works of well-established academics, specializing in RAF history, while the contemporary three case studies illustrate the analysis of personal insights of doctrine writers, official assessment of operational performance, textual analysis of doctrines and some theoretical frameworks.

This book is an analytical history. It seeks to demonstrate the re-establishment of RAF doctrine in post–Cold War environment. This book shows the evolution of air power doctrine at a time of rapid changes in national politics and in the international arena. Changes in strategic thinking regarding air power are explored through the development of new concepts, evaluation of operational experience, the political environment and budgetary cuts, and the role of academics and personalities in the development of air power doctrine. Moreover, this book investigates the influence of jointery (the process of cooperation between the three services: army, navy and air force) on thinking, conceptualizing, teaching and using air power in recent operations in Afghanistan, Iraq and Libya. The three case studies presented in this book demonstrate how the authorship of doctrine shaped content and vision of air power in each doctrine. The book also suggests critical views of the future of air power, its new conceptual component, organizational innovations in the RAF and the place of the service in British defence.

The main analytical approach applied in this book is historiographical analysis, meaning the situational factors that shaped air power doctrine at different stages of its development are analysed. To this end, the four-layer approach introduced by Dr Oliver Daddow is used. Daddow argues that doctrine should be treated as a historical document of its time, which reflects the influences of a wider historical environment including intellectual and political atmospheres, review boards and networks, as well as the contributions of individual doctrine writers.[1] Daddow suggests that doctrine is shaped in accordance with the writers' views, experiences and inspirations. They explain 'the orientation of doctrine'.[2] Although writers are the final arbiters of what comes into a final draft, 'they have to work in the context of military and political structures that can affect both what they write and how they go about it'.[3] Daddow outlines three potentially influential elements within networks: academics, editorial boards and review structures. First, authors are involved in cooperation with academics, exchanging ideas and opinions about the existing strategic environment and how each service functions in it. Editorial boards and review structures provide the unanimity of common values and new trends in conceptualization of military force according to the doctrine writing process in the UK. This is particularly the case of doctrine writing in joint environment.

Regarding the third factor, Daddow suggests that 'doctrine cannot be isolated from the domestic political context of its time … [and that it is] affected by the nature of the domestic political environment within which it was written'.[4] The major component of this influence would be strategic culture or the national way of warfare. This would inevitably affect writers and their way of writing; resource allocation (meaning the correlation between public policy and military budgets); and ministerial/official input. The final factor is the international context, which influences doctrine in two fundamental ways. First, the impact of world events affects doctrine through the previous conflicts in the form of operational experience. The second way in which international context affects doctrine is, more directly, at the writers' level 'and pertains to the transmission of both technology and doctrinal concepts across states borders, especially between the US and Britain'.[5]

Oliver Daddow's approach was chosen for a few reasons. This framework provides a systematic vision of factors shaping doctrine. The four criteria provide an opportunity for a detailed comparison of case studies within different stages of jointery. Strictly from an academic perspective, his approach has been successfully applied in various research projects on doctrine development.[6] However, this is one of the first research designs that uses his methodology for comparison of different editions of the same doctrine emphasizing doctrine writing process *per se*.

For the holistic purposes of this book, Daddow's four layers of influences on doctrine writing were distilled to four exact factors that could be traced in the doctrine writing of each case study: operational experience, domestic politics, the role of academics and doctrine writers. All three case studies are structured accordingly. The reverse order was chosen to show how wider factors affected the narrow ones. In other words, the exploration of external and internal environments could explain the atmosphere in which academics, practitioners and authors wrote doctrines. The actual analysis is conducted using diverse methods aimed at cross-verification of data and viewpoints. They include textual analysis, top-level interviews and comparative analysis of the three case studies. Case studies were chosen to illustrate distinctiveness of doctrine writing at each stage of institutionalization of jointery.

This book consists of seven chapters. In Chapter 1, 'Theory', the notions of doctrine and key supporting terms are explained. The main functions of doctrine, its relation to policy and strategy, doctrine hierarchy, doctrinal dilemmas and the changing role of doctrine are identified. The emphasis is placed on official documents as sources of relevant, trustworthy and up-to-date information. Some critical materials on the use of doctrine are presented to demonstrate the place of doctrine in contemporary military practice. Also, the main purposes and roles of doctrine are examined, paying attention to the primary (military personnel) and secondary (other stakeholders) audiences. Moreover, key academic and military debates on the utility of doctrine are presented, illustrating the complexity of the doctrinal phenomenon in contemporary military practice. In other words, this chapter answers the question 'what is a military doctrine?'

Chapter 2, 'The Historical Context', explores the history of RAF doctrine and sets the context for the research which follows. The development of air power doctrine is explored through the histories of the RAF and of air power. The history of the RAF provides an insight into how doctrine, its roles and the perception of it among airmen and women evolved together with the service. This chapter traces the history of doctrine from the first doctrine, CD 22, the Operations Manual (July 1922) up until AP 3000, second edition (1993). In particular, the reluctance of the RAF to accept doctrine in the 1990s is explained by its previous misuse as a political tool for self-justification and explanation to a wider audience. This chapter also provides an insight into the organizational culture and the place of doctrine in this culture.

Chapter 3, 'Case Study of the Third Edition of AP 3000 (Part I)', is devoted to the first case of AP 3000, third edition (1999). The chapter covers the time frame from 1994 to 1999, when the previous doctrine was published and the preparation for a new edition took place. Attention is paid to two major factors influencing doctrine writing. The first is the external environment, which includes the operational experience of past campaigns (the lessons of the Gulf War and Peace Support Operations (PSO) in Bosnia). The second factor is internal politics outside the RAF. The consequences of the Labour Government's SDR of 1998, and the introduction of a cost-efficiency approach and jointery are analysed.

Chapter 4, 'Case Study of the Third Edition of AP 3000 (Part II)', is a continuation of the first case study. Unlike the previous chapter, this one concentrates on two other factors in doctrine writing: the roles of networks (academics and review boards) and authors in the process of doctrine preparation. This chapter illustrates that the involvement of academics in doctrinal workshops is secondary.

However, collaboration with academics encourages critical, innovative and systematic thinking on air power. This collaboration also assists in the adaptation to a rapidly changing external environment. Moreover, academics and review boards have influenced authors' decision-making on the content of first drafts. The impact of the authors' background on the intellectual nature of doctrine under consideration is also explained in this chapter.

Chapter 5, 'Case Study of the Fourth Edition of AP 3000', is devoted to the fourth edition of AP 3000 (2009). This chapter explains the driving forces of a new edition of AP 3000 and how the doctrine writing process was different from that of the previous editions. The main feature of this edition was the relatively small number of people involved in its preparation, mainly the Chief of Air Staff and Director for Defence Studies for the RAF, and a few specialists. This edition had the precise purpose of reflecting upon eight years of fighting counterinsurgencies in Iraq and Afghanistan and the upcoming Strategic Defence and Security Review (SDSR). The rationale for the size and content of this edition is explained by the authorship, prevailing tendencies in teaching courses at that time and the strengthening of vertical jointery.

Chapter 6, 'Case Study of JDP 0–30', discusses the most recent edition of air power doctrine, JDP 0–30, *UK Air and Space Doctrine* (2013). Unlike previous doctrines, this edition was prepared under joint authorship. This chapter explains which factors influenced the process of doctrine preparation of this edition. Operational experience in Libya and the impact of the SDSR on budgetary arrangements were analysed. At this time, structural and functional changes in jointery had a more profound impact on the process of doctrine preparation. The systematization of doctrinal cycles with respect to the SDSR is only one aspect to mention. Thus, the chapter also demonstrates the tendencies in the contemporary process of doctrine writing. It also illustrates current trends in the North Atlantic Treaty Organization NATO-oriented approach to reforming the British Armed Forces and the place of doctrine in it.

Chapter 7, 'Air Power Today and the Future', seeks to demonstrate where air power stands now and what future is predicted for the RAF and air power. Particular attention is paid to the civil–military gap and the necessity of engaging the public in the process of air advocacy. The role of doctrine in the organizational transformation of the RAF is examined. Attention is also paid to the transformation of the RAF after the SDSR 2015 and the launch of a new conceptual component. The main points of the RAF's innovative initiative Thinking to Win is examined. This chapter concludes with suggestions for the future of air power and the place of doctrine in shaping it.

1

Theory

Just as every story has its beginning, and every game has its rules, so does every research has its own starting point. One needs to distinguish the key concepts, terms and definitions used, to understand the nature of research. Thus, identification of relevant terminology and the place of doctrine in military practice are essential for exploring the development of doctrine. This chapter explains military and formal doctrines; the purposes and functions of doctrine; doctrine hierarchy; the relationship between doctrine, policy, strategy and technology. This chapter also includes traditional debates on doctrines and changes in its primary and secondary audience. Here, the basis for understanding the field of doctrinal studies is laid out.

The definition of doctrine

'Doctrine' is often confused with 'dogma', meaning prescription of behaviour and rigidity of mind and actions. A reader without any military background is likely to assume that a military doctrine is like a religious doctrine, meaning dogma, but applied in a military context. To avoid further confusion, a distinction between the two is worth making. Even the dictionary meaning of the word 'doctrine' does not impose obedient following of prescribed norms. *The Oxford Dictionary* gives the following definition: 'Doctrine/ˈdɒktrɪn/noun: a belief or set of beliefs held and taught by a Church, political party, or other group: e.g. the doctrine of predestination.'[1] This definition corresponds to the origins of the word, which comes from the Latin '*doctrina*' meaning 'teaching, learning'. However, the word 'dogma' stands for 'a principle or set of principles laid down by an authority as incontrovertibly true.'[2] Therefore, the two words cannot be substituted. Doctrine is a set of perceptions and ideas of a particular institution. Dogma prescribes norms that should be followed unconditionally. The word 'doctrine' has preserved its original meaning of 'teaching'. On the contrary, 'dogma' has evolved from its initial Greek meaning of 'opinion' and 'suggestion'. Linguistically, both doctrine and dogma reflect a set of principles established by a certain institution. However, the term 'dogma', rather than 'doctrine', has a higher degree of prescription, unarguable authority and denial of deviation.

Most doctrines include definitions of military doctrine and its utility in military practice in order to address the difficulty in distinguishing between doctrine and dogma. These definitions are useful in explaining the meaning of doctrine to a wider audience. They also makes it more accessible and acceptable for the military audience. No matter how strange it may seem, unlike the historical religious use of the word 'doctrine', in military terms, the phenomenon of doctrine is more flexible in its contents and application. The most commonly used definition of doctrine is derived from NATO joint discourse: 'Military doctrine is fundamental principles by which military forces guide their actions in support of objectives. It is authoritative, but requires judgment in application.'[3]

This definition reveals that doctrine is not about indoctrination of traditional thoughts and old-fashioned behaviour. It is about the provision of common ground for officers and staff to act in different operational settings. Accordingly, a military doctrine seeks to provide potential ways of task accomplishment. However, it is up to an individual to decide how a certain doctrinal principle is applicable to a situation. In other words, unlike dogma, doctrine provides a common ground for adaptability to the rapidly changing environment of warfare. Moreover, doctrine serves as the glue that sticks different branches of military organizations together. It educates people of different backgrounds with military principles and historical best practice for the military institution to absorb them. It also supplies them with a common frame of reference to boost both their conceptual and practical knowledge of national strategic and organizational cultures.

Historically, doctrine, as a set of principles existed in the form of best practice and expertise passed from one generation of serving personnel to another.[4] Doctrine was rather oral or semi-oral, while certain principles of action were written in service manuals. However, in contrast to historical or regiment-based doctrinal traditions, there is also a written or formal doctrine. The distinguishing features of the latter are that it is often written in a single document, issued by an authoritative body, and reflects top-to-bottom delivery of general principles and best practice. A formal doctrine is more authoritative in its nature than an unwritten and informal one. Although it usually contains the same principles, it is more centralized in its dissemination. Formal doctrine also reflects the official position of military institutions. It is also universal in its application. Although oral and written doctrines might often correspond to each other, this book examines only formal and written doctrines.

The purposes of doctrine

There are different approaches to the functions of doctrine. In this section attention is paid to the functions or purposes of doctrine that are outlined in the actual texts of doctrines and those that are defined by academics who study doctrine and its utility in organizational transformation. Harald Høiback approaches purposes of doctrine from an institutional perspective. According to him, doctrine serves three purposes within an organization. First, doctrine is a means of education. As mentioned previously, it is used to drill the organizational ways and principles into the minds of personnel. It provides them with the common ground to learn the national way of warfare. Second, it is a tool of operations, meaning that doctrines influence the way militaries plan their campaigns and how they implement them in the battle space.[5] The degree of doctrine's authority and influence is very situational. The first two purposes illustrate what authors of doctrines wrote in manuals, while the third purpose is distinctive for an organizational outlook. Høiback suggests that the final purpose of doctrine is to be a means of change and transformation: 'as a tool of change, it says authoritatively what to be.'[6] In other words, doctrine may contain the service's vision of its future in a new strategic environment. It may also demonstrate the change in service's role with the acquisition of new technologies changing the character of contemporary warfare. It may be suggested that doctrines contain the conceptual commitment of an organization to adapt to changes in the external environment.

Thus, the aim of any military doctrine is to deliver knowledge to a target audience, in order to stimulate action. The sole purpose of military doctrine is to 'describe how the Armed Forces go about military activities but not why they do what they do (which is the realm of policy).'[7] Joint doctrine writers outlined two purposes of doctrine: educative and informative,[8] based on the two different target audiences it pursues to reach. The first audience comprises military personnel in their early career, who need to learn the basics of a service's principles and best practice. The second audience consists of various stakeholders interested in how the Armed Forces go about their business. They include journalists, politicians, academics, public figures, allies and even adversaries, since doctrine explains the principles the Armed Forces fight for.

The military audience

According to the Joint Warfare Publication (JWP) 0-01, 'military doctrine is targeted principally at members of the Armed Forces.'[9] Doctrine seeks to educate military officers in the initial stages of their careers. It should stimulate creative thinking, improve situational awareness and informed decision-making. Doctrine usually includes an explanation of national strategy and the relationship between strategy, policy and military objectives in a strategic environment. It also contains a detailed explanation of the national way of warfare and how it is implemented under changing circumstances. It identifies similarities and distinctiveness of operations in which the Armed Forces may be involved.[10] Historically, the first military doctrines were more prescriptive and uniform in their nature. They aimed at formation of a uniform way of thinking and therefore acting. The first RAF doctrinal manual declared: 'The Royal Air Force will be trained in peace and led in war in accordance with the doctrine contained in this volume. The principles of this doctrine should be so thoroughly impressed on the mind of every commander that, whenever he has to come to a decision in the field, he will instinctively give them their full weight.'[11]

Gradually the perception of doctrine's purposes changed. Nowadays, the essence of doctrine is to give general guidance, based on experience, best practice and universal principles of warfare, which remain relatively the same, despite technological or environmental changes. In other words, doctrine provides the Armed Forces with basic knowledge of how to plan and conduct a potential mission. This is what Høiback calls the tool of command. Therefore, the contents and perceptiveness of doctrine depend on the evolution of the Armed Forces and society. In the last two decades, new doctrinal trends were distinguished: doctrinal texts included ethical and moral discussions, paying attention to incorporation of the Armed Forces into the civil society. Doctrine is also a means of expressing and thus understanding a service's philosophy. Colin Gray suggests that doctrine can be used to understand a military institution itself: 'Doctrine may not provide a thoroughly reliable guide to probable military practice, but it does provide clues, and more, to understanding the current credo of military institutional stakeholders.'[12]

Although doctrine is based on best practice and thus is directly connected with past events, it is not a retrospective account of how wars were fought. In contrast, it aims at the application of relevant and accessible knowledge 'today and in the immediate future; it is dynamic and is constantly reviewed for relevance'.[13] This phrase reveals the position of military institutions and doctrine writers in the critical discussion of the relevance of a doctrine. This statement refutes the first argument against doctrine that it is about the past, and thus is irrelevant for the future. Colin McInnes argued that what was considered the British way of warfare was the main limitation on doctrine. He opposed the idea that since previous campaigns were successful, the techniques by which they were won could still be relevant in subsequent decades. McInnes also added that the national strategic culture or prevalence of the British approach made doctrine 'positivist and ahistoric understanding of the nature of war'.[14] He was convinced that doctrine represented mere 'cherry-picking' of successful campaigns in support of the British approach.[15] On the contrary, other academics argue that history is vital for military education. Charles Grant emphasized that, in the development of doctrine, historical lessons are a foundation stone for understanding what needs to be achieved.[16] Eliot Cohen paid attention to the meaning of history in shaping the 'historical mind' of militaries.[17] According to Cohen, the role of doctrine is in educating personnel in how to use historical experiences in evaluation of contemporary situations.[18] Douglas Porch argued that militaries should learn from history. However, he suggested a new threat that invocation of history might pose – incorrect interpretation of history or its misuse for political reasons.[19]

Like any other historical document, doctrine is a document of its time. Furthermore, it is also timeless since it contains enduring knowledge on continuity of the nature of warfare, reflected in the principles of war. Whether doctrine is dogmatic, retrospective- or forward-looking, intellectual or easy to understand depends on the particular circumstances in which it was written and to what purpose. Doctrine is studied not in an attempt to justify a political or military position but to explore how to improve its efficiency in application using its fullest capacity. Without constant revisions, it might stimulate rigid thinking and adherence to outdated traditions. Doctrine aims at showing how wars can be fought today utilizing all available experience and knowledge, but it does not provide an exhaustive guidance of actions in all possible situations. The relevance of theory and doctrine for a practitioner was well defined by Clausewitz. He argued that a positive doctrine was unattainable: 'We must remind ourselves that it is simply not possible to construct a model for the art of war that can serve as a scaffolding on which the commander can rely for support at any time.'[20] In other words, doctrine cannot be universally applied for all cases of war. Instead, it suggests certain modes of behaviour that have proved to be successful in the art of war. Nevertheless, they might not be applicable under all circumstances. In contrast to doctrine, theory is helpful because it is not situational and provides a wider variety of alternatives. Theory is a learning tool, not an action manual:

> Theory then becomes a guide to anyone who wants to learn about war from books; it will light his way, ease his progress, train his judgement and help him to avoid pitfalls … Theory exists so that one need not start afresh each time sorting out the material and plowing through it, but will find it ready to hand and in good order. It is meant to educate the mind of the future commander, or, more accurately, to guide him in his self-education, not to accompany him to the battlefield; just a wise teacher guides and stimulates a young man's intellectual development, but is careful not to lead him by the hand for the rest of his life.[21]

Consequently, both doctrine and theory seek to educate one's mind in fighting wars and provide options for actions, but they are different. Theory is wider than doctrine. It provides more alternatives than a doctrinal document. Doctrine suggests the best practice and a framework for military thinking within the national way of warfare, while theory tends to be more neutral to the national context of fighting wars.

The wider audience

The UK Joint Doctrine stressed that the second purpose of doctrine is to inform. In fact, the purpose is the same – to educate. However, the audience and the way it uses this knowledge are different: 'BDD has a wider secondary purpose. Members of Parliament, academics, industrialists, journalists and members of the general public, all of whom have a legitimate interest in the way the UK's Armed Forces go about their business, will find BDD of interest.'[22] Doctrine is used as a source for explaining the British way of warfare to a wider audience within the ruling authority, internal and external parties. In this context, ministers and governmental departments that deal with military affairs use doctrines to understand how certain military activities are conducted. JWP 0–01 addressed such departments as the Foreign Office (FO), the Department of International Development (DFID), the Home Office, the Department of Trade and Industry (DTI)[23] and the Treasury.[24] From a public perspective, doctrine serves as a portfolio of the Armed Forces. It explains the services to academics, journalists, entrepreneurs, potential recruits and the public. Doctrine explains not only what war is, but also the means of its conduct by the Armed Forces in accordance with national ways. It can help both a better understanding of militaries' jobs at home and improve business interactions between governmental and private sectors.

Regarding the wider stakeholders, doctrine describes military strategy, ethos and the national way of warfare for traditional allies and potential partners in order to achieve a better mutual understanding: 'Doctrine is of value to allies and potential coalition partners who will benefit from an understanding of the UK's military ethos and general approach to strategic and military issues.'[25] Accordingly, doctrine seeks to harmonize coalition cooperation and subsequent joint operations. Often, doctrine confirms Allied commitments. In the case of the British defence doctrine, it should not contradict NATO doctrine.[26] The harmony between the national and Allied doctrines is achieved in a number of ways. First, the main conceptual framework and general contents of the national-level doctrines should correspond to the Allied framework. Second, doctrine hierarchy is often explained within the text of doctrine.[27] In terms of a wider audience, doctrine is also aimed at potential adversaries: 'It also conveys a message to potential opponents and adversaries that the UK is military well-prepared; by doing this BDD contributes to deterrence in the broadest sense.'[28] Therefore, doctrine itself is a means of enhancing security. JWP 0–01 stated that although the secondary purpose is relevant, 'doctrine has to be written around the principal purpose of conducting effective military operations.'[29] Military doctrine should aim at educating military personnel for more effective performance in future operations. Thus, the stretching functionality of doctrine can threaten its ability to achieve the primary role – reaching a military audience.

Where does doctrine fit in the structure of fighting power?

The Armed Forces must preserve a high level of fighting power and warfighting excellence in order to secure the achievement of posed objectives, credibility and utility of military force.[30] Fighting power means ability to fight, which comprises of multiple components and enabling factors. It consists of three components: a conceptual component, a moral component and a physical component. The conceptual component is a thought process. In a narrow sense, it refers to thinking about how wars should be fought in a new strategic environment, how available capabilities should be used and which skills are required. In a wider sense, this process combines more systematic thinking on how the lessons of past warfare can help in fighting wars of the future, and how new technologies change the character of wars, leaving its nature unchanged. While the first approach is more goal oriented, the second is more systematic and strategic in its nature. The conceptual component includes the principles of war, doctrine and conceptual innovation. The moral component is the will of people to fight. It illustrates the motives that drive people in fulfilling their military service, such as leadership, morale and core values. The physical component refers to the means to fight and includes specific categories like manpower and equipment, but also more abstract notions such as sustainability, readiness and efficiency of collective performance.[31]

These components are placed in their logical order, outlining that, first, there should be a strong intellectual foundation for developing strategies and training courses. They require a credible and authoritative system of values for military personnel to believe in and to identify with. Leadership, morale and core values provide a frame for the strong will to fight. Finally, the physical component comes last, because, as the history of warfare shows, without a strong strategy and soldiers' will to fight, even the best capabilities are undermined. However, for a fighting power to be effective, all three components should be well balanced. The connection between these components can be explained by Paul Wilkins' words: 'an attitude of mind which translates perceived ethereal conceptual thinking into relevant day-to-day RAF activity by all personnel who contribute to its outputs'.[32]

Overall, the conceptual component seeks to provide the Armed Forces with an intellectual view on their potential roles within different strategic settings and different ways of using force. Moreover, it helps in transferring past experiences, know-hows and organizational culture from one generation to another, resulting in continuity of a national and organizational way of warfare. While the principles of war explain the continuity of the nature of war and changeability of its character, doctrine contains the most recent conceptual framework for the use of military force. Finally, the conceptual innovation refers to the analytical process of realizing how new technologies, threats and sociocultural factors influence military thinking. Conceptual innovation seeks to achieve a systematic self-reflection, looking for gaps and ways of filling them in. Moreover, both doctrine and conceptual innovation show how military force adapts to the constantly changing character of war.

Doctrinal instrumentalism and organizational transformation

Looking at the matter from a more instrumental perspective, Colin Gray emphasized the purposes of doctrine in terms of its utility for the service as an institution. He argued:

> Doctrine provides a common basis of understanding of what its issuing organization currently believes to be best military practice ... doctrine provides

guidance, in some military cultures it provides mandatory guidance, not merely strong suggestions, on how soldiers should proceed on the basis of lessons learnt from historical experience, sometimes on the basis only of deduction from first principles, while occasionally it reflects nothing more solid than the commander's intuition.[33]

In other words, doctrine embodies the strategic culture absorbed and processed by the issuing institution. Doctrine can distil the useful of the strategic culture for the institution's personnel. Therefore, doctrines of two services would emphasize different lessons, mainly because of different experiences in their inherent environments warfare. The purposes of doctrine depend on existing practice, historical tradition and strategic culture, not only within the Armed Forces of a particular nation, but also in each service within that nation. For a researcher, it is crucial to understand that doctrine is not only a historical document, reflecting the strategic environment of its time. It is also an instructional and cultural document of an issuing service. It reflects how the service responds to particular threats posed by the existing strategic environment. These two characteristics of doctrine should always be kept in mind. Each doctrine should be analysed in terms of the historical (strategic) situation and distinctive institutional political framework.

The shift of a target audience or the substitution of functionality

Despite the obvious representative benefits, an instrumentalist approach to doctrine might have rather negative and counterproductive affects. Military personnel as the primary audience should be educated in the ways of the service and the national strategic culture. If that primary audience is substituted with a wider secondary one (politicians and members of the public), the doctrine might become a single-purpose political document. The single purpose of such a document would be the service's self-justification. Thus, doctrine would not explain the service to a wider, secondary audience, but would justify the service under particular conditions. In such circumstances, doctrine becomes a simple bureaucratic tool for getting a bigger piece of the budgetary cake. The main issue is not stretching doctrine's purposefulness, but substitution of one purpose for another. Thus, doctrine's purpose of educating personnel in how to fight and win wars is substituted for a political purpose of resolving certain interservice budgetary issues within national defence. Major Andrew Methven comes to a very gloomy conclusion:

> Culture sets the managerialist context, to which doctrine is a response. Doctrine is no longer for the practitioner. It is there to satisfy the demands of those above for auditable, hence written, method. It is a bureaucratic tool, primarily in the field of acquisition. The doctrine industry is now less concerned with fighting and winning on the battlefield today; instead it provides ammunition for the bureaucratic process of winning in the imaginary battlefields of the future.[34]

This statement shows the negative side of doctrinal instrumentalism. If doctrine is developed in the closed environment of bureaucratic domestic politics and interservice rivalry, it may lose its credibility and validity for the serving personnel. To overcome this obstacle, doctrine should adopt the experience gained in previous and ongoing operations. Moreover, cross-verification and subordination of doctrines in a joint hierarchy is required to secure consistency of conceptual framework. In other words, if doctrine is not revised according to operational experience, it can become not only dogma but also a situational political document. New operational experience becomes the driving force for doctrine to remain what it is intended to be – a guide for military personnel on how to fight present wars and potential future ones in the framework of the existing strategic culture. Inevitably, it has to reflect each service's place in national defence and serve as a means of preserving its unique strategic culture. However, adopting new operational lessons, doctrine becomes a means of adapting traditional strategic culture to new strategic, political realities. Thus, it can become the means of preserving the common ground of the past, while reaping the benefits of contemporaneity. Despite widespread criticism of strategic culture,[35] it is a ground on which the national Armed Forces can build their training courses and into which new practices can be incorporated. Thus, instrumentalist functionality of doctrine is somewhere in-between self-explanation of a service's traditional way of warfare and adoption of contemporary lessons learned in a new strategic environment. However, in both cases, military personnel should remain the primary audience.

Relationship between policy, strategy and doctrine

If doctrine answers the question of how services should go about conducting military operations, it does not explain why and how exactly they should act in situations that are not envisioned by doctrine. Although from a systematic perspective, these questions are crucial for assessing the application of doctrine in particular situations, the answer to the why question is given by policy, while strategy answers the how exactly question. The aim of policy is to embody 'the nation's response to the prevailing strategic environment, reflecting the Government's judgement of what is necessary and possible in pursuit of the national interest'.[36] Policy can be both fluid and enduring. In terms of its impact on the military field, this might mean a rapid review of military strategy and the roles of the Armed Forces, or continuation of certain trends in handling threats with a subsequent shaping of a traditional strategic thinking.[37] The relationship between policy and doctrine is direct. The American guidance on joint doctrine development gives the following explanation:

> Policy can direct, assign tasks, prescribe desired capabilities, and provide guidance for ensuring the Armed Forces of the United States are prepared to perform their assigned roles; implicitly, policy can therefore create new roles and a requirement for new capabilities. Conversely, doctrine enhances the operational effectiveness of the Armed Forces by providing authoritative guidance and standardized terminology on topics relevant to the employment of military forces.[38]

From this description of the policy–doctrine relationship, it can be concluded that policy drives doctrine. However, a particular capability might also trigger the development of a subsequent policy. In any case, it is the requirement of doctrine writers to ensure that doctrine is consistent with the established policy. Regarding rapidly changing political situations, doctrine's ability to cope with political volatility is different at each level of doctrine hierarchy. The most sensitive to political changes and thus less enduring are joint doctrines, which have to be modified when crucial political changes occur. The chain reaction of changes can follow. However, before the introduction of the most recent doctrine preparation cycle, if the change in political objectives was not fundamental, single-service doctrines could remain without modifications. Conversely, the lower the level of doctrine, the more enduring and immune to political changes it will be. In other words, no matter how policy changes, the number of flights a single jet can fly and the number of targets it can physically reach cannot change, without changes of technologies and actual capabilities. Therefore, different levels of doctrine would change in different ways depending on how close they are to the political dimension. Regarding the relationship between policy and doctrine, it does not mean that policy statements should be quoted throughout a doctrinal document. The NATO doctrine development guide suggests the following: 'Policy guides doctrine development by providing the baseline for the doctrinal principles or fundamentals. It is the job of the custodian to interpret that policy guidance and elaborate upon it in such a manner that it becomes doctrine.'[39]

Therefore, policy identifies goals and delegates subsequent roles to the Armed Forces, while doctrine accepts these goals and roles and explains how they can be achieved on the basis of existing practice and national military capabilities. Therefore, policy answers the 'why' question, while doctrine answers the 'what' question. The mediator between the two is military strategy: 'The UK's military strategy draws together Defence Policy (which must reflect the realities of the strategic environment) and military strategic doctrine (which provides guidance on the military means of support of policy). An alternative way of defining military strategy is to describe it as the bridge linking policy and operational effects.'[40]

In the general public discourse, the terms 'strategy' and 'policy' are often interchangeable. However, in a military discourse, such substitution is a huge mistake and undermines the understanding. The main difference between defence policy and military strategy is that defence policy 'establishes the ends of military strategy and, in the normal course of events, shapes the structures and capabilities of the Armed Forces within resources and other constraints.'[41] The role of military strategy is to evaluate the use of force in terms of potential advantageous or harmful political consequences and tackling threats.[42] Military strategy aims at selecting the way of using force from the existing arsenal and best practice, suggested in doctrine, to suit situational political objectives in a particular operational environment. Thus, as Colin Gray has stated, doctrine is one of the dimensions and components of strategy.[43] In this context, military strategy should consider available ways of achieving posed political objectives. It should also evaluate their cost-efficiency. Through doctrines, military strategy can evaluate services' correspondence to a particular objective, with subsequent preference of the most suitable or cost-effective option. The joint doctrine of 2008 clearly states: 'Military strategy is concerned with the allocation, prioritization and balancing of military resources between concurrent and competing operational demands.'[44] In this case, the main problem is to keep the balance between long-term implications, immediate restraints in resources and short-term contingencies.

Relationship between doctrine, technology and policy

Another important element in military practice is technology. The development of technologies is important, because it can define future military capabilities and roles each service can play. In turn, new capabilities can widen the range of potentially achievable objectives, both political and strategic. From a conceptual perspective, development of new technologies can support implementation of new concepts or can undermine the existing conceptual framework. From a doctrine perspective, technologies trigger changes in strategic thinking, modification of political objectives and, as a result, prompt changes in doctrines: 'Policy is developed in response to changing circumstances in the political-military strategic environment, agreed political guidance, practical lessons learned or new technology and is essentially prescriptive. Among other factors which influence the development of doctrine, it primarily evolves in response to changes in policy, warfighting capabilities and/or force employment considerations.'[45]

While official documents concentrate on explanation of general connections between elements, academics look into a cause–effect relationship. In terms of technology and doctrine, three potential scenarios of interaction are possible. First, doctrinal requirements can speed up certain tendencies in technological development. Second, emerging technologies might force changes in doctrines. However, a certain symbiosis of cooperation between the two is possible, which results in balanced and gradual shaping of future capabilities.[46] In a retrospective analysis, Roger Thomas drew a few conclusions. First, developing technologies help in improving military capabilities, but their subsequent correct application requires an appropriate doctrine. Second, emerging military technologies are often derived from private sector research. Collaboration with the private sector carries its own challenges: security breaches and information espionage, difficulty in delivering of the final product and the need for additional transparency in financial transactions. Moreover, with the spread of new sophisticated weapons and systems in conflicts of different intensity, collaboration with the private sector may bring additional uncertainty of commercial competition.[47] Third, although the experience of air power development in the First World War suggests that the experience of war can be vital for boosting and testing new technologies and analysing their impact on warfare,[48] Roger Thomas argued that a war was not needed for testing new technologies. Consequently, the relevance of technological improvement was in its correspondence to strategic concepts, political objectives or the national interest, in general.[49] On the other hand, absence of operational verification of technologies might lead to procurement of platforms that might fit political preferences rather than military requirements. Fourth, while the comparative advantages of a new technology are short term and the competitive advantages for militaries are seldom calculated, appropriate doctrine with a long-term evaluation is of a particular use. Finally, an emerging technology ought to be financially sustainable.[50] No matter how advanced and promising technology might be, it does not mean it is universally applicable. The gap between technical feasibility and operational utility should always be taken into account: 'That a given capability is technically feasible does not always mean that it is operationally useful in the demanding world of actual combat.'[51]

Doctrine can also be a means of covering this gap. Existing on the borderline between past and future, doctrine also brings together old and new experiences for the benefit of future achievements. From a technological perspective, doctrine unites the lessons of historical experience with the theory of technological change. Doctrine describes not only the lessons history teaches about the general principles of war, but also operational best practice and human experience of dealing with technologies in their various stages of development. In turn, this experience shows both the utility of new technologies and their limitations through the operational history of the Armed Forces. Doctrine can serve as a means of sobering overenthusiastic perspectives on the immediate adoption of ultra-new technologies. However, it is not always the case.

From another perspective, in terms of systematic guidance reflecting historical best practice and contemporary acquired technologies, doctrine serves as a mediator of human experience and machine technologies. In its essence, doctrine brings together centuries of human knowledge of warfare, together with new means of its conduct. This provides military personnel with a flexible framework of potential actions applicable to a given situation. In other words, doctrine serves as 'a dialogue between the past and the present for the benefit of the future'.[52] It contains enduring principles of warfare and guidance for application of new technologies under the conditions of unpredictability and situational character of warfighting. Another substantial function of doctrine in terms of technological discourse is that it reminds us of the permanence of war. Despite the means, the cornerstone of warfighting is a human being. Until the futuristic Star Wars of clones and robot battles, fighting for opposite sides, become the reality, the nature of war will remain human-centred and thus enduring. Doctrine will have to reflect this trend.

Doctrine hierarchy

A person not acquainted with doctrinal studies might become convinced that doctrine might be something of a military bible, applicable to all situations. It may seem that doctrine is a single book, like Tolstoy's *War and Peace*, meaning that all military wisdom and advice are contained in a single volume. In reality, British military doctrine is contained within numerous publications, which explain the specifics of a particular service, operational requirements, detailed logistics and tactics. The diversity of doctrinal publications is the outcome of a variety of military specializations and subsequent requirements of the relevant knowledge for day-to-day efficient performance. Depending on the needs of the target audience, doctrine has different contents, language and degrees of prescription. The diversity of doctrines is not chaotic. There is a certain hierarchy, which is based on the three levels of warfare: strategic, operational and tactical. The highest authority is at the strategic level, and publications of the next few levels should correspond to the general principles of the strategic level.

The substantial differences between doctrinal levels are the issues they address. A higher-level doctrine describes 'the philosophy and principles underpinning the approach to conflict and military activities'.[53] This type of doctrine generally explains the nature of military instruments and their efficient application in the evolving strategic environment. However, tactical-level manuals reveal the practices and procedures applicable in specific operations and particular theatres of warfare.[54] Subsequently, tactical manuals and procedures are larger, more detailed and concrete. The correlation between different levels of doctrine and tactical manuals refers to the connection between philosophy and procedures. Philosophy as an interdisciplinary, conceptual and descriptive matter aims at understanding. In this respect, principles are the key points of the philosophical thought on war. Just as war is enduring, so is its philosophy. As a result, the most continuous components of joint doctrines are the Principles of War. However, 'practices describe the ways in which activity is conducted. Procedures link practices together. Both are intended to be prescriptive'.[55] The prescriptive nature of tactical manuals and procedures is conditioned by the continuity of physical characteristics of possible and impossible actions. For instance, AP 3000 third edition outlined the universal principles of war and armed conflict, which are derived from centuries of experience. It also incorporated the manoeuvrist approach, which was introduced in joint doctrine and was detailed in subordinate publications, according to specific environmental requirements of the service. It also contained a modernized concept of air power for strategic effect.[56]

The best way to look at doctrine hierarchy is through the Army example. In the post–Cold War era before the final stages of joint reformation, British joint doctrine hierarchy consisted of capstone, keystone, functional, environmental, and thematic doctrines and tactical manuals. The top-level, capstone doctrine was British Defence Doctrine under the code of Joint Doctrine Publication (JDP) 0–01.[57] The essence of the publication was the description of defence philosophy, the correlation between national power, strategy and military capabilities, explaining the British way of warfare and its correspondence to the contemporary threats and use of military means as a response to those threats. It also emphasized the importance of a comprehensive approach to efficient accomplishment of new security tasks. This type of doctrine was closely connected with both political and strategic publications. Unlike subordinate doctrines, the joint capstone doctrine entwined with the National Security Strategy, Strategic Defence and Security Review, Defence White Papers and so on.[58] It set a tone for the subordinate doctrines to follow.

The next in the hierarchy was a joint keystone publication, *Campaigning* (JDP 01).[59] Its main function was to outline a framework for joint campaigning in terms of the comprehensive approach. It was 'based on enduring principles and good practice, updated to reflect recent experience, it provides guidance to JFC on contemporary military operations and how best to understand operational level challenges'.[60] At the operational level, the joint keystone publication was complemented by joint supporting publications, which were categorized as functional, thematic and environmental doctrines.

❖ Functional doctrines (J1–J9 categories) were intended to deal with the joint approach at the operational level. Each specific doctrine described a certain aspect of accomplishment task. For instance, functional doctrines described the importance of knowledge-based approach (JDP 2–00 *Understanding and Intelligence*[61]), principles of execution (JDP 3–00 *Campaign Execution*[62]), logistics (JDP 4–00 *Logistics for Joint Operations*[63]), planning (JDP 5–00 *Campaign Planning*[64]) and importance and use of communications and information systems (JDP 6–00[65]). JDP 3–00 paid separate attention to harmonization of joint operations within national tri-service and multinational Allied operations in the framework of military execution and further assessment.

❖ Thematic doctrines contextualized the functional doctrines for a specific operation or for contingency. For instance, JDP 3–40 *Security and Stabilisation: The Military Contribution*[66] brought the functional doctrine of Campaign Execution into the specific requirements of a thematic operation, in this case the security and stabilization type. Doctrine explains not only the means of operational execution but also their historical context and impact on the current strategic environment. Thus, the text of doctrine was divided into three chapters – the current context, an approach to stabilization and stabilization planning and campaign management.[67] Another example of this type of doctrine was JDP 3–50 *Military Contribution to Peace Support Operations*.[68]

❖ Environmental doctrines contextualized functional and thematic doctrine principles into distinctive environments: the maritime, land, air, space, information, cyberspace and electromagnetic environments.[69] Examples included BR 1806 *The Fundamentals of British Maritime Doctrine*[70] and AP 3000 *Air Power Doctrine*.[71]

❖ Tactical-level manuals further detailed practical implementation of the earlier-mentioned doctrines through prescription of the best ways of efficient accomplishing tasks and procedures efficiently. In the Army case, the lower-level doctrines are Army Field Manuals (AFMs), from which flow 'tactical doctrine notes, tactical aide memoire and handbooks, and standard operating procedures and instructions'.[72] One of the most prominent examples was Army Counterinsurgency (COIN) field manual Army Code 71876.[73]

Although this hierarchy seems to be exact and clear, its practical implementation over the last two decades had proved to be more complex. For example, different resources mean different things by environmental doctrine. The aforementioned definition of environmental doctrine was taken from the Army Doctrine Publication (ADP) *Operations*, which emphasized the following distinction between environmental and single-service doctrines: 'It describes doctrine within the context of the surroundings of conditions within which operations occur. This distinguishes environmental doctrine from single-service doctrine. However, a single-service's doctrine may be dominated by one environment in particular, so that service may take the lead – as it does with ADP Operations – to turn the result into its own capstone publication.'[74]

In other words, the main distinction between single-service and environ mental doctrines is that single-service doctrine concentrates on the activities of a single service, which might pay attention to the particular environment of its activity. However, ideally, environmental doctrine should concentrate on the environment itself and the activities of all three services within this particular environment. In other words, joint efforts within this environment. Theoretically, the distinction is exact; practically, the situation is rather complex. On the one hand, single-service doctrines concentrating on the particular environment of services' functionality existed and were revised accordingly. On the other hand, environmental doctrines that would reflect proportionate three-service, joint actions within each environment were scarce. Due to this, in the general doctrinal discourse, a single-service doctrine is sometimes referred to as an environmental one. This is the case with the studied AP 3000 editions. The third and fourth editions of AP 3000 *Air and Space Power Doctrine* were written under a single-service authorship of the RAF. It conveyed the RAF's vision of how air power could be used in strategic circumstances of the time.

From a practical perspective, there were two more reasons AP 3000 was referred to as environmental doctrine. First, as noted earlier, there was no three-service environmental doctrine until the publication of JDP 0–30 *UK Air and Space Doctrine*,[75] authored by the Development, Concepts and Doctrinal Centre (DCDC), and published on 17 July 2013. Second, according to practitioners and academics, despite single-service authorship and an emphasis on RAF role in air and space environments, the efforts during doctrine writing were three-service and joint.[76] The two other services were consulted about their views on the use of air power and its functionality. This was illustrated in chapters on joint operations within AP 3000 editions.[77] Although there are different sides to this argument, for the purpose of this book, the AP 3000 editions are treated as environmental doctrines, which is a generally accepted practice of the last two decades.

From a multinational perspective, national doctrines should correspond to the Allied NATO doctrine. This subordination is achieved by introducing an umbrella joint publication – Allied Joint Publication (AJP) – 01 (D) *Allied Joint Doctrine*, which is a capstone doctrine for Allied joint operations:

> Commonly accepted and allied doctrine is necessary for effective coalition building. A common NATO doctrine is essential to enhance interoperability, both at the intellectual level, allowing commanders from different nations to have a common approach to operations, and at the procedural level (so that, for example, land forces from one nation can request and direct air support from another).[78]

However, when certain aspects of doctrine differ from AJP – 01 (D), then national doctrines 'remain the authoritative source of doctrine for UK Operational level commanders'.[79] Apart from sharing common doctrinal specifics with NATO, the Ministry of Defence (MOD) emphasized the importance of framework doctrinal correspondence for efficient implementation of American, British, Canadian, Australian and New Zealand Armies (ABCA) programme, which aimed 'to improve current and future interoperability, mutual understanding and commonality of doctrine and concepts, in support of coalition operations'.[80]

Thus, doctrine can also be a means for improvement and harmonization of coalition activities.

Debates on doctrine

The phenomenon of doctrine is quite complex, and its efficiency depends on the situational characteristics of its writing, teaching and application. Depending on the combination of factors affecting doctrine and changes in the military environment of its introduction, doctrine might have diverse effects. Thus, it can cause various disputes on its purpose and application. The most common controversies over doctrine refer to concern bias in its writing, its form and its application: dogma versus creative thinking, asset versus liability, brief versus long, detailed versus accessible, written versus tacit, static versus dynamic.

Dogma vs. creative thinking

As explained previously, doctrine is not the same as dogma. It is not intended to create a rigid mind. However, its very aim of presenting a unified perception of best practice, the principles of warfare and the national way in warfare, caused multiple debates. Both military practitioners and academics explored whether doctrine was boosting creativity or unified organizational thinking. As stated earlier, Colin McInnes suggested that doctrine tied military doctrine with the national way of warfare. He argued that as an envelope for the British way of warfare, doctrine contributed to rigidity of mind and concentration on past rather than present and future operations.[81] He considered that the very recommendation of certain principles was prescriptive by nature, since there were no alternative options.[82] Andrew Methven concluded that the dominance of the managerial approach in national culture causes dogmatization of doctrine and a shift of its functionality towards bureaucratic purposes.[83]

Colin Gray suggested that while strategic theory aimed at creation of intellectual structure for rational and justified decision-making in the military field, 'doctrine states beliefs'.[84] He opposed the official perception of doctrine as a guide on how to think and not what to think. He argued that doctrines of various levels were about what to think, and therefore what to do. The rationale of his conclusion was revealed in the following statement: 'Military organisations have to develop and employ doctrine – whether written, or culturally transmitted orally or by example – if they are to train large numbers of people with equipment in sufficiently standard modes of behaviour for them to be predictable instruments of the commander's will.'[85] In this case, Colin Gray viewed doctrine from an institutional perspective, suggesting that it reflected the Armed Forces' desire for and, in fact, the vital necessity of unifying personnel's thinking, providing them with an equal amount of knowledge and subsequent development of skills. Colin Gray was entirely correct in suggesting that doctrine was about providing equal training and incorporating newcomers into the national approach to warfare. He was also right in suggesting that military personnel should be predictable and follow the orders of their commanders. After all, the Armed Forces are about subordination and following orders.

However, the crucial element of the British approach is mission command. In this context, 'the fundamental guiding principle is the absolute responsibility to act or, in certain circumstances, to decide not to act, within the framework of a superior commander's intent. This approach requires a style of command that promotes decentralised command, freedom and speed of actions and initiative, but which is responsive to superior directions when a subordinate overreaches himself.'[86] It may seem that mission command contradicts Colin Gray's definition of doctrine's functionality. On the contrary, this concept aligns with his stance. Doctrine functions as a means of teaching the basics and making sure a lower-level subordinate knows how to use this basic knowledge. However, since the most characteristic feature of warfare is uncertainty, it is vital for subordinates to know the intent of the commander, the expected outcome and that their creative and adaptive approach according to circumstances will not be punished afterwards. Doctrine provides both informal knowledge and scope for creativity and flexibility – mission command.

Approaching the question from a different angle, doctrine teaches both how and what to think. At the initial level, an individual learns the basics for a certain behaviour under known circumstances with little uncertainty. So, Colin Gray stressed that doctrine contributed to standardization of group behaviour to accomplish a task effectively. However, based on the initially acquired knowledge and mode of thinking/acting, one applies 'how knowledge' to circumstances that were not envisaged by a doctrine or a specific principle. Thus, one would act according to the circumstances, but within the learned experience of doctrine teaching as a guiding light rather than the Bible. Accordingly, each decision and action can be judged only within each situation and individual outcome. In the doctrinal discourse, the aforementioned dilemma can be summarized by the phrase, 'thinking outside the box', meaning 'thinking in an original and creative way'.[87] In terms of an institutional perspective, Colin Gray suggested that doctrine was, in fact, an empty box which military institutions filled with whatever was required for their subordinates to know: 'doctrine *per se* is a box empty of content until organisations decide how much of it they want, and how constraining they wish it to be.'[88] However, Neville Parton argued that in order to think 'out of the box' one should realize that the box exists to think outside.[89]

Another aspect to be considered is the existence of informal doctrine, which is a specific 'know-how' passed from one military generation to another at levels as small as squadrons or interpersonal contacts. Barry Watts writes, 'because no one goes to war with a blank mind – with John Locke's *tabula rasa* ("blank slate") – informal doctrine is inescapable.'[90] In this case, the practical experience details the knowledge taught by the formal doctrine. Subsequently, this knowledge is brushed further by individual judgements in a particular situation. Inevitably, the knowledge of previous generations is passed to the new ones. The formal doctrine complements the individuals' personal experience and informal operational know-how with the official practice and principles of behaviour. Due to its adaptability and development, each doctrine is a box of different characteristics. With each new edition of a particular doctrine, new ideas are incorporated according to changes in the surrounding environment. If doctrine is changed in due time, it provides a sufficient box to store knowledge for a time before the next one is published. Accordingly, if doctrine updated in alignment with changes in strategic realities, that is, if it keeps up to date, then doctrine contributes to the expansion of the existing box with each new edition. The revision of the box, according to the requirements of the time, also demonstrates what set of skills and the depth of knowledge the personnel should have.

Asset vs. liability

Despite personal preferences or background, sceptical or favourable attitude towards doctrine in one way or another, doctrine says something about the Armed Forces and how they go about their business. As was mentioned earlier, doctrine might not be used. Its influence might be limited. However, it still serves as the Armed Forces' means of communication with various audiences, including potential adversaries. Despite the official position that doctrine serves as a means of deterring potential enemies, some scholars argue that doctrine can become a threat to national security because it could expose the practical aspects and ways of conducting warfare. Thus, it can be used as intelligence and be an asset to an enemy. Doctrine is viewed in terms of its military purpose, as a means of bringing military personnel to a common ground. Doctrine contains the national ways of transforming military theory into potential practice. Although it does not prescribe specific actions and case-sensitive details of operations, it can be used to understand the way of thinking of the national Armed Forces. If so, it might help in predicting their future actions.

Addressing this, Colin Gray analyses a paper by a former head of the military intelligence for the Israel Defence Forces, Yehoshavet Harkabi, who argued: 'Doctrine cannot be kept secret, for doctrines are means to socialisation of an army, especially since complying with their precepts is by definition repetitious. Doctrine would thus serve to divulge the commander's plan to the enemy, much as an enemy intelligence agent would. Doctrine may also impoverish thinking and creativity by diverting attention from alternative courses of action.'[91] The focal point in this argument is the predictability of actions, which is derived from repetition and dogmatization. However, dogmatization and repetitiveness can be avoided by timely revision of doctrine and incorporation of required changes. Thus, under the conditions of constant updates, the wider overview and creativity in application would be inevitable.

Nevertheless, although Colin Gray agrees with Harkabi, he argues that the main reason doctrines are not 'fuel for failure'[92] is due to the human factor, meaning a reluctance of commanders to follow doctrine that they consider to be irrelevant or simply do not agree with.[93] In this context, doctrine may be ignored for a number of reasons. First, it might represent ideas and certain principles of policy that do not reflect existing practice at the tactical level. In other words, there is a difference between strategic doctrines and tactical manuals in their very essence and purpose. Second, the doctrine might not have yet been incorporated into existing practice. Finally, the circumstances may require a different action than doctrine had envisioned. This returns us to the point that doctrine should not be prescriptive or dogmatic in its nature, leaving enough space for flexibility and adaptability of actions and correspondence of these actions to the situational requirements. In this context, doctrine can be altered in the battlefield.

Apart from the aforementioned pros and cons, there is another perspective to consider within this debate. It was mentioned in the section referring to doctrine hierarchy that there are different levels of doctrine, and each level has a different degree of openness. The more joint and general the doctrine is, the more widely spread and open it is. On the contrary, the closer the doctrine is to the ground and tactical level, the more classified it becomes. Tactical-level manuals are classified and accessible only by the personnel of the Armed Forces. Therefore, adversaries cannot predict specific operational and tactical manoeuvres from the doctrines that are available to a wider audience. Joint, strategic, operational and environmental doctrines do not contain such information. Peter Gray explains this phenomenon in the following way:

> When doctrine transcends the barrier between the general and the fundamental principle into the realm of technology, tactics and procedures, the reach of damages is correspondingly greater and the material is classified accordingly. Supplementary to that, the more the high-level doctrine has been influenced by network production, when they have according input, the more likely it is that they had been published and the thinking was exposed to wider audiences. Arguably, it is in a field of official histories when academic authors have had an access to privileged information, that there is any sensitivity at all. The same may be said about academic work that has been published by authors who had been influential in the field of policy formation and from this work are more aware explicitly or intuitively of which areas are the most sensitive.[94]

Formal written vs. informal know-how

Another controversy about doctrine is its form. The main point of discussion is not doctrine *per se*, but two different approaches to learning in the Armed Forces. From an institutional perspective, personnel need to learn how to do business through training courses. In this case, a formal doctrine serves as means of transferring the distilled wisdom of practitioners through an institutional lens. On the contrary, military personnel can also learn from their superiors, who have practical knowledge that often might not be reflected in various formal documents and teaching curricula. In other words, the form of doctrine depends on the interaction between various levels in the command structure. Historically, the most common form of doctrine in the British Armed Forces was usually oral. Best practice was communicated within the regiment or squadron. Written guiding documents in the form of tactical-level manuals standard operational procedures (SOPs) were published only when a situation or environment required such publications. To an extent, these different approaches to the form of doctrine, tactical manuals and learning explain the development of different types of culture. Formal doctrine helps in establishing distinctive organizational culture within a single service, while the practical knowledge of superiors contributes to the development of sub-service cultures within each regiment or squadron. This way of knowledge transfer was influenced by various factors particular to each service. For instance, in the Army, the existence of 'verbal doctrine' was conditioned by the practical existence of two armies. There was the Continental Army with conventional tasks of Cold War deterrence and potential war fighting in Europe. There was the specialized Army, which concentrated on expeditionary, low-intensity and COIN operations in the colonies.[95] Thus, the lack of a unified doctrinal framework for actions was due to the different functions and subsequent requirements laid upon each army within their traditional operational expertise. Thus, each army was likely to develop its own wisdom and best practice of task accomplishment.

In the case of the Royal Navy, excessive prescriptions were considered counter productive. Historically and culturally, the ideal standard of organizational performance was Admiral Nelson's mission command approach to the command structure. The 'Nelson effect' was in the supremacy of charismatic leadership, which Nelson exercised so effectively that his subordinates knew exactly what was expected from them. They were capable of independent and efficient performance without detailed directions on task accomplishment.[96] So, Markus Mäder argued that organizational culture of the Royal Navy was characterized by 'widespread aversion against written doctrine'.[97] It does not mean that the Navy did not have the experience of written doctrines and tactical manuals. Various procedures and tactical manuals of naval warfare were numerous. The missing element was a strategic-level doctrine that would conceptually frame the service's performance. From a perspective of naval commanders, the introduction of a doctrine would result in additional prescription of the suggested concept. It was even considered dangerous for the Admiralty to be bound by a certain framework.[98] On this specific issue, Eric Grove stated that higher strategic-level doctrine was not supported, because it could endanger two primary principles of the maritime environment: flexibility and freedom of action, which were incorporated into a decentralized approach to command and control of the Royal Navy.[99]

Finally, in the RAF, written doctrine was opposed for three reasons. First, the very nature of the service required prescribed behaviour and subordination in the air. Additional documents restating what was practised on an everyday basis, with some variation from squadron to squadron, was again viewed as bureaucratic redundancy.[100] The second reason for opposition to formal/written doctrine was the 'complex of the junior service',[101] which has developed throughout the history of the RAF. Accordingly, the reintroduction of written doctrine could be considered as an attempt to diminish the freedom of the RAF and fit it into a narrow theoretical framework.[102] The final reason was the previous negative experience with written doctrine of 1957, which was published during an interservice competition for a nuclear deterrence role.[103] Written doctrine was also associated with the subordination of the RAF to the Royal Navy.

After almost three decades of written doctrine, the contemporary British militaries and academics still discuss the purposes and utility of doctrine. However, the emphasis of these debates has changed. In the first post–Cold War decade, the question was whether written doctrine is needed and whether it is productive or counterproductive for services' operational performance and organizational development.[104] However, in the next two decades, the essence of debates was the functionality of existing doctrines. The main points of controversy were: do single-service doctrines contribute to general jointery or are counterproductive in its establishment?[105] Should single-service strategic level doctrines be written by a single-service or joint authorship, meaning the DCDC?[106] Does the establishment of jointery mean potential redundancy of single-services' impact on their conceptual component and subsequent importance of independent services? To what extent does doctrine emphasize a service's identity, efficiency and overall contribution to joint operations?[107]

Short vs. long/detailed vs. general

One of the crucial debates on doctrine *per se* refers to the efficiency of its content and language in reaching the target audience. As was mentioned earlier, the target audience is the personnel of the Armed Forces. One of the main problems in teaching military personnel is that people come to the Armed Forces from different backgrounds, and go to different services, which have their own ways of doing business. Afterwards they proceed with different careers within these services or approach a joint path. Under such conditions, doctrine has to accommodate all these differences and achieve a common outcome – basic knowledge for all. Doctrine writers have to balance between a brief but too general doctrine and a long but too detailed one, in order for the personnel to get the most from what they have. The brief versus long discourse is complicated by the struggle between intellectuals and tacticians within each service. Since the aim of this research is to explore RAF doctrine, it is logical to concentrate on the RAF example of this struggle.

The history of RAF doctrine is discussed in the next chapter. However, it is worth mentioning here that complex history of the service resulted in the formation of two schools of thought and distinctive approaches to air power. Intellectuals encouraged creative thinking on air power and thus suggested wider education for RAF personnel. On the contrary, the tacticians with pilot background argued that training courses should be more practical and tactics oriented. Practitioners argued that over-excessive intellectualism distracted from the main aim of training courses – teaching air power skills. Philip Sabin argues that 'this was attributed primarily to the more highly technological nature of the Service ... the skills needed to perform missions and other tasks at the tactical level were seen as more distinct from the demands of operational and strategic warfighting than was the case in the Army'.[108] In terms of doctrine, the intellectual approach argued for more depth and systematic evaluation of air power. Doctrines were usually longer and concentrated on cooperation with other services and the adaptation to the changes in the strategic environment. In other words, the intellectual approach to doctrine writing aimed at not only teaching ways of using air power but also an understanding of its implications and connections with wider strategic objectives and political considerations.[109] Thus, the intellectual approach advocated diversification of the basic knowledge taught and application of a systematic approach to air power.

Practitioners suggested that doctrine had to be less intellectual and easy to understand. However, it was not meant to be a manual of tactical procedures either. The main concern was the diverse audience that had to digest information within a short period. Thus, practitioners argued that a long, over-intellectual document was redundant. It could not reach the audience and they had no time to spend on its prolonged study. Since proponents of both approaches still exist within the service, preparation of each doctrine document went through this debate. In each doctrine, dominance of one or the other argument can be traced.

It may seem that an institution decides what it wants its new personnel to know. However, the knowledge integrity is not at stake, but the efficiency of unified training. In this context, training provides a general, uniform basis for future members of the Armed Forces. Chris Finn suggested that people coming to the RAF College Cranwell differ in their background, age, career goals and physical training.[110] Therefore, the nine-month programme might be easy for one category of students, but more challenging for others. However, the result is the same – the preparation of the future members of various branches of the RAF. Documents like doctrine should be precise and short, in order to achieve common ground and transfer basic knowledge of the service.[111] In this case, they can reach the audience and be accepted by individuals with different backgrounds. However, the challenge lies in finding the middle ground between detailed contents and accessibility. Either this is resolved on a case-to-case basis or one is sacrificed for the sake of the other. The implications of this struggle will be shown in the analysed case studies.

Static vs. dynamic

Finally, there is a question of the tempo of doctrine's adaptability to the requirements of a new strategic environment. It is often disputed whether doctrine is static or dynamic in its nature. Subsequently, there are two views: doctrine contributes to the institutionalization of traditions or it is one of the driving forces of modernizing everyday military performance. One line of argument is that doctrine becomes irrelevant the moment it is published, mainly because it represents the reality of the last few years and not the immediate requirement of the day.[112] This view is informed by the time required for initiation of a new doctrine writing, preparation of the draft, publication, dissemination and final introduction of the document into military practice in terms of both training and use in combat. Accordingly, although doctrine might reflect the strategic reality of the time when it was initiated, it might be outdated by the time it is read and applied.

As a response to this idea, it should be first mentioned that various levels of doctrine were revised in different time frames. Joint doctrines were more directly connected with policies and more frequently changed according to shifts in priorities of foreign and defence policies. They are more likely to change every five to six years.[113] However, tactical-level manuals were directly influenced by technologies and best practice of the previous campaigns, which were incorporated into new manuals depending on the experiences. Another aspect of this argument is that any kind of doctrine is not the same as a political manifesto. It cannot be written, published and disseminated in a week. Doctrine publication has a consequential impact on the military field. It is aimed at not only informing a commander, but also teaching further levels of command. It should also be incorporated into educational programmes. Accordingly, for a doctrine to be recognized and used time is required. From a sceptical perspective, since doctrine cannot provide immediate reflection of the recent and ongoing operations, then it is useless and thus fails. However, doctrine is not about description of what is happening in the field of ongoing operations. It is about updating the existing knowledge on the subject in the context of the new strategic environment and identified lessons of the recent operations.

Within this debate, doctrine fits in between the static and dynamic. It is not static because it is not written once for good, because the nature of war is enduring, while its character changes together with the technologies. However, it is not inherently dynamic. It may remain outdated and even counterproductive,[114] if it is not revised according to the new experiences and changes in the strategic environment. Professor Richard Overy argued that 'doctrine tends to solidify like a slowly moving lava flow'.[115] Thus, for doctrine not to become a dogma, it should be revised and modified according to changes in the strategic and political environments.[116] Overy's historical analysis of doctrine shows that the development and application of doctrine are influenced by five factors. First, wide politics are usually the main reason for a doctrine not to work properly, since strategic objectives and priorities change faster than doctrine. However, there is also an issue of interservice relations, which is usually more complicated than the general politics. Second, doctrine cannot remain the same and relevant, due to technological changes, which became decisive in modern warfare.[117]

Third, effective doctrine requires lessons of experience, which are derived from past events. In this context, the main danger is that experience requires a certain mindset, which corresponds to the specifics of a single situation in the past. Thus, teaching and passing on these experiences become extremely difficult without a context. Fourth, doctrine should be modified and reviewed when the need arises. It should be reviewed only when the military environment and technology change, but not because the time of the next review has arrived. Finally, Overy outlined that there is the 'eccentricity factor', meaning the presence of abnormal individuals in the sense of intelligence and strategic thinking, who are beyond the normality of the doctrinal level.[118]

A wider perspective of doctrinal functionality

At the end of the Cold War, many aspects of military performance and functions were fixed in stone. Substantial changes were required and were on the way after 1991. In terms of military doctrine, the lack of continuous doctrine publications was due to the constancy of the Cold War strategic environment. With the end of the Cold War era, doctrine became a necessity for services' transformation and adaptation to rapid changes. Doctrine was crucial because there was no longer a contingency of the Cold War. Moreover, doctrine was a response to the problem of uncertainty. The end of the bipolar world created an environment of unpredictability and uncertainty about potential adversaries, and unconventional conflicts. Under these conditions, the return to doctrine can be viewed as a means of services' adaptation to these changes. The main role of the first post–Cold War doctrines was not the usual adaptation of best practice and learning the lessons of the previous operations. The functional aim of these documents was to equip the services with means to deal with unpredictability. At a time when policy was still quite uncertain and vague, doctrine had to inform personnel of the vital questions of where and how to fight. Thus, the doctrine was meant as a vision of service's future roles and place in a new world order, which was still establishing. Over the last three decades, doctrine has had to deal with the intensification of media and public involvement in military sphere, caused by improvement in media technologies and social networks. From a sociopolitical perspective, doctrine became a certain facilitator of the Armed Forces into society. The necessity of explanation and incorporation into society was due to the assumed pacification of international relations and hopes for peace dividend, conditioned by the end of the Cold War and normalization of relations in Europe. The lack of a direct threat from nearby or from a state like the Soviet Union was a convincing evidence that Cold War military structures had to be reduced.

Although the transformation of the Armed Forces was inevitable, social pacification reached extreme levels, resulting in the phenomenon of 'marginalisation of Western military culture in their host societies'.[119] In this context, the public perception of the Armed Forces' importance diminished due to the shift from generalization to personalization of war.[120] In other words, public opinion became more interested in the human side of warfare. Seeing war in terms of tragedies of individual people resulted in a desire to make war bloodless and more civilized instead of a means for achieving political objectives. The inconsistency between the public idealized perception of war and the continuing, unchanging, bloody nature of war put additional pressure on the Armed Forces in terms of 'the CNN effect'.[121] In the light of the postmodern public perception of militaries, the Armed Forces needed to explain themselves better and make the public understand what they dealt with in the battlefield and in which operations they were involved. Joint, single-service and some operational doctrines kept the necessity of this dialogue in mind.

The potential disadvantage of such a tendency would be the substitution of the primary audience with the secondary and transformation of doctrine into a sociopolitical document rather than the guidance for military personnel. Tony Mason argued that the functionality of doctrine has not changed, but rather its significance has increased due to diminishing resources, existential threats, post–Cold War reorganization and the fact that 'we fight wars away from home'.[122] Moreover, he argued: 'All these factors increase doctrine's importance as socio-political phenomenon, but I would not say that doctrine loses its primary functionality. Doctrine provides the cohesion, determines the practices in which the operations take place. It provides an intellectual framework, it does not exist in isolation, and it is not static, so it does not become simply a socio-political document.'[123]

Conclusion

Overall, this chapter has explained what military doctrine is and where it fits in the practice of the Armed Forces. Doctrine is a multipurpose official document, which has substantial internal or external functionality, depending on the changes in the environment of its creation. Doctrine can be more directed towards serving personnel, or wider stakeholders, depending on what the issuing body requires. It can be used exclusively for teaching the principles of the service or as an explanation of the national way of warfare. Doctrine can be abused and become a dogma, or it can be timely revised and stimulate systematic learning and training of personnel for the changing character of war.

Doctrine can be written with the intention of boosting creativity and systematic learning or it can stop at teaching general basics in order to achieve a unified level of knowledge. Thus, it can be long and complex or brief and simple in substance. Doctrine can be an asset if it contains the right information for the right audience, or it can become a danger if the rules of classified information are not followed. Doctrine can exist in various forms, and can be spread in horizontal or vertical ways, incorporated into training courses or become a condition for further career development. All those aspects depend mainly on who prepared a doctrine, for which purpose and under which situational restraints. In other words, the characteristics of a particular type of doctrine can be understood through the process of its writing.

It is not enough to explore the doctrine preparation process alone, to understand the success or failure of doctrine. The understanding of why some doctrines are accepted within the services, while others are ignored can be achieved through the exploration of the prevailing organizational culture within a studied service. Each service has its own traditions, unwritten modes of behaviour and characteristic perceptions, which originate in services' history. The role of doctrine in the organization's history should be examined, in order to understand the organizational perception of doctrine. The next chapter is devoted to the history of RAF doctrine.

2

The Historical Context

In the contemporary world of advanced technologies, digitization of information and spreading of cyberspace into every aspect of human life, it is easy to forget the knowledge of the previous generations and the lessons they have to teach. Each culture values the lessons of the past, suggesting they provide some clues to understanding contemporaneity. Confucius said, 'Study the past if you would define the future.' A few millennia later, another man who shaped the future of the Western world clarified this idea: 'The farther backward you can look, the farther forward you are likely to see.'[1] Learning from the past may seem an easy and logical idea. However, in the age of overabundance of information about today and predictions about tomorrow, it is easy to disregard the lessons of the past. While in personal decision-making, the consequences might be undesirable, in warfare disregarding the past can have disastrous implications. Thus, the author of this book is a strong believer in the importance of history for understanding where we are right now, why we are here and where we are going. This chapter describes the development of RAF air power doctrine through the entire history of the service. Attention is paid to doctrinal manuals, the historical context of publications, situational functionality and subsequent implications for the service. This historical discourse should help in understanding the role of doctrine in RAF history and its reforming in the post–Cold War era. This chapter also demonstrates how doctrine might be misused and become a dogma. Eventually, this account should assist in understanding the contemporary scepticism towards doctrine *per se* within the service and the difficulty of its revival in the post–Cold War period.

Preconditions of the first RAF doctrine

The history of the RAF as an independent service should be explored in order to understand how a service could exist without a founding guiding document for four years. In the beginning of the First World War, air power was young and was hardly recognized as a crucial military capability. In the UK, the first official aeroplane flight was conducted by an American, Samuel Franklin Cody, on 16th of October 1908, and entered history as British Army Aeroplane No 1.[2] Neither the War Office nor the Treasury viewed air power as a crucial military capability. No centralized actions were taken to incorporate its potential. The old Balloon Section of the Army was expanded into an Air Battalion in 1911. The next year, in 1912, the importance of aviation was realized, and the Royal Flying Corps was created on 13th of March 1912.[3] The lack of conceptual and practical knowledge on the potential of air power and budgetary considerations resulted in the introduction of supplementary units into two traditional services – the Army and the Navy. The pre-war government endeavoured to create a centralized institution of the Royal Flying Corps (RFC) with separate Naval and Military Wings.[4] However, the war experience resulted in a complete separation of the two wings: the Royal Naval Air Service (RNAS) was subordinate to the Admiralty, while the Army Wing became the RFC, subordinate to the War Office.[5] This differentiation accounts not only for the supplementary status of both wings, but also for them being assigned entirely different roles. The main purpose of the RFC was to assist in expeditionary missions: 'The Military Wing concentrated on building a reconnaissance force to work closely with the Army, and on convincing the Army staff that the aeroplane could get accurate and quick information to the land commander – not an easy task when the Cavalry still dominated the War Office.'[6]

The main function of air power was limited to reconnaissance. The very ability to observe panoramas of the battlefields, the location of troops, railroads and supply stores made aeroplanes the main source of the most up-to-date information.[7] A further function of aeroplanes was in spotting for artillery. The Naval Wing took a different direction – the air offensive, and, consequently, long-range bombers were developed. The practical application of the air offensive was demonstrated in the Battle of the Somme in July 1916.[8] Just as the reconnaissance function of air power was developed in practical cooperation with the Army, so was the offensive in terms of practical consideration of the Admiralty: 'Thinking in terms of the offensive use of military aircraft as long-range bombers, especially against the Zeppelin bases, since the Navy's own dockyards and arsenals at Chatham and Portsmouth appeared to be open invitations to Zeppelin raids should war break out with Germany.'[9]

Therefore, this division resulted in concentration of the RFC on land warfare while the RNAS cooperated with allies in expanding pre-emptive strikes on enemy aircraft and 'the long-range bombardment of enemy resources'.[10] The Air Force remained divided throughout the war. The status of a proto-service meant the lack of resources and subsequent constant possibility of a wing being cut back or even abolished. It was also unpopular because of the high rate of human losses among the RFC.[11] There was also a debate about what should be prioritized, homeland defence or long-range attack. The head of the RFC, Major General Sir Hugh Trenchard, regarded the Admiralty's focus on long-range attack as likely to drain resources from the RFC, and thus opposed it.[12] Accordingly, without consulting the RFC, the RNAS worked with the French on common long-range bombing operations. As a result of this interservice friction, RNAS' No. 3 Naval Wing, responsible for long-range bombing operation, was abolished.[13]

The First World War is an example of how the situational requirements of war boosted adaptability, development of technologies and unconventional use of air power. Apart from air reconnaissance, stimulating the development of communication technologies[14] and air offensive boosting the evolution of bomber aircraft, further improvement of technologies and new roles of air power were stimulated by operational experiences. The initiative of reconnaissance planes to strafe trenches during the Battle of the Somme introduced ideas for Close Air Support (CAS) and a need for a ground-attack aircraft.[15] Further on, the Battlefield Air Interdiction (BAI) as 'ground strafing missions' was practised on the Western Front.[16] BAI also proved to be decisive in the air campaign against Turkish forces in Palestine.[17] Consequently, apart from air superiority achieved on the Western Front,

> Several other doctrinal air power roles had been established during this bitter conflict including Counter Air (both defensive and offensive), Close Air Support, Air Interdiction, Tactical Reconnaissance, Photographic Reconnaissance, Maritime Patrol and Air Supply. Supporting roles had also been developed that included Air Command and Control, Intelligence, Tactical Communication, Engineering Support and Logistics.[18]

Thus, the First World War was a starting point for the development of air power in both technological and conceptual frameworks. During this war, tactics constantly changed and adapted to the technological modifications of aircraft.[19] Tactical manuals could change on a monthly basis.[20] From an institutional perspective, the potential of air power was recognized after the Gotha Raids of 1917. It prompted the transformation of British air power. The conclusion of the two Smuts reports on 17th and 19th of August 1917, praised the efficiency of air power as a new military force that provided the government with the ground for an immediate reforming of air structure and the establishment of a single service, the RAF.[21] The legal framework of the initiative was the Air Force Constitution Act, which was passed in November 1917, followed by composition of the Air Council in January 1918 and subsequent formation of the independent RAF in April 1918.[22] Hugh Trenchard was appointed the first Chief of the Air Staff (CAS).

Once independent, the RAF had to establish itself in the national defence. However, the next twenty years were characterized by 'the fight for survival against the government economy cuts and the desires of the other 2 Services to see their air arms returned to them; this conflict reached its climax in 1923'.[23] Only two years after its creation, the service suffered tremendous cuts of personnel and the dismantling of some of its units, such as the Women's RAF and the RAF Nursing Service: 'More than 23,000 officers, 21,000 cadets (potential pilots) and 227,000 other ranks had been demobilized.'[24] The next three years 1920–1923 were characterized by paper wars in ministries, where each service justified its existence and role in British defence. It was precisely the time when the first RAF doctrine was published.

The first RAF doctrine

The first RAF formal doctrine was Confidential Document (CD) 22 under the official title of *Operations Manual, Royal Air Force*.[25] According to Neville Parton, the document was 'well under way by mid-1921'.[26] Diverse senior officers took part in writing process. However, the authorship is attributed primarily to two junior officers: Flight Lieutenant C.J Mackay and Squadron Leader E.L. Tomkinson.[27] They both worked within the Directorate for Operations and Intelligence. The divided nature of the service and its day-to-day cooperation with the other two services were reflected in doctrine writing and division of duties between the authors. Tomkinson was responsible for the Navy section, while Mackay wrote the rest.[28] This feature of doctrine writing confirmed the divided nature of the RAF and its junior status. Accordingly, the acceptance of common principles and tactical procedures of cooperation required the approval of the other services. For instance, the Navy insisted on keeping the document classified, while the Army agreed mainly on 'the tactical level issues, in terms of strategical and operational level considerations, it is evident that there was considerable disagreement over whether there should be separate Air Force'.[29] Thus, from the very beginning the document was doomed to reflect interservice rivalry. CD 22 was meant to unify and re-establish the main principles of services' actions and training of their personnel. Instead, CD 22 exacerbated divisions within the service and illustrated its inferior position to the other two services. On the one hand, the document was truly historical and reflected the reality of its time. On the other hand, it was not very efficient as a doctrine because of its initial political purpose and targeting political decision-makers instead of military personnel. These considerations are explained in the further analysis of the text.

As already mentioned, doctrine writing was characterized by the need to influence opinion and to obtain the agreement with the other two services. The structure of the document confirms this. Some chapters referred to the practical training of RAF personnel, like quarters, orders and reports in the field, aerial operations and aerial fighting. However, most of the document was devoted to the division of roles between the three services, emphasising the importance of the Navy. The document was distinctive because it outlined the independent role of air power in counterinsurgency and peacekeeping operations. The successful use of air power in British Somaliland and further in Iraq and Transjordan was analysed in the brief final chapter of the document, *Aircraft in Warfare against an Uncivilised Enemy*.[30]

At first glance, CD 22 emphasized cooperation with the other two services. For instance, the support of tanks or cooperation with the Navy. Conversely, the independent and unique environmental nature of air power was defined in indirect statements. For instance, the third paragraph of the introduction stated: 'The independence necessitated by aerial warfare tends ever to increase the responsibility of subordinates.'[31] This is a good example of the gradual attempt to distinguish air power and airspace from the other two environments. Reading between the lines, the document suggests that, although the new service had been established and it was independent in its status, practically, it had to show that it was capable and eager to work with the other two services. Such caution in wording and emphasis on cooperation were essential in order for CD 22 to be approved. That is why it is not surprising that CD 22 relied heavily upon publications of the two other services: the British Army's Field Services Regulation and Royal Navy Confidential Air Orders. Only three out of eleven chapters were written by the RAF.[32] Thus, as the first doctrine of an independent service, it failed to show the independence and distinctive functionality of the service. For instance, even in the last chapter, which justified a new role for air power in establishing the imperial policy of preserving order in the overseas territories, the wording was cautious: 'The role of aircraft in operations of this nature will be a major one, though it is unlikely that they will be in a position to undertake a campaign entirely independent of military assistance.'[33]

It may seem that the main role of doctrine is to serve as a guide for training courses. Thus, it should not justify the service's independence or have any other political purpose in an interservice discourse. However, this doctrine had more holistic purposes. Like a contemporary doctrine, it targeted two audiences: RAF personnel and a wider audience. In regard to the primary audience, this document was intended to unify the divided personnel of the service, showing that the RAF could cooperate with the other two services and still preserve its independence and uniqueness. For the secondary audience of the other two services and political decision-makers, the doctrine had to demonstrate the eagerness of the service to cooperate in a united interservice environment, while expressing its distinctive potential in contrast to them. At that time, air power could deliver what no other service was capable of – the outreach of strategic bombing. Thus, from a political perspective, doctrine was more useful in interservice struggle than in teaching serving personnel. Doctrine achieved two substantial goals at the time. First, although the general discourse of the document did not express the independent role of the service and proclaimed cooperation with the other two services, it was published. Thus, the first official conceptual framework of an independent RAF saw daylight. Second, although it was classified, it succeeded in proclaiming the RAF-centred concept of strategic bombing, which would work as a justification of the service's existence and expansion in the next sixteen years. The document materialized and further indoctrinated this concept within the service.

Conceptual perspective of the time and its reflection in CD 22

The introduction of an independent single service was not only about the merging of two branches from within two sister services, but also about establishment of a service with a distinct philosophy, role and purpose. It required a unique conceptual framework for its existence. In his report, Smuts paved the way for the conceptualization of independent air power and future RAF doctrine:

> There is absolutely no limit to the scale of its future independent war use. And the day might not be far off when aerial operations with their devastation of enemy lands and destruction of industries and populous centres on a vast scale may become one of the principal operations of war, to which the older forms of military and naval operations may become secondary and subordinate.[34]

Clearly, the elder services could not accept this. A more detailed and fresh concept was required in order to establish the RAF as a self-sustained service. As the first CAS, Hugh Trenchard was the person to establish such a core concept and to make sure it was followed within the service. The functional approach of Hugh Trenchard as applied to the service's conceptual framework can be demonstrated by the change of his attitude to this concept with time. At first, he opposed the concept of strategic bombing when the RNAS initially developed it, because it was counterproductive for the force under his command. However, for the new service, a concept suggesting a unique role could unify it, provide required funding and secure its survival. On the other hand, Trenchard's change of heart to this concept was also conditioned by practical technological reasons. He initially opposed the concept of strategic bombing because it was highly ineffective at the time technologically and had a high cost in human lives. Later on, he concentrated on the offensive because his pilots could not climb quickly enough to intercept the adversary. Moreover, further dogmatization of the concept in the years to come can be associated with the inability of this concept to keep up with the development of technologies in the 1930s, including monoplane fighters and radar.

Trenchard's approach to air power and what was later called the 'Trenchard doctrine' concentrated on the sociopolitical implications of strategic bombing rather than on its destructive impact on the enemy's industrial infrastructure and military targets.[35] He argued that the main purpose of air power was to destroy the enemy's 'morale' and willingness to fight. No distinction was made between moral and industrial targets but a preference for the former was emphasized. Bombing the adversary's territory aimed at destroying his will to fight.[36] The main task for the RAF in the interwar years was to decide how air power should be used to its optimum effect. The main argument within the service was whether air power should concentrate on the development of offensive or defensive capacity. Trenchard was the CAS, had most of the authority within the service and was known to be quite a strict and charismatic person. In decision-making, he listened to the opinions of various levels of officers, even junior pilots.[37] Personally, Trenchard did not believe in air defence. He considered that only offensive action such as bombing the adversary's territory would result in the demoralization of the enemy's will. Consequently, his followers or 'bomber purists'[38] argued for less investment in defence and for paying more attention to the offensive. Thus, the entire argument was boiled down to the number of fighters devoted to defence and the number of bombers used for the offensive. Accordingly, the first RAF doctrine practically embodied Trenchard's conceptual vision of air offensive. In the very first pages of the document, one of the identified principles of war (actually the second one) was offensive action: 'Victory can only be won as a result of offensive action; the adoption of any other policy re-acts not alone on the morale of the force itself, but on that of all other arms.'[39]

Chapter VII is entirely devoted to *Aerial Operations and Aerial Fighting*.[40] This is probably the only chapter where the word 'aerial' can be easily substituted for 'independent', since they are so often used together. Once again, this illustrates Trenchard's symbiosis of strategic bombing and the service's independence:

> Independent operations comprise the destruction of the aerial forces of the enemy either in the air or on the ground, or on the other hand, attacks on ground objectives such as munition factories, strategic railway junctions or other suitable targets, the destruction of which will influence the course of the war ... The destruction of his [enemy's] air forces at their bases on the ground is the most effective method of attaining the main object ... Munition factories and other targets are, therefore, subsidiary to air objectives and should not be included in the aerial offensive until a serious reverse has been inflicted on the enemy.[41]

The implications of CD 22

What can Trenchard's concept as a cornerstone of the main chapter on air power use tell about the doctrine itself? First, it means that the document reflected the predominant conceptual framework of the time and corresponded to the political intentions of CAS, stressing his authority in the doctrine preparation process. Second, the document was a part of Trenchard's political campaign of the RAF's self-explanation both as an independent service and as a very eager team player, which in the eyes of the government was a favourable move. Third, the dominance of the concept of strategic bombing in the doctrine as the main interpretation of air power's independent role also reflected rigidity in strategic thinking. Eventually, this concept and the doctrine associated with it became a dogma.

It does not mean that there was no alternative thinking on air power. The main proponents of air defence were Air Commodore Thomas Charles Higgins and Air Commodore Sir John Adrian Chamier. Having experience in homeland defence and air support in India, they both identified limitations of strategic bombing. They argued that under the conditions of fast development and improvement of technologies, eventually aircraft would be forced into individual combats.⁴² Thus, strategic bombing might not prove to be effective until an adversary's air fleet was destroyed. Contrary to Trenchard's idea of the moral effect of strategic bombing, Higgins argued for what is called today air control. He considered that the bombing of targets could be achieved only if supported by fighters during the air combat: 'As a result of these battles [between fighters] one side would probably in time obtain a fighting superiority, which would carry with it a concomitant bombing superiority.'⁴³ On the one hand, the conceptualization of air power was going beyond existing technological and material capacities. On the other hand, this conceptualization was the driving force for further improvement of technologies and materialization of air power potential.⁴⁴ Wing Commander and later Marshal of the RAF Sir John Slessor, in his work *Air Power and Armies*, argued for joint campaigns, in which air power served in support and protection of land forces attaining land warfare objectives.⁴⁵ In this work, he described air superiority and air intelligence in detail. However, the most important contribution of his work to strategic thinking was his statement that air power was not simply a tactical means. It had a huge strategic potential achieved through 'concentration on disruption, destruction and neutralisation of enemy armaments and supplies'.⁴⁶ Thus, he argued for a different set of targeting priorities than Trenchard.

Although different conceptual ideas in professional discourse and the inclusion of aerial home defence and aerial fighting roles into doctrinal text suggest that a more systematic and holistic approach was adopted, the reality of training courses was far from that. The systematic approach was doomed to defeat due to the dominance of Trenchardian ideas among the leading teaching staff of the RAF Staff College, established at Andover in April 1922. Alan English argues that 'the first courses at the Staff College, followed a syllabus that reflected the preferences of the commandant, Brooke-Popham'.⁴⁷ Both he and the second commandant, Ludlow-Hewitt, argued that the main aim of the Air Force was to target vital centres in order to effect the morale of the enemy's population. In its turn, population would force their government to seek peace.⁴⁸ Thus, the Trenchardian approach was still predominant in strategic thought within the RAF.

Nevertheless, it should not be assumed that RAF doctrine was the only publication to reflect conceptual thought on air power, at the time. Various aspects of air power use were embodied in minor doctrinal publications such as Air Staff Manuals (ASMs) and the CD series. According to the results of Neville Parton's research, over the first five years of the service's existence, thirty-eight ASMs were published, four of which belonged to the CD series.⁴⁹ These findings show that, despite the prevalence of a single idea in the main air power discourse, conceptual and tactical thinking on air power did not stop. Slowly but constantly the field was evolving. However, the progress was quite slow in contrast to the other two services. Consequently, RAF officers' contribution to *RUSI Journal* was only 6 per cent at the time.[50] Neville Parton concluded that despite what was written in the doctrine, the service was developing in an entirely different direction. He asked a few very profound questions: 'Why the RAF would produce doctrine if it was then going to ignore it – and as second order issues, if it did produce bad doctrine, why did it do so, and if the doctrine was in fact reasonable, why was it not followed?'[51]

The answers might be found in the lessons of the first RAF doctrine. First, although the document targeted diverse audiences (RAF personnel, the other two services and policymakers), the purpose of the doctrine was unusual. Its principal aim was unification of the service through the conceptual embodiment of strategic bombing. Inevitably, this resulted in the dogmatic nature of the first doctrine and establishment of rigid thinking. In terms of the wider audience, the doctrine was used to promulgate service's independence rather than stimulate mutual understanding and effective cooperation in a future war. The serving personnel of the RAF considered doctrine *per se* a dogma, because too many roles were attributed to doctrine. Second, instead of guiding personnel, the first doctrine had too many roles to play and scopes to cover. This was also partly because different levels of warfare were mixed in a single document. Accordingly, a single document referred to aerial policy, campaign strategy, operation planning, including cooperation and division of duties with other services, procedures of orders, and report submission in the field. In other words, strategic, operational and tactical levels were combined in one document, regardless of their relevance for the audience. Therefore, RAF personnel could not adopt such a multifaceted document effectively, not to mention that only three chapters were RAF oriented.

The RAF doctrine was not in itself a bad political document. It was a doctrinal document aimed to achieve political objectives, when the service was in a constant fight for its survival: 'The most desperate years of the struggle to maintain independence were 1921–1923. In this period, there was no shortage of acrimony and bitterness amongst the 3 Service Chiefs as they presented their own views of the proper way for an air service to be organised.'[52] Nevertheless, the first RAF doctrine set a precedent for the dogmatization of a single concept, rigidity of strategic thinking and the substitution of practical doctrine functionality with political purposes in interservice rivalry. In retrospect, the experience of the first doctrine paved the way for an anti-doctrinal attitude within the service and partly contributed to a division of RAF personnel into two groups: intellectuals and tactic-oriented thinkers.

Air Publication (AP) 1300

In the next few years, RAF performance in support of colonial rule in overseas territories proved to be sufficient and more cost-effective than Army presence.[53] As a result, the service experienced a modest expansion in 1925–1926: twenty-five squadrons were formed. More importantly, 'in 1925, the first 4 of the Auxiliary Air Force squadrons were formed thus bringing into being Trenchard's idea of an RAF reserve similar to the Territorial army, and the first of the University Air Squadrons (UASs) was formed at Cambridge; London and Oxford UASs followed soon afterwards'.[54] This expansion was significant not only in terms of numbers but rather in political spheres of influence, subsequent public and academic recognition, which improved the status of the junior service and attracted talented individuals.

With the further development of the RAF, the discourse of offensive prevailed. The concept of strategic bombing was considered the main role of air power in British defence. Although, as mentioned earlier, certain independent thinking on air power existed in informal discourse, the concept was meant to shape air power thinking leading to its successful implementation in battlespace. The cause–effect relation between thinking and practising this concept was explained in Trenchard's address to the Imperial Defence College on the war aim of the Air Force Staff, known as CD 64.[55] First, he discussed the difference in tri-service views on the functionality of air power in the war. He argued that the main reason for inconsistency of views was an inability to understand that in the next war, air power was not going to be 'confined to the armed forces, but will also be directed, as they were by all sides in the last war, against the centres of production of war materials and transportation, and communications, and of the war control and organisation of the country'.[56] In this way, he reemphasized the independence and self-sufficiency of the service and its ability to perform military tasks on its own. The potential of other significant roles of air power, except for a strategic offensive, were ignored:

> And it also seemed to me that in some quarters an idea was held that the main efforts of the air forces should be directed to attack the opposite air forces, a view

with which the Air Staff strongly disagree. The aim of the Air Force in concert with the Navy and Army is to break down the enemy's resistance. The Air Force will contribute to this aim by attacks on objectives calculated to achieve this end in addition to direct co-operation with the Navy and Army and in furtherance of the policy of His Majesty's Government at the time.[57]

In this speech, Trenchard illustrated the existing air power thinking environment – complete prevalence of a single concept in official discourse and expectation of unquestionable implementation. It is not surprising that the next doctrine contained the same conceptual framework.

The next version of RAF doctrine was the AP 1300, *the Royal Air Force War Manual*[58] of July 1928. Just as the service saw expansion and certain settling down in the national defence, so did the doctrine, as the reflection of this process. Although cooperation with two other services was included in this publication, as in CD 22, the chapters devoted to air power and air warfare expanded and became more service oriented. Various parts of the text were identical to the CD 22, yet the contextual interpretations and meaning were more purposeful and directed towards the service's equal status with two other services and subsequent role in a future war: 'The aim of a nation at war is to compel the enemy as quickly and economically as possible to conform to its purpose or will. Thus, the ultimate aim of all armed forces is identical, though the means to achieve that aim may differ.'[59] Furthermore, air power was argued to be capable of overcoming defences of both land and sea environments, achieving a preliminary victory.[60] Once again, this interpretation corresponded to Trenchard's vision of the effects of strategic bombing on morale. The capability of aircraft suggested that the 'bomber will get through': 'Unaffected by the configurations of the earth's surface, aircraft have the ability to move freely in three dimensions; they are thus able to strike rapidly and directly at the vital centres of the enemy which may be any centre essential to the maintenance of any or all of the enemy forces.'[61] In other words, the doctrine suggested that aircraft were capable of reaching all forces, while the other two services were limited to their own environments. As well as Trenchard, the doctrine argued for the inability of air defence to prevent direct attack. The best defence and the use of air power was again the air offensive:

> To this direct air attack it is extremely difficult for an air force itself to offer an opposing barrier, because the wide space of the air and the condition of cloud and wind confer unique powers of evasion on the attacking aircraft and renders their timely interception uncertain. Even should interception be effected, the

defenders cannot be said to possess absolute stopping powers, and cannot altogether prevent the attackers reaching their objective if the attack is made with sufficient determination.[62]

Preceding the explanation of the principles of war campaign planning, the introduction stressed upon the roles of air power in future wars – the unique potential of air offensive. This message of the introduction set the tone of the entire document and was reflected in its structure. The first six out of fourteen chapters referred to general considerations of the principles of war, policy and plans, command, leadership and morale, the fighting services, movements and protection. The remaining eight chapters were devoted to air power, three of which corresponded to aircraft cooperation with the Navy (Chapter XI[63]), the Army (Chapter XII) and combined operations (Chapter XIII). Thus, five chapters were dedicated exclusively to air power, which was a progress compared to CD 22. These chapters corresponded to the introduction and general theme of the air power offensive. The chapter on air warfare distinguished between offensive and defensive actions, air superiority and defensive actions had their own subsections. However, the essence could be summarized in one sentence: 'The maxim that offence is the best defence applies even more truly to air warfare than to any other operation of war.'[64] In this discourse, chapters on bombardment, air fighting and air attacks on aerodromes were logical to follow.

Successful experience in overseas operations[65] resulted in an expansion of the final chapter on *Air Operations in Undeveloped and Semi-Civilised Countries* (Chapter XIV). This chapter is important because it corresponded to the content of contemporary doctrines. Taking into account previous operational experience, the chapter explained 'semi-civilised enemy operations', the functionality of aircraft and their role in these operations, tactical considerations of the most effective actions (methods of air attack), cooperation with other services and employment of air forces in support of civil administration.[66]

Overall, the significance of the first edition of AP 1300 was that it reflected the strengthening of the service and the atmosphere prevailing within it. Despite the lack of systematic or creative thinking on air power, this document showed a more profound consideration of air offensive. The doctrine was more service oriented than its predecessor. In the meantime, like CD 22, the line between levels of warfare was still quite vague. Tactical instruction could be in the same paragraph as strategic justification of air power. Thus, the notion that 'the bomber will always get through' prevailed in conceptual and doctrinal discourses. The enduring nature of the conceptual framework was also due to external factors.

Almost a decade after its formation, the service found itself struggling for means to survive in peacetime without precise objectives and a specific enemy to fight. Constant budgetary restraints originating from the 'Ten Year Rule' resulted in relatively the same level of RAF development in 1928, as in 1918.⁶⁷

The early doctrines showed the rigidity of RAF's strategic thinking and limitation of actions. In other words, the doctrine of the air offensive and strategic bombing became a dogma.⁶⁸ Scot Robertson commented on the situation as follows:

> The pattern that remains is of disjunction between theory and doctrine ... What the strategic bombing advocates had been expounding for the better part of two decades was a theory. A doctrine for strategic bombing was virtually non-existent. Yet doctrine is essential to the conduct of operations, be they strategic bombing or any other. In the albescence of a well-developed doctrine, Bomber Command as condemned to feel its way forward in war. Although it was sustained in this arduous task by its almost fanatic belief in the pre-war vision of Sir Hugh Trenchard and his disciples, vision was not enough.⁶⁹

However, this dogmatic framework was necessary to build an independent service with its own strategic, conceptual and doctrinal traditions. Doctrine served as a means of unification and establishment of the service as an independent and self-sufficient actor in the national defence. This conceptual permanency served as a demonstration of the service's validity and the rationale for its existence. On the other hand, a shift in doctrinal functionality from its primary guiding role, towards a political manifesto, created an atmosphere of suspicion regarding its purposefulness as an authoritative guide for practitioners and as means of training the new generations of RAF personnel.

The relevance of doctrine would be even more compromised during the Second World War, which showed inconsistency between politics-oriented concepts and the reality of warfighting. The interwar doctrinal experience of the RAF also showed how dangerous rigidity of mind and the service's self-perception might be in warfighting. In this context, the 1930s showed new tendencies in air power development. First, new technological improvements of fighter aircraft manoeuvrability proved that, after all, the bomber might not always get through. Without fighter support, they might become easy targets for enemy fighter squadrons.⁷⁰ Second, British bombers lacked precision and bombing capabilities. Finally, the RAF lacked any practical experience of joint operations under the conditions of actual warfare. On the contrary, the Luftwaffe gained that experience in Spain.

According to James Corum, 'there were two primary reasons for the German success in Spain: good strategic leadership and a superior war doctrine'.[71] There were considerable differences in the way the RAF and the Luftwaffe viewed that application of air power. At the operational level, the Germans learnt how to plan support operations in protection of land forces. Despite the difference in technological strategic cultures, they also managed to cooperate efficiently with an international contingent of Italian and Spanish allies.[72] They had also verified the concept of the moral effect of bombing and concluded that, instead of fear, bombing of civilians might result in an increased willingness to fight. From a tactical perspective, the Luftwaffe used its *Condor Legion* fighters to provide coverage for its bombers.[73] Another essential modification was a switch from a 'v' structure of air units to a pair. This modification made it easier for the wingman to concentrate and protect the main aircraft. Such modifications provided an advantage of surprise in a battle. The achievements of the Luftwaffe were largely contingent upon their previous investment in the analysis of the First World War experiences and subsequent modification of air power doctrine.

On the example of successful night-time bombing of industrial targets in Coventry, in November 1940, James Corum argued that 'putting 450 bombers on target in the dark is scarcely the trademark of an air force that had been designed purely for army support'.[74] Thus, the Luftwaffe's concentration on itself as a self-sufficient service might be one of the reasons for a straightforward development of its doctrine and its application. However, as Williamson Murray points out, a sound military doctrine does not guarantee victory: the inconsistency between grand strategy, logistics and actual capability would impair even the most detailed and practice-oriented doctrine.[75] Furthermore, Murray noted that the Luftwaffe's defeat in the air war in Europe was due to its inability to provide aviation production in the required numbers in 1940–1941.[76] Consequently, although Luftwaffe doctrine embodied the analysis of best practice and suggested guidance for the lessons to be learned and applied under favourable conditions (this is exactly what doctrines should do), its doctrine could not overcome the reality of material scarcity and the mistakes of grand strategy.

AP 1300, second edition (February 1940)

The new edition of AP 1300[77] was issued soon after the beginning of the Second World War, in February 1940, although the work on an initial draft took place a few years before the war. This time, the emphasis was placed on both the defensive and offensive use of air power. The whole tone of the document was different from the previous editions since it was more oriented at the exact war. Chris Finn notes: 'The second edition of AP1300, published in 1940, dealt with the context of war at the strategic level in terms of the main roles of air warfare: the strategic air offensive; the strategic air defensive; and operations in support of the Navy and Army.'[78] The introduction was concise and stated that the document explained the strategic level of warfare and contextualized air power into it. First, such a distinction made the doctrine more intelligible. Second, it demonstrated a practitioner-oriented approach to the content. It also suggested the existence of a certain hierarchy in doctrinal documents within the service, which again demonstrated further development of the service and doctrinal practice. The doctrine no longer concentrated on the explicit proclamation of the service's independence. Instead, it was systematic in explaining the current war, diverse implications of bombing targets and consequences of civilian casualties in war. The description of features of war for the nation and division of roles between the Armed Forces were included. Thus, the doctrine read like a contemporary environmental doctrine outlining the context first, details and means afterwards.

The most crucial change in the doctrinal discourse was the introduction of a chapter on strategic air defensive. Although it can be considered a breakthrough in terms of strategic thinking, it was rather the need of the strategic environment of that time. Although the emphasis was still placed on the dominance of strategic offensive, it was reluctantly admitted that 'air offensive measures will not afford immediate protection from the enemy's air attacks upon our territory. Therefore, other steps must be taken to achieve the maximum defence practicable against air attack.'[79] Accordingly, the chapter did not only state commitment to defensive actions but was practical in its nature. It looked into potential defence strategy, constitution of a force for air defence and strategic use of fighters.[80] The main components of air defence included a force of fighter aircraft, anti-aircraft artillery, aircraft warning organization, searchlights, balloon barrages and intercommunication system.[81] General considerations of roles and potential obstacles of each component implementation were addressed. Another practical advantage of the new doctrine was its attention to the importance of information and intelligence for air operations: 'The basis of all plans for air operations must be good information. Only if full, accurate and up-to-date information concerning the enemy is available can our air forces be economically and effectively employed against the enemy.'[82] Furthermore, it paid attention to practical means of collecting accurate data and the ways of their processing and transition, including such details as duties of an Intelligence Section. However, the relevance of radar in the information was not mentioned, because it was still classified at that time.[83]

The increased attention to the information role of air power was due to the importance aerial intelligence during the war. As a result, the changes in intelligence gathering and organizational adjustment of the Air Ministry intelligence unit, or AI, to the war requirements followed.[84] Considering the interwar rivalry between the services and consequent paper wars, aerial intelligence was not paid due attention. Before the beginning of the war, the AI consisted of forty people distributed within twenty-five units. It was structured according to the geographical principle with Director of Intelligence (DI) and three deputy directors in charge. While the first deputy director (DDI1) was responsible for liaising with the MI5, DDI2 dealt with the Europe and DDI3 with all other countries of the world.[85] This approach reflected the peacetime convenience instead of preparedness for the war: 'This geographical organisation of intelligence was designed to meet peacetime requirements and largely reflected peacetime sources and needs.'[86]

Another feature of peacetime mindedness of AI was that the primary sources of intelligence were diplomatic channels, open sources and friendly intelligence. Moreover, these sources were analysed on country-by-country basis instead of systematically. Even signal intelligence was analysed in terms of signal patterns and not the actual meaning of the messages.[87] Both organizational structure and diversity of sources of information had to be changed in order to fit the war requirements. The shift from stovepiped information resources to the multichannel fusion took place. In the contemporary military discourse, fusion is defined as follows:

> The blending of intelligence and/or information from multiple sources or agencies into a coherent picture. The origin of the initial individual items should then no longer be apparent ... Fusion melds information from a variety of diverse organisations into a coherent entity. It requires agreement on a common set of rules and procedures between the agencies involved, as well as the will to make it happen.[88]

Since the official channel and diplomatic sources were no longer a valid source of intelligence, the tendency towards collecting hard evidence via the aerial photography became evident. The best illustration of this shift in intelligence gathering was the success of Operation Crossbow that aimed to destroy Nazi's V-weapons. The intelligence based on aerial photography was cross-checked through the intelligence gathered from another channel – human intelligence collected through spying and interrogation of prisoners of war (POWs).[89] Change of approach to data gathering and processing required further structural changes in AI, which was reorganized to thirteen subunits. Initially, all but one unit (AI3, dealing with Germany) were structured according to geographical principle. However, further, into the war, the functional structuring of AI3 was spread across the entire organization.[90] This transformation reflected the significance of another crucial principle of situational awareness and understanding – collaboration.[91] Shifting the emphasis from a geographical structure towards the functional and systematic structure of AI, the RAF improved the degree of information dissemination, its productivity and consequent timeliness of information.

None of the aforementioned achievements of the intelligence would be possible without the development of scientific air intelligence and pre-war military-academic collaboration which resulted in the invention of radar and improvement of analysis of signal intelligence. The Tizard Committee, or, as it was officially known, the Committee for the Scientific Survey of Air Defence (CSSAD), was established in 1934. The first and the most important research project of the committee was initiated with the memorandum 'The detection and location of aircraft by radio methods', which was discussed at the first meeting in February 1935.[92] This project gave birth to a radar that drove not only the further development of aircraft technologies and intelligence countermeasures but also the way the war was fought. The activity of this committee was an early example of productive collaboration between scientists and military practitioners. The work of this committee later allowed Prof R.V. Jones to develop further scientific intelligence during the war.[93]

These features of the development of AI during the Second World War illustrate a few considerations. First, despite the significance of air power in the First World War and establishment of an independent service, the RAF was still considered a junior service. Second, although various sources of information were available, there was no mechanism for its systematic multichannel collection, cross-verification and dissemination. The AI illustrated flexibility in adapting to the war requirements by implementing a functional approach to reorganization and multichannel fusion to data collection. Moreover, the shift towards the improvement of both vertical and horizontal dissemination of information improved the timeliness of information and situational awareness. Third, the classified status of radar technology resulted in its ommision in the text of the doctrine. Finally, the improvement of intelligence system was largely conditioned by the development of scientific intelligence, which illustrated the necessity for a close collaboration between scientists and military practitioners.

In general, doctrine written during a war is inevitably directed towards practical considerations dictated by the necessities of the wartime. This wartime doctrine was case specific. It aimed at explaining how to fight an exact enemy and not preparing for the potential diversity of adversaries. Although the first drafts of this doctrine were written before the war, its final draft was amended and published during the war and had to address the urgent matters of the ongoing war, instead of considering the preparation of the personnel for future ones. In terms of the evolution of doctrine from a policy-oriented to a training, practical document, this doctrine was a step forward. It demonstrated understanding of the application of air power and the required training. Nevertheless, the doctrine was far from a systematic evaluation of air power potential, since it was still leaning towards strategic air offensive. As was previously mentioned, besides the necessity of explaining the role of air power in the ongoing war, the doctrine reflected the dogma of strategic bombing. Thus, this edition could not keep up with rapid technological changes of the time and multifaceted roles air power played during the war itself. Tami Biddle was precise in explaining the Second World War RAF doctrinal discourse as follows: 'While RAF wartime and post-war rhetoric was influenced by its organisational and bureaucratic context, it was also shaped by genuine perceptions of the day – all of which were oriented to the future, and all of which seemed to be heavily conditioned by expectations about behaviour of civilians in war.'[94]

AP 1300, third edition (January 1950)

From an operational perspective, the Second World War was an immense test of air power. The previously emphasized introduction of CAS into air warfare during the First World War was far from efficient and well coordinated at the time of the Battle of France.[95] This was mainly due to the lack of effective communication technologies and the consequent coordination of action between services.[96] However, by the end of the war, CAS cooperation was improved through the establishment of RAF Army Cooperation Command and Forward Air Support Links to coordinate interservice cooperation and procedures for request of air support.[97] On the other hand, the example of the Luftwaffe in the Battle of Britain demonstrated that a conceptual component should align with physical and morale components in order to establish a sufficient fighting power:

Perhaps the most glaring is the doctrinal bankruptcy of the Luftwaffe, which led it to emphasise battlefield air support to the detriment of more significant strategic air operations, together with its failure to develop an adequate force structure, acquisition system and training apparatus to ensure that it got the right weapons and the right people in sufficient numbers to do the job.[98]

The Battle of Britain and the war in general demonstrated the importance of air superiority and interdiction for strategic objectives. Tony Mason suggested 'air superiority was essential to permitting friendly concentration of forces and supply while denying them to an enemy. The battlefield had to be isolated by destroying enemy access to it: the process of interdiction.'[99] The war also demonstrated another aspect of services' cooperation apart from CAS – airborne troops. A British airborne division was formed in 1941 after the Battle for France. Airborne Forces were involved in the Italian campaign and the Battle of Arnhem.[100] Consequently, the war tested air power *per se* and the full spectrum of its potential.

Inevitably, the war put to the test the service's conceptual framework. As the Battle of Britain showed that air supremacy was essential for defence and victory. The cornerstone of RAF doctrine and the function of the RAF, the concept of strategic bombing, used in a few bombing operations of 1941/42, proved to be less effective than the Trenchardian doctrine had envisioned.[101] Night-time bombing of German cities confirmed the Luftwaffe experience in Spain – contrary to the expected results, the bombing of civilian or industrial targets did not undermine the will to fight. Instead, it caused anger and desire for vengeance.[102] The controversy over civilian casualties during the bombing of Dresden in February 1945 weakened support for the strategic effect of air power.[103] Walter J. Boyle commented on the evaluation of strategic bombing after the Battle for Britain in a very precise way:

> Although the British were aware of just how imprecise the German bombing had been, how relatively little critical damage had been done, and how their British morale had been maintained during the Blitz, they did not profit from their knowledge. Instead Britain embarked upon a night bombing campaign against Germany, believing somehow that RAF bombers would bomb accurately, and that the German people would not be as morally tough as the British.[104]

This simple observation confirms the dominance of strategic bombing in the RAF. Another significant implication of the Second World War for air power and the RAF was the introduction of a new capacity of air power – a nuclear attack. It did not only make strategic bombing complete in its moral and material destructive capability, but also proved that air power might be able to win wars on its own.¹⁰⁵ Whether the benefits of using it outweighed the destructive consequences was an entirely different matter. From the RAF's perspective, the time for selfre-examination had arrived. Although the service had proved its defence capacity during the War, it needed a new conceptual framework to function in the post-war environment. The new strategic environment required the service to reconsider its role and find a place where it could belong. The third edition of AP 1300¹⁰⁶ was a good attempt at doing so. The new doctrine reflected the RAF's experience and functionality during the Second World War and its potential in the new strategic environment. The structure used in the previous edition of AP 1300 was further complemented with a more detailed explanation of the meaning of war for the nation after the two world wars, characterization of the Armed Forces and the place of the RAF at that time. For the first time, the notion of air power was defined, and the whole of Chapter 4 was devoted to it:

> Air Power means the use of the air to enforce the national will. It is a compound of air forces themselves and of all those things upon which air forces directly or indirectly depend such as the aircraft industry, civil aviation, the air traffic control system with its communications, the meteorological service, secure fuel supply, and so on.¹⁰⁷

Further, the chapter explained the history of the RAF, arguing that, despite its young age, the service and air power had managed to achieve a lot in the last war and that air power was 'the determining factor'¹⁰⁸ in modern warfare. Although cooperation with the other two services and the necessity of diverse roles of air power were emphasized, the main conclusion was still unchanged: 'But the basic weapon of the Air Force is the bomber, and the basic strategy of Air Power must be offensive.'¹⁰⁹ Although this document was once again institutionalizing the same concept of strategic bombing, it also reflected a widened functionality of air power. Considering the roles air power played during the Second World War, subsequent chapters were devoted to air defence, air transport operations, air reconnaissance and air operations in the undeveloped world.¹¹⁰ Technical aspects of air power support were also included in terms of protection of the Air Force on the ground, intelligence considerations, signals and administrative factors affecting operations.¹¹¹ Thus, a more systematic analysis of air power roles and their necessary support was conducted.

Taking into consideration operational experience of the two world wars, a more systematic approach to air power could be more beneficial for the service. However, this document reflected the historical and political situation when it was written. In the environment of peacetime reorganization, by April 1947 nearly a million personnel were demobilized, resulting in an overall strength of 300,000.[112] In terms of political changes, the first post-war years witnessed the withdrawal from the Empire.[113] From the RAF's long-term perspective, the emphasis on air power functionality exclusively in peacekeeping and counterinsurgencies in overseas operations would have been unimaginable if the service wanted to secure a stable position in the national defence. Ironically, the approaching Cold War suggested the necessity for strategic bombing to deliver nuclear weapons 'alongside the draw-down of the RAF's strength, and in spite of the financial and economic problems, plans were made to re-equip the RAF with modern jet aircraft and atomic weapons: in 1947 the Government decided, in great secrecy, to develop a British atomic bomb which could be delivered by an RAF jet bomber'.[114] Doctrine could not emphasize any other function than the one that could provide the service with a central place in the national defence. The irony of history is that Trenchard's strategic bombing achieved its goal and secured a dominant role of the RAF in the British nuclear programme. However, a short-term success paved the way to a long-term disappointment in this concept and doctrine as its vessel.

A nuclear aspect and the fourth edition of AP 1300 (March 1957)

Duncan Sandys' Statement on Defence 1957 initiated a new wave of post-war reforms. The paper addressed maintaining nuclear deterrent and 'a comprehensive reshaping of policy'.[115] For the RAF, this paper meant centralized prescription of a single purpose of air power. The minister of defence, Sandys, wrote: 'The V-Force was to be "supplemented by ballistic rockets" … The fighter force, responsive only for the defence of V-Force bases since a more general task of air defence was thought impossible, was to be "in due course replaced by a ground-to-air guided missile system"'.[116]

This time was particularly disadvantageous for the service, due to the failure of the UK's nuclear programmes. The British project, the medium-range ballistic missile Blue Streak, was cancelled in 1960 due to its inflexibility, 'having already cost £100 million, in favour of the American-built Skybolt air-launched missile'.[117] Unfortunately, Skybolt was the last nail in the coffin of RAF's nuclear role. American counterparts cancelled it due to major problems in its development. On 22 December 1962, the Nassau Agreement for British participation in the

Polaris programme was signed.[118] Thus, 'within 18 months, the RAF had lost its 2 future nuclear weapons, Blue Streak and Skybolt'.[119] Furthermore, in seven years, on 30 June 1969, the service lost its nuclear role to the Navy, with the approval of Polaris missiles for British nuclear-powered submarines. Although the RAF would continue to carry the WE 177 nuclear bomb until the 1990s, the national deterrent capability at the strategic level was entrusted to the Navy.[120] According to Eric Grove, this failure to secure the most crucial strategic role 'caused perhaps the fundamental role of the RAF to disappear'.[121]

Although doctrine was treated with scepticism inside the service, the RAF elite did not forget its self-explanatory and mediating role. When the new Defence Statement was published in 1957, a new edition of *AP 1300 Operations 4th edition*[122] followed. The essence of the document was in explaining the roles and potential of air power particularly in the environment of the Cold War. In the introduction note, the then CAS wrote:

> Providing the great deterrence is the primary function of air power today. Responsibility for providing the United Kingdom's contribution to the deterrent rests with the Royal Air Force. This is our major task … In addition the Royal Air Force has to hold itself ready to exercise air power in all its forms against minor aggressions and subversive activities throughout the world in support of the United Nations and in defence of the Commonwealth.[123]

This straightforward note practically summarized the entire document. In terms of doctrinal development, this edition was characterized by a greater number of historical operational examples and future role of air power. A distinctive feature of this document was that different roles of air power were explained using examples of diverse types of operations. For instance, air operations in the undeveloped countries were examined in terms of control of undeveloped territory, air control, air operation in support of land forces in undeveloped countries, the value of intelligence and knowledge of the country and employment of air forces in jungle country.[124] In general, the presentation was systematic and well linked to the particular strategic discourse of the Cold War and a potential global war. The nuclear role was explained mainly in terms of the wider use of air power in a global war:

> The aim of air power in the context of global war is therefore: (a) To maintain a level of nuclear striking power that will cause a potential aggressor to have grave doubts as to his ability to achieve his war aims without incurring devastating retaliatory damage; and (b) Should this deterrent fail, to destroy the enemy's nuclear offensive power and his means of continuing the war.[125]

In terms of the evolution of doctrinal texts, this edition was closer to the contemporary symbiosis of theory and practice. However, in terms of achieving RAF's political objectives, this doctrine was unsuccessful. The explanation of multiple tasks air power could achieve was masterful. Nevertheless, it failed to secure a nuclear role for the RAF, mainly because doctrine, by its very nature, was never meant to fulfil such a role. Military doctrine should guide personnel and not political decision-makers. However, the political aspect of RAF doctrine was threefold: to secure the deterrent role, funding and the independence of the RAF. Since the RAF lost the nuclear role to the Navy, any incorporation of doctrine into the ongoing political discourse to promote and safeguard the service had rather a counterproductive effect towards general personnel's scepticism about utility and validity of doctrine *per se*. Serving personnel considered doctrine a dogma, due to the negative experience with the first doctrines. However, after the nuclear chapter in the RAF history, doctrine lost any relevance for the RAF, and thus was completely abandoned by the service. Although it was reissued twice, in 1964 and 1971, eventually the publication was withdrawn and entirely substituted by NATO's tactical air power doctrine.[126] On the other hand, 'it was still used as a "C" promotion exam (from flight lieutenant to squadron leader) primer as late as 1977'.[127] In the long run, the failure of doctrine to fulfil a political function 'contributed to the RAF's anti-intellectualism in the subsequent decades, characterised by a widespread reluctance within the Service to formulate grand concepts on paper'.[128]

Doctrinal vacuum in the 1970s–1980s

Despite the active involvement of the RAF in handling colonial nationalism, after the loss of nuclear role, the 1960s were characterized by cuts in defence spending and dropping numbers of serving personnel. The RAF has suffered substantial reshaping:

> At its peak post-1945 strength in 1952, total RAF manpower was over 270,000 of which about one third were National Servicemen; in 1962, with barely a trickle of National Servicemen remaining, it was 148,000; in 1968, when the first large scale changes were announced, it was 120,000; and in 1976, when the second major defence review had been completed and more cuts made, the RAF was only 90,000 strong (in total less than the number of officers in the USAF).[129]

As a result of substantial cuts in numbers and preservation of its commitments in Europe, changes affected the command structure, which witnessed simplification in the years to come. Moreover, with the withdrawal from Empire, the Far East, Middle East and Near East Air Forces were dismissed, making RAF Germany the only overseas command.[130] Despite the national strategy of retrenchment, the RAF was still responsible for the Allied commitments in Europe within NATO's strategy of 'Flexible and Appropriate Response'. One of the RAF priorities in that time was monitoring and protection of the Atlantic and the North Sea. Nimrods and Buccaneers performed this role carrying both nuclear and conventional weapons. Moreover, the withdrawal from Empire resulted in the relocation of all combat and combat-support aircraft to NATO.[131] Despite the budgetary cuts and constant simplification of command structures, the RAF fulfilled all four roles of Allied deterrence identified by British Defence Forward Policy Statement regarding NATO's flexible response strategy in the 1970s–1980s. Tony Mason wrote: 'British air power contributes to the theatre nuclear forces; it is the mainstay of the direct defence of the United Kingdom homeland; it is the major contributor to the European mainland commitment; and a major partner in the maritime capability in the Eastern Atlantic and the Channel.'[132]

Despite the multifaceted duties and activities within the Allied framework, the 1970s can be considered a challenging period in the RAF history. Except for budgetary cuts and structural changes, one of the problems of the time was miscommunication and disconnection between the RAF and the public. In 1976, the Air Force Board argued that the service was not viewed for what it was capable of, but the lens of V-Force and its contribution to deterrence. After the loss of the deterrent role, withdrawal from Empire and compulsory redundancy, the main question was, what is left of the Air Force and the purpose of its independence? In July 1976, CAS Air Marshal Sir Neil Cameron argued that 'somehow we have grown shy of talking about air power … about the critical importance of the Air Force in our defences'.[133] His public comments stimulated the discussion of the matter in the Parliament.

Moreover, this stage of the RAF history was characterized by a complete absence of the national single-service, strategic-level, environmental doctrine and the prevalence of NATO tactical doctrine. In terms of the NATO strategy of 'Flexible Response', the RAF had become 'a low-level tactical air force tailored for high intensity operations in Europe against Warsaw Pact forces'.[134] From one perspective, the service concentrated on the Allied objectives due to the threats posed by the Cold War adversaries. Consequently, all members of the Alliance were attributed regional roles. From another perspective, it can also be explained by the decline of interservice struggle after the RAF's failure to preserve a nuclear role. In this context, the argument was about the provision of a carrier-based role in joint operations.[135] Accordingly, the RAF's concentration on NATO doctrine looked like another attempt to keep its independent status in the interservice rivalry.

The doctrinal experience until 1971 not only left the service without a framework document on a strategic level, but also resulted in anti-intellectualism and decline of creative and strategic thinking on air power.[136] The general impression was that, the service existed, but it was practically mute about itself. It functioned primarily in the Allied environment and was driven by procedures. In order for the service to get a second life, it required stimulation of intellectual thinking on air power. The starting point was 1976, when the post of the Director for Defence Studies (DDefS) for the RAF was established by CAS Air Chief Marshal Sir Neil Cameron. The role of this position was 'to be responsible for reviving and maintaining an interest in the study of present and future uses of air power in its various military applications'.[137] The first DDefS was the then Group Captain Tony Mason. His contribution to the subject was the following:

> My personal contribution, at the time, was in the stimulation of thinking on air power in the new era. I did not exclude strategic bombing but supported synergy in air power use. Another contribution is the introduction of the definition of air power which is used nowadays, and was used in the recent doctrines: 'Air power is the ability to project military force by or from a platform in the third dimension above the surface of the earth.'[138]

Tony Mason's activity was far-reaching and stimulated cooperation between the military and academic communities, which developed into the first symposium on air power, titled *Air Power in the next generation*, taking place in April 1977, at the University of Southampton.[139] This initiative merged military practice with scholarly creativity. Further on, master courses for serving officers were introduced to boost intellectualism within the service, contributing to its modification according to the new global tendencies in air power development. This is the time when the contemporary close collaboration between the RAF and the University of Cambridge originated. As the future practice will show, most of the appointees on the post of DDefS would receive an MPhil at Cambridge, acquiring wider academic up-to-date knowledge of the time. Another important aspect was that the RAF began to think on air power in a wider, global framework. External operational experiences were incorporated into the national discourse. Based on the analysis of past and future challenges: 'This is generally speaking a symposium about the future, and about air power and its part in the future. If we want to look at the future, we can learn much from the past, and in the history of air power the one constant has been – paradoxically – that of change.'[140]

Although the doctrinal vacuum of the 1970s illustrated the reluctance of the service to revive doctrinal momentum, it also showed that RAF elite was conscious about the necessity of bringing intellectualism into organizational practice and widening personnel's overview on air power. This period in RAF doctrinal history had a few implications on the revival of doctrine in the post-Cold War environment. First, Cameron's initiative to establish the post of DDefS formalized the intellectual and creative thinking on air power. It provided a link to unite military practitioners and academics in critically evaluating the current state and future trends in the development of air forces across the world. Second, stimulation of critical and creative thinking on air power in 1976 paved the way for the revival of doctrine in the 1990s in a few ways. The post of DDefS was well established, and Andrew Vallance could count on the role his post had within the RAF and international air power community. Air power was included in training syllabi, and the connection between the RAF and Cambridge was forged to strengthen intellectualism within the service. DDefS could speak to various public audiences. Andrew Vallance also followed the Cambridge path and did his MPhil there. Cameron's initiative stimulated critical thinking on air power and showed its acceptance within the service. Without the DDefS post, there would have been no platform for doctrinal enunciation. It was like preparation of the soil for the seeds to grow and bloom. It can be argued that Neil Cameron and Tony Mason prepared that soil; Andrew Vallance grew the seeds, revived the doctrine and made it bloom as the first post–Cold War doctrine. Third, the RAF was not the only service that realized the necessity of reformation and innovation in strategic thinking at the end of the Cold War. Right after the introduction or the DDefS post in the RAF, the other two services followed the example and established similar posts.

Finally, Cameron's initiative also showed the significant role of personalities and CAS in stimulating innovations and reformation in the RAF. While various CASs, including Trenchard, had significant impact on shaping the service and its future outlook, Neil Cameron shaped the future of the RAF for decades to come. He filled the vacuum of strategic thinking on air power in the 1970s not by initiating a new edition of doctrine but by establishing the post of DDefS and enabling 'the RAF to acquire a comprehensive doctrinal base which would support it in a new era of widely differing operations and enable it to avoid the resurrection of bomber dogma that infected the 1990s elsewhere.'[141] Moreover, in the long run, it can be argued that his far-reaching vision of the role of intellectualism in the RAF paved the way for the most recent innovative initiative of Thinking to Win.

Despite the revival of intellectualism and critical thinking on air power within the RAF in the 1970s, the first steps in post–Cold War writing of military doctrine were made by another service. The fundamental changes in doctrinal practice started with the Army and Bagnall's reform. The Army doctrine written closest to the end of the Cold War, in 1989, was *Design for Military Operations – The British Military Doctrine*.[142] It was characterized by the orientation on NATO's Central Front and Cold War discourse. The spirit of innovation and change in the post–Cold War reformation of the Army is associated with the name of Sir Nigel Thomas Bagnall, who promulgated the necessity of changing the culture of two armies within the British Army and reforming the Army according to the requirements in strategic environment. Already in 1989, Bagnall argued that one of the means of providing importance and complementing nuclear deterrence was 'the conventional capability to make it credible'.[143] Bagnall suggested reforming the Central region to allow each division conducting its own battle. He aimed at expanding the coordination of actions far beyond the divisional level towards stimulation of corps' battle. Thus, he envisioned more manoeuvrable warfare.[144] Bagnall realized the necessity of an intellectual approach to the implementation of his ideas for reforming the Army. For this reason, he created an informal group of co-thinkers who supported his vision of the Army reforms. They became known as the 'Ginger Group'.

Bagnall initiative was important for the Army and British doctrine, because he revived the interest to doctrine in reforming the Armed Forces. He was convinced that one of the ways of understanding the best ways of the contemporary development of the Armed Forces was to study military history and analyse the operational lessons. Although it was admitted that 'history could be a double-edged instrument for doctrine development as the line between its use and misuse was thin',[145] it was also acknowledged that systematic analysis of the past was the key to reforming the contemporary Army. Thus, Bagnall's reform was a focal point in history of the British military doctrine. He brought back its credibility in the military practice and emphasized its crucial role in the adaptation of the Armed Forces to the new post–Cold War strategic environment.

At the same time, in the 1980s, the Royal Navy continued its formal mission with NATO in the context of the potential global war, the ten years of the Armilla Patrol in the Gulf suggested slightly different realities. Markus Mäder argues that the conceptual debate within the Royal Navy shifted from discussion of the nature and duration of the NATO mission towards evaluation of the results of expeditionary operations.¹⁴⁶ The regionalization of naval operations raised a question regarding the balancing of the maritime force that could and was expected to tackle various threats. Regarding the use of force, given the types of tasks the Navy would have to perform, they required 'flexibility and versatility, as the spectrum of tasks ranged from "show of force" and embargo enforcement to fully-fledged warfighting'.¹⁴⁷ Mäder suggests that the Royal Navy had envisioned the type of operations, which would be required in the first post–Cold War environment, meaning the shift from sea control towards maritime power projection particularly functional in the cases of stability projection and crisis intervention.¹⁴⁸ Thus, the naval discourse demonstrates that the influence of creative thinking on the service's performance can be functional without doctrine. However, in the post–Cold War environment, where doctrine gained its place in the national Armed Forces reformation process, a service without a formal conceptual framework could find itself in a disadvantageous position in contrast to the other two services. Mäder states that the late publication of the high-level doctrine by the Royal Navy in the post–Cold War period was conditioned by the inner ongoing changes within the service, which seemed not to require the formal recognition. However, 'confronted with inter-service rivalry, the Royal Navy gradually acknowledged the need for a written statement of its role in the new strategic environment'.¹⁴⁹

A new chapter in the history of RAF doctrine

At the end of the 1980s and beginning of the 1990s, the service without a conceptual framework for the national air power was losing its self-sufficiency, particularly when American allies began to question their concepts in the light of the post–Vietnam experience.¹⁵⁰ Although the attitude to doctrine remained generally quite hostile, RAF practitioners did not stop thinking about conceptualization of air power and the place of the service in future wars. Although at the time, there was no formal single-service doctrine publication in use, 'there was some published writing available on the subject which provided guidance for those prepared to look'.¹⁵¹ The RAF magazine *Air Clues* was a forum for practitioners to discuss various ideas and share experiences and best practice. However, there was no official, systematic framework document to direct the service's development and facilitate it in the future of British defence. Following the tradition established by Cameron in the 1970s, the holder of the position of DDefS for the RAF was at the forefront of intellectual initiatives and creative thinking on air power. Thus, it is not surprising that the initiative to revive service's doctrine came from a group of intellectuals and DDefS. One of next DDefSs, Group Captain Andrew Vallance, argued that the main rationale for his interest in RAF doctrine was due to the inquiries of American colleagues:

> At that time, US doctrine was well-established, and American colleagues became interested in the British experience. That is why Chris Bowie initiated a research to find out what is meant by RAF doctrine. The finding was quite surprising for him – 'we simply do not have one'. Chris wondered how we structure our forces if we have no doctrine. Personally, I became interested in the topic and convinced RAF Chief to send me to Cambridge, where I explored the development of RAF doctrine in Post-World Wars period.[152]

The result of his study in Cambridge was an MPhil thesis on *The Evolution of Air Power Doctrine 1957–1987*.[153] In this work, Andrew Vallance explored doctrinal experience within the service in order to 'chart the way ahead for doctrinal evolution'.[154] In the article which followed in *Air Clues* in May 1988, he stated that a single-service framework document had become essential in the environment of centralization and merging of all colours into purple, meaning proto-jointery, which was on the way. In 1984, with Heseltine's reorganization of the MOD, which 'aimed to eliminate the effects of inter-Service rivalry over the allocation of defence resources',[155] and the introduction of a 'vertical perspective' into concept studies, one of the main obstacles was 'the trend towards ever greater role specialisation, when combined with the lack of a unifying central doctrine, meant that many civilians, politicians, and even military men tended increasingly to consider each role in isolation'.[156] The RAF needed to express itself clearly and 'as a whole' from the horizontal perspective, in order to make the vertical approach more productive. A single-service doctrine could fulfil this role. In other words, in the development of proto-jointery and reorganization of the MOD, the framework document could explain the role of air power to decision-makers and secure a more exact division of duties, avoiding duplication. However, it also suggested that the service had to re-establish its originality/authenticity in an age of reform. Thus, doctrine was necessary because of the changes in the internal environment rather than a new operational experience or factors in the wider external environment of global politics and international relations.

As well as bringing attention to doctrine in the professional realm, Andrew Vallance showed that thinking on air power also existed informally. He compiled relevant essays and published them as *Air Power: Collected Essays on Doctrine* in

January 1990.[157] This was an anthology of experts' opinions on various practices of air power use. It aimed to stimulate thinking in the Air Force. Andrew Vallance called it 'a doctrinal balloon: punch it and see where it will fly'.[158] Later, this semi-official publication became the essence of the first edition of AP 3000,[159] published in 1991. The main rationale for publication was not only the lack of a single-service doctrine. The service needed a guide to adapt to new trends in air power development. In this context, Andrew Vallance argued: 'The new doctrine had to go away from strategic bombing; in Europe, its role was in air superiority. Therefore, the Air Force was going for a dominant role of the contemporary scale – air strategy and command of the Air.'[160]

The RAF had been without a distinct conceptual framework for a considerable period. The new doctrine was not only meant to summarize the relevant best practice of the past and how they could be applied in the new environment. It also had to explain what the service was at that time, and where it belonged in terms of British defence and global security in the evolving strategic environment. Unlike contemporary doctrines, the first edition of AP 3000 was not future looking, but a reflection of contemporary problems. It excluded lessons of the Gulf War, mainly due to the time when it was published. Andrew Vallance argued that the driving force behind the first edition was a need to understand where the RAF was located post–Cold War: 'The first edition was looking at where we are now, in 1990s, the end of Cold War, experience of the Gulf War. It was waging of war on a grander scale, which still proved a Cold War direction. There were three main types of air campaigns outlined in the first edition: Close Air Support (CAS), strategic effect and anti-surface.'[161]

Unlike its predecessors, a new doctrine was primarily aimed at practitioners and not just political decision-makers or a wider audience. Attention was paid to the understanding of the role of doctrine *per se*, as a means of explaining air power and teaching of conceptual component to the service's junior officers. This tendency was well illustrated in the foreword by the then CAS Air Chief Marshal Sir Peter Harding:

> This manual does not lay down a rigid set of rules; rather, it identifies guiding principles which can be used to ensure that air power is employed to best effect in national and multi-national defence. It has three aims. First, to foster a more cohesive approach to air power education within the Service; second, to be the foundation of our contribution to the formulation of joint-service doctrine, and alliance doctrine with NATO or other allies; and, finally to enhance the understanding of air power within our sister-Services, the Civil Service, Parliament and the general public. This is the document for all branches of the

Service and is as relevant to the administrator and the engineer as it is to the pilot. I expect all officers, irrespective of their branch, to familiarize themselves with its contents.[162]

The tone of the address persuades the audience that doctrine was relevant to all personnel of the service. Thus, it tried to overcome the environment of scepticism and misperception of doctrine, which had formed after thirty years of its absence on a strategic level and a dogmatic history of strategic bombing. The fact that CAS wrote a foreword to the doctrine gave it official recognition and authoritative status, which was quite an achievement at that time. The necessity of doctrine and its place in RAF practice was reflected in the text. Apart from chapters on operational considerations of air power use, two separate chapters and one appendix were dedicated to military doctrine *per se*.[163] They explained the definition and role of doctrine, levels of doctrine, which are traditional for contemporary publications, doctrine application and doctrine writing. The whole doctrinal discourse of the text can be summarized in a couple of paragraphs:

> Doctrine is in essence 'that which is taught'. It is in accumulation of knowledge which is gained primarily from the study and analysis of experience. As such it reflects what works best ... The function of military doctrine is not to detail a set of rules but to provide direction as an aid to understanding. The importance to an armed force of this was put by Major-General Fuller as follows: '"what to think" supplies us with the bricks and mortar, "how to think" with the craftsmanship'. It is that craftsmanship which formal military doctrine seeks to develop.[164]

Apart from various ways of showing the relevance of doctrine for personnel and its further application, this publication also assessed how doctrine should be prepared and when it fails to be relevant. The most important connection was between doctrine and operational experience. Operational experience should serve as a source of knowledge for doctrine and also as means of its validation and further modification.[165]

Overall, the first post–Cold War doctrine paved the way for a new chapter in RAF history, where doctrine was part of the service's modification and experience assessment. Although the publication of the first doctrine would have been more systematic and practice oriented if it had waited for analysis of the Gulf War experiences, it was published in due time to explain the relevance of doctrine *per se* for the service and incorporate it into RAF practice. Although the doctrine was still Cold War oriented and thus could not be progressive in its nature,[166] it was the onset of the service's conceptualization in the post–Cold War era. Explanation of where the service is at a particular point of time is a good start for its thinking about where it wants to be and how to evolve. Therefore, the main aim of the first post–Cold War RAF doctrine was to become the inception of the service's self-realization in a new strategic era. It was still too early to speak about its future, since the lessons of the new post–Cold War operation had not yet been analysed. The driving force for a next edition was the operational experience of the Gulf War.

AP 3000, second edition, 1993

Just as Bagnall's reform was crucial for Army doctrines, so was the Gulf War for the new RAF doctrine. Accordingly, the second edition of AP 3000[167] summarized the service's experience in the Gulf and outlined the potential framework of the use of air power in the post–Cold War era. Whilst this war showed a crucial necessity for technological and tactical improvement,[168] it also had an impact on the conceptualization of air power and understanding its place in a new strategic environment. Although the traditional function of air power – strategic bombing – was revived in the war, this time, it struck the balance between precision and political objectives. Air power had not only proved useful in supporting the ground forces, but it had illustrated the main advantages of reach and speed within a limited time. No other service could do this at that time.[169] It had also re-established the importance of air superiority in conventional conflicts like the Gulf War. Another lesson was the efficiency of interservice cooperation, particularly air–land integration.[170] Finally, this operational experience suggested the importance of technology in the new age of warfare.[171] All these aspects can be traced in the second edition of AP 3000.

First, despite the prevalence of the Cold War orientation of the military, the international response to the Iraqi threat was viewed as sufficient and rapid. It could not be provided by any other service.[172] At that time, the deployment of F3 squadrons, forty-eight hours after the British government had committed itself to the conflict, was considered as the political confirmation of the 'special relationship'. Also, it illustrated the potential of air power to provide such means for decision-making.[173] Although the advantages of air power are permanent, speed and reach were emphasized, reflecting the reorientation of the RAF and air power to the national strategic discourse instead of the Cold War Allied context. In other words, the war and the subsequent analysis of air power use argued for the importance of air power as the 'means of first use' for political decision-makers.[174] In this context, doctrine explained the campaign in terms of air offensive:

> During the Gulf War of 1991, Coalition Strategic Air offensive operations achieved major results. The attack disrupted Iraq's nuclear research and production capabilities and severely damaged its chemical and biological warfare facilities. Half of Iraq's oil-refining capacity was destroyed, the national electricity grid was 'broken', transport feeder routes to Kuwait cut by half and communications were severely disrupted. Baghdad was short of food and without electricity and mains water.[175]

This paragraph from the doctrine demonstrates in a very delicate and precise manner how strategically efficient the air offensive can be and how many centres of gravity it could reach if applied at the strategic level. As the following decades showed, in distant regions air power confirmed national commitments to regional allies. In other words, the logistics, political imprint, financial considerations and strategic implications are different for using air power compared to the deployment of the ground forces. Although the British response to the conflict was rapid, the immediate deployment was partly due to the ongoing training of two F3 squadrons on Cyprus. They were ready operationally because of the training they were involved in at the time.[176] Nevertheless, this experience proved the high efficiency of air power, combining combat strength and deployability in distant battlefields within a relatively short period.[177]

Second, the war had proved the vital necessity of air superiority for any campaign. It was not the concept of air superiority that was new to the operation. Initially, the plan envisaged four phases. The role of air power was exceptionally supportive – to clear the area for the large-scale ground operation. In other words, the campaign was planned according to the principle of linear warfare. However, merging of stages resulted in simultaneous use of air power and ground forces in a parallel manner. The successful air–land integration showed that air power was an equal partner in the campaign.[178] These were not simple tasks of destroying land targets and letting the Army do the 'real job', but a case of joint interservice cooperation. The doctrine addresses this aspect as follows: 'Strategic air offensive operations can be carried largely independently of other air and surface operations, but they tend to be very much more effective, when fully integrated into theatre campaigns.'[179]

Since air power fulfilled both independent and joint roles in the achievement of strategic objectives, the Gulf War had various implications. First, it demonstrated effective functionality of different services, regardless of their natural environment. Second, it had resulted in excessive expectations from jointery. Although operational cooperation between services and nations proved to be effective, despite some minor contradictions,[180] the same expectation from peacetime cooperation during the post–Cold War transformation was rather a dream than reality. Thus, a contextual judgement was essential. Third, the concept of strategic bombing was not only revived and modified according to the new strategic discourse, but was finally vindicated: 'The precision of the Coalition air attacks was of a completely different order from that achieved during previous wars; this enabled Coalition air forces to attack successfully a large number of strategic centres of gravity within a single wave, thus achieving strategic paralysis of the enemy.'[181]

This was due to the correspondence of the available technologies to almost century-old concepts. The improved precision and application of unmanned aerial vehicles (UAVs) and laser sighting contributed to a relatively surgical character of the war.[182] The significance of stealth technology was particularly emphasized within the doctrine: 'The Gulf War also witnessed the usefulness of stealth technology in strategic air offensive operations. Stealthy F-117As flew hundreds of sortie without loss. Though comprising only 2.5% of the Coalition force, the F-117s struck 31% of the strategic targets and 80% of the targets in Baghdad.'[183] Precision gave an opportunity to attack a wider choice of targets depending on their strategic relevance. In other words, the experience of the Gulf War was the empirical onset of the concept of 'effects-based targeting', which prevailed in the strategic discourse throughout the 1990s.[184] The core of the conceptual changes was not in semantics. It was the transformation of the functionality of air power from the large-scale bombing of the Second World War to the expeditionary roles of the twenty-first century.

Finally, the doctrine was beginning to look forward and adapt to the new global security discourse, which included peace support operations (PSOs). Although the development of PSO doctrine was still far from its completion,[185] RAF doctrine addressed this topic from the perspective of air power. Andrew Vallance argued:

> In the second edition we started to get involved in PSO. This edition included five categories of air campaigns. In reality, PSO was a variation of surface attack operation. This time we had PGMs, which showed that air power was able to deliver what it has always promised. PGMs also raised another question – you do not need so many combat forces, if you have those [PGMs]. On the other hand, the counter-force was the importance of ISTAR, which meant a necessity

of diversity of combat forces. Thus, Air Power was not just for mass effect but for selective targets. Enemy casualties mattered. You could not wage the war by a simple statement 'they are enemies – will kill them all – we win the war'.[186]

Consequently, success in the Gulf War and the revival of doctrine in the service resulted in the introduction of a new doctrine writing process. From 1994, regular air power workshops between the RAF Staff College and the Centre for Defence Studies were established.[187] The main aim of these workshops was to reflect on ongoing operations to promote creative and unconventional thinking on air power and the role of the service in national defence. The main topics of the time were the contribution of air power to PSOs, influenced by NATO's Operation Deliberate Force of 1995 in Bosnia, the impact of the Revolution in Military Affairs (RMA) on air power and so on. The next step in encouraging exchange of ideas was the establishment of the service's own journal on air power debates – *Air Power Review*, in 1998.[188] Accordingly, doctrine reflected the service's evaluation of operational experience. It served a tool of incorporating operational lessons and organizational culture into training courses and formal means of the service's self-explanation and manifestation to a wider audience, in that order of priorities.

The lessons of history

Looking at this chapter, one might ask reasonable questions – so what does all that mean? What does the history of the RAF teach us and what has it to do with doctrine? From all discussed earlier, the main conclusion would be that history is crucial for doctrinal studies. From a pragmatic perspective, history provides doctrine with experience from which to learn and train new generations. It gives understanding of what was done before and from which assumptions contemporary ideas and concepts are derived. On the other hand, history provides practical evidence of doctrine application and pitfalls of misinterpretation. The history of doctrine development provides an opportunity to explore a connection between the enduring concepts, establishment of the organizational culture, roles of air power, the reasons for doctrine writing and changing functionality of doctrine *per se*. Thus, knowledge of history is a key to unravelling the meaning of a formal doctrine in situational historical settings, its purpose and evolving role in the military-political dichotomy. It is also a key to understanding doctrinal dilemmas and potential failure – the human factor (over-reliance on prescribed methods and the lack of creative thinking). Therefore, the history of RAF doctrine has the following lessons to teach.

Doctrine can become a dogma if it is not revised and adapted according to the strategic environment and technological trends. Trenchard's experience with doctrine was doomed to failure because doctrine was initially associated with the service's independence. Consequently, it was considered that the psychological effect of strategic bombing was a cornerstone of air power. This concept justified the existence of the service and its potential role in war. Thus, the supporting concept had to remain permanent in order to secure the permanency of the service's status. Subsequently, the formal doctrine, new editions notwithstanding, remained almost the same. Instead of reflecting changing strategic and technological realities, doctrine was used to secure the material embodiment of the conceptual framework. From a perspective of survival, as a newborn service, the constant search for alternative concepts of air power could result in mistrust and dissociation within other services. Without a precise conceptual framework identifying the unique role of air power, the service would not be able to explain the rationale for its independence and the role in the national defence to other services and the government.

While in warfare, services cooperate in order to achieve posed objectives; in peacetimes, rivalry prevails. However, the first RAF doctrines were written in peacetime, as a preparation for war. The severity of interservice struggle might affect doctrine even more than experience of previous and ongoing operations. Since peacetime is a time of preparation for the next war, if time is wasted on dividing the defence budgetary cake and not on the development of new approaches to mission conduct and planning of joint operations, then services might find themselves unprepared for the next war. Under those circumstances, the cost of wasted time might outweigh the privileged position of any service. From a doctrinal perspective, the lesson is that, while exploring the formal doctrine of a particular time, the state of interservice rivalry should not be forgotten. The wider political, defence and interservice situation should be explored in order to understand the full complexity of tasks imposed on a given document. Another lesson to learn is that, although doctrine can be associated with a service's independence and self-justification, its main purpose as guidance to the Armed Forces should not be substituted by the secondary ones. Thus, history shows that in order to understand a given doctrine, exploration of its historical framework is essential.

Interservice rivalry is an important factor in doctrine writing, because it helps to trace how and why the purpose of doctrine as a guidance for military personnel is confused with a political purpose of advertising a service and attracting more funds. In other words, the doctrine might lose its initial purpose and become a means of manipulation. Depending on which threats and thus which service dominate the national defence discourse, the doctrines of the other two services will emphasize cooperation with the dominant service. Interservice rivalry is an inevitable component in the Armed Forces interactions. On the other hand, the factors affecting doctrine writing should not be reduced to a single factor of interservice rivalry. Many factors influence the final content of the doctrine. The situational configuration of these factors in the dominant context of interservice rivalry shapes the doctrine. In other words, the atmosphere of rivalry is a constant factor, while the others can vary depending on the historical context. The essential point regarding this factor is that in a cause–effect relationship, it is not a cause or a trigger for the RAF position regarding its doctrine and the manner it is written. The main motivation for the RAF doctrine writing and emphasizing the strategic role of air power is the necessity of preserving an independent status of the service.

Taking into account previous lessons, there is another consideration that should be acknowledged: When doctrine stops being a guide to military personnel, what does it become? The experience of RAF doctrine shows that, when the primary audience of military personnel is substituted by the secondary, meaning a wider audience of policymakers, doctrine functions as a political document. As a political document, it expresses a certain purpose, which is as short-lived as the political situation for which the document was written. Under such conditions, doctrine is incapable of securing the endurance of the long-term experience of the service, but rather provides material justification of conceptual claims for further funding. Doctrine fails to carry any educative role and subsequent relevance for serving personnel, and therefore it loses any practical relevance and validity. In other words, the same document could have been called a report to the government: 'The service's justification of its existence and money spending.' It should be emphasized that military institutions do have to report and justify their spending to the government. However, RAF doctrinal history shows that doctrine is the wrong document to do so. Thus, the lesson to be learned here is that doctrine should target military personnel and be a guide to desired operational performance first. Only as a secondary purpose, should it explain the service to a wider audience.

From the perspective of doctrine evolution, the lesson is that, although doctrine should be revised according to changes in the strategic environment, the driving forces for reviewing doctrine vary from time to time. The rationale for each doctrinal revision is different. The first RAF doctrine was written due to the necessity of a formal framework document to reflect the existence of an independent service. Although the subsequent editions were not characterized by substantial conceptual changes, the revision of AP 1300 after 1945 was prompted by failure of the expected psychological effects of strategic bombing and diversity of operational experiences of the Second World War. In this context, the new doctrine was crucial for explaining the previous failures and providing new guidance in the entirely new environment of the nuclear age. However, while the doctrine of 1945 was more apologetic and explanatory in its narrative, the doctrine of 1957 was a justification of the strategic offensive in the framework of the new nuclear strategic environment and the necessity to preserve the role of strategic nuclear deterrence. In other words, doctrine was again used as a means to political ends. In this case, it is evolution of the service. Finally, the doctrine of 1991 aimed to reform the service due to the new realities of the post–Cold War era. Starting from AP 3000 (second edition), the main reason for writing doctrine became the necessity of absorbing new operational experience and introducing them into training courses. Overall, it can be concluded that doctrine is rewritten when substantial changes in the strategic and political environments occur.

One crucial lesson of doctrinal history is particularly relevant for this book. The decades of doctrinal dogmatism created a doctrine-hostile environment within the RAF. It did not only mean that Andrew Vallance had to fight the reluctance of RAF personnel to produce and even read doctrine. The service's inner culture, which was formed during these decades and which is passed to the new generation, is doctrine-sceptical, at best. Therefore, it should be kept in mind that there were diverse groups within the service that considered doctrine to be another means of bureaucracy and that tactics-oriented thinking was the most functional within the RAF. Thus, the struggle between intellectuals and tacticians should not be forgotten. This lesson is relevant for this monograph because this struggle and the service's anti-intellectualism were reflected in the studied doctrines and thus indicated tendencies within the service's development. These lessons will become more vivid when the case studies of contemporary doctrines are studied. The first one will be the third edition of AP 3000, which is the subject of the next two chapters.

3

Case Study of the Third Edition of AP 3000 (Part I)

The previous chapter set a scene for the exploration of the development of air power doctrine in the post–Cold War environment and within the process of jointery. This chapter seeks to explore the doctrine writing process of the third edition of AP 3000. Attention is paid to two major factors influencing doctrine writing. The first is the external environment that includes the operational experience of the lessons of PSOs in Bosnia and multinational operations. The second factor is internal politics outside the RAF. Thus, the consequences of the Labour Strategic and Defence Review (SDR) of 1998 and the introduction of a cost-efficient approach and jointery are analysed.

The third edition of AP 3000 was published in 1999. The edition was required because of two primary reasons. First, a more future-looking evaluation of the previous operational experience including the Gulf War and Bosnia was required. Second, a new doctrinal framework for explaining air power capabilities in the new joint environment was essential for further understanding and actual strengthening of jointery. As in the first two editions, the main responsibility for the preparation and publication of doctrine was with DDefS. However, unlike before, the main protagonist and initiator of doctrine writing was CAS, Air Chief Marshal Richard Johns. In his memoire, Richard Johns argued that a new edition was needed to explain air power capabilities in the upcoming new century:

> SDR debates brought home to me the simple fact that not only senior officials but colleagues in the Royal Navy and Army had no informed understanding of the complexity of contemporary air operations and attendant risks. But, first we needed to put our own house in order. Air Publication 3000, Air Power Doctrine, was first published in 1990 to set out the characteristics of air power, both strengths and limitations, and fundamental tenets for its employment. The end of the Cold War and Gulf War I prompted an update of AP3000 in 1993

but in my judgement it did not go far enough in attempting to define the core capabilities of our national air power as we look forward to the 21st century. Nor did it consider changes in the strategic environment and how we should address change in the concert with our sister Services. I thus commissioned a complete rewrite of AP3000 that took full account of jointery and multinational operations. I had just the man for the job, Group Captain Stu Peach, the then Director of Defence Studies (RAF).[1]

This edition of AP 3000 was prepared under the supervision of Group Captain Stuart W. Peach (DDefS for the RAF), as the principal author and editor, and Wing Commodore P.J. Greville (SO1 Defence Studies, RAF), as an assistant editor.[2] However, CAS was also directly involved in the actual preparation process. Various warfare specialists from all three services were involved in discussions during doctrinal workshops and review process. Compared to the previous two editions, the structure of a new document changed slightly. First, the doctrine no longer tried to explain to either practitioners or a wider audience what doctrine *per se* was. Instead, this edition concentrated on the nature of doctrine, its relevance for the service and the history of air power doctrine. Therefore, such chapters as *Military Doctrine, Applying the Doctrine, The Doctrinal Process* were substituted with such chapters as *The Nature of Doctrine* and *History of British Air Power Doctrine*. The use of air power was explained not within air campaigns, as in the case of the second edition, but in terms of capabilities. The document was divided into three parts. The first part explained the strategic context contained in three chapters: *The Nature of War and Armed Conflict, Air Power* and *The Command and Control of Air Power*. The second part referred to the core capabilities of air power. This included chapters such as the following: *Information Exploitation, Control of the Air, Strategic Effect of Air Power, Joint Force Employment 1: Indirect Air Operations and Direct Air Operations, Joint Force Employment 2: Combat Support Air Operations, Joint Force Employment 3: Force Protection*, and a chapter on *Sustainability*. The third part explored the evolution of air power doctrine, followed by definitions and a chapter on further reading.

Factors of the external environment

The third edition of AP 3000 was separated from its predecessor by five years. This period was characterized by the development of the post–Cold War strategic environment and spreading of unconventional conflicts. Accordingly, a new doctrine was needed in order to reflect the new operational experience of Bosnia and the role of air power in PSO environment. In the foreword, the then CAS Air Chief Marshal Sir Richard Johns stated: 'Today the generation of Air Power must take into account both "jointery" and multinational operations – themes that are reflected in the focus of this document and its title. Thus, the third edition of British Air Power Doctrine stresses the need for our Armed Forces to be trained and ready to meet an enormous variety of tasks which in turn requires our doctrine to be relevant, dynamic and flexible.'[3] The doctrine had to reflect the continuous revision of conceptual framework, operational experience and roles of air power, in order to preserve its continuous relevance.[4] While the experience of the Gulf War showed the continuity of conventional warfare, the experience of Bosnia suggested the rise of more intricate and less identifiable conflicts; air power had to be conceptualized to cover both. Consequently, its utility was to be determined by experiences of two entirely different types of conflict. The First Gulf War had much to do with the preparation of the battlespace, bombarding Iraqi ground forces before the engagement of the land forces. Thus, the integration of land and air forces in a manoeuvrist way took place. However, in the Balkans, the adversary was different. His response to coercion differed as well. The Bosnian conflict showed just how complex operations could be when military means were used to attain humanitarian goals. This suggested the need for a new operational framework – PSOs. Bosnia showed that pursuing humanitarian objectives could not be entirely effective due to the limitations imposed by exceptionally strict rules of engagement (ROE). For instance, during Operation Deny Flight, the targeting approval process was particularly strict. For a NATO aircraft to hit Serbian artillery striking Sarajevo, approval was required from the UN Secretary General. Obviously, by the time approval was granted, the artillery was under cover.[5] In other words, although technological advancement allowed militaries to hit certain time-sensitive targets, humanitarian considerations either slowed them down or undermined their efficiency altogether.

Another issue with Operation Deny Flight was inconsistency between actual strikes and the political message sent to the belligerents. After the first strikes of Deny Flight, UN officials declared that these measures were necessary due to the deterioration of the situation, but that it took no sides. Afterwards, in order to reduce the risk of the United Nations Protection Force (UNPROFOR) personnel being taken hostage, the UK and France blocked plans for new strikes.[6] What might be viewed as adequate political and diplomatic action under certain circumstances was counterproductive and disastrous in military/ tactical terms. Interrupted strikes allowed the Serbs to recover and regroup their forces. Although the UN tried to resolve the problem through diplomatic means according to international law, the belligerents treated UN observers as hostages, chaining them to bunkers and main infrastructure targets like bridges and communication towers.[7]

Another crucial factor that restrained the utility of air power was sensitivity to collateral damage. As a result, the ROEs were exceptionally strict and prescriptive: 'OPLAN 40101's ROE annex, Security Council Resolutions, and the general feeling that even small levels of collateral damage would undermine political support tightly restricted what NATO air men actually could do.'[8] Moreover, these ROEs identified the targets that could be hit, and accountability to civil authorities, which could interrupt the air campaign at any stage of its conduct.[9] The problem here was not missing time-sensitive targets, but that 'highly restrictive ROEs, useful for preventing unwanted escalation, can also increase the risks to the forces involved in an operation'.[10] Overall, the experience of Bosnia was bringing practitioners to the conclusion that the conflicts of the post–Cold War strategic environment, particularly characterized by the peace support element, would undermine traditional use of military capabilities.[11] Tony Mason commented that there were two views of the conflict:

> Those who argued that Air Power could bring the Bosnian tragedies to a speedy conclusion were opposed by those who were concerned about collateral damage, retaliation against civilians and UN forces on the ground, and the apparent lack of suitable targets for air attack in a confused patchwork of relatively small military confrontations; nor was topography of Bosnia as Air Power friendly as in Iraq.[12]

Regarding tri-service cooperation, much improvement was required. Synergy was back on the table of discussions, although the concept itself was not new.[13] Andrew Lambert stated that 'as a buzz-word of the 1980s, "synergy" came to be applied to any interaction deserving approbation; it became hackneyed, and any two successful combinations were frequently labelled a "synergy". However, the true effect was often one of increasing numbers producing increasing results, when, in reality, the extra forces reacted in contrary, or perhaps only complementary, ways with one another'.[14] While Operation Desert Storm showed 'an unmistakable operation-level synergy, demonstrated by the ease of the land offensive',[15] the lack of consistent coordination between forces in Bosnia had negative synergetic results.[16] One of the lessons of Bosnia was that synergy should be used in order to prevent UN soldiers or any other land forces being taken hostage in response to air strikes. Depending on the characteristics of the operation, when synergistically used, air power could decrease the enemy's power, leaving the land forces to tidy up the rest of the battlespace. Alternatively, it could be used as a means of supporting peacekeeping and peace enforcement operations, thus securing its role in the PSO environment.[17]

Operational experience in doctrinal discourse

The unconventional nature of Bosnia and its difference from the Gulf War meant that existing air power doctrine was not enough to reflect the new strategic reality and the role of air power in both conflicts. This does not mean that AP 3000 (second edition) was wrong, rather that it was still more oriented to the experience of the Gulf War and employment of the Armed Forces in conventional warfare.[18] The striking difference between the two conflicts showed that doctrine could not predict development of the strategic environment and be fully prepared for it. Also, it should not rest solely on the experience of a single operation, even if it was the most recent one. Thus, a more systematic approach was still required. The new doctrine had to develop a new conceptual framework towards the improvement of synergy based on operational lessons from the two recent campaigns.[19]

Moreover, the new edition had to align with the doctrines of other services or, at least, not contradict their concepts of PSO. It also had to take into account the changing nature of the domestic political and public opinion, and be a means of preserving support at home.[20] Consequently, it is not surprising that the new edition of AP 3000 was not published immediately after the Bosnian conflict. There were simply too many variables to consider. Not only a detailed analysis of the use of air power in the recent operation was required, but also harmonization of PSO concepts among all three services. The post–Cold War development of the Army's PSO doctrine had a significant influence on AP 3000 third edition.

PSO doctrine and the RAF

During the first post–Cold War decade, the Army was discussing which way peacekeeping was meant to go, and whether a new concept and consequent changes were needed, in the first place. According to the traditional approach, the national contribution should be conducted only within the UN framework, with the use of force only for extreme cases of self-defence. Consequently, the consent of all participating parties was required.[21] However, the reality of Bosnia showed that this approach was insufficient. Post-operational analysis demonstrated the inconsistency between tradition/dogma and the operational requirements, which stimulated a debate on the new PSO conceptual framework and doctrine. The essence of the debate was to distinguish between peacekeeping, peace support and peace enforcement. The group of traditionalists, together with Colonel Allan Mallinson and Lieutenant Colonel Charles Dobbie,[22] argued that the main distinguishing feature between peacekeeping and peace enforcement was absolute consent and that peace enforcement equalled warfighting.[23] The opposite group of thinkers, represented by John Mackinlay, Richard Connaughton and Philip Wilkinson, argued for a more progressive common ground between PSO and COIN approaches. Wilkinson, as the author of this doctrine, suggested that although peace enforcement, like warfighting, had no consent, the main difference was meant to be in means and objectives. Peace enforcement aimed to return consent and required limited use of military force.[24] On the other hand, warfighting envisioned substantial use of force in order to achieve a particular political objective. Regardless of this debate, the first post–Cold War PSO doctrine – Wider Peace Keeping (WPK) was written following the traditionalist approach.[25]

Therefore, it is not surprising that such a single-minded approach to doctrine writing caused a wave of criticism. First, the empirical utility of the doctrine was highly doubted since it was based on vague notions like consent, which could be interpreted differently in interstate or intra-state contexts.[26] Second, the document was written more as a plan of actions rather than doctrine. In this context, Connaughton suggested that instead of broad principles applicable under the conditions of any operation characterized by a PSO component, the document reminded him of prescriptions derived exclusively from the Bosnian experience.[27] On the other hand, referring to Connaughton's criticism, Mallinson suggested that expectations from this interim and tactical doctrine were pushed to the operational level. He argued that consent at the tactical and operational levels had a different meaning. While, in the field, consent might be lost for various reasons, it should not be dismissed at the operational level.[28]

Moreover, Mallinson argued that while a new doctrine on peacekeeping was required, WPK was not the right one. Its main purpose was exclusively tactical, illustrating long-existing Army practices that could be applied in PSO environment.[29] In other words, the main negative aspect of the document was its situational nature. It reminded more of tactical prescription rather than generic principles of military conduct in PSO. In his book, Markus Mäder drew the conclusion that the document served a political purpose, rather than a military guide: 'In short, the doctrine had a clear political function serving specific Service interests: the justification of its behaviour vis-à-vis Bosnia.'[30] Since this document had a political purpose, an introduction of new concepts in volatile domestic and international environment would be unwise. Thus, the Army decided to play safe in its interpretation of the new operational realities. Consequently, the first doctrine illustrated service's readiness for the new challenges with the resources it had at that time. From one perspective, the Army showed that it had a fully functional doctrine as a response to the new PSO environment, which could be used in justification of the service's performance in the next defence review. Thus, conceptual innovation was not the priority. From another perspective, introduction of a doctrine with an entirely new approach to identification of peace enforcement and warfighting without due long-term political support could be counterproductive for the establishment of Army's role in the post-Cold War British defence. It may seem that since Wilkins' approach proved to be accurate and was the cornerstone of the next Army PSO doctrine, it should have been adopted already in 1995. However, it is easy to judge retrospectively. In 1995, the path of national defence reform was less clear, and required caution while writing formal framework documents.

It may seem that debates on Army doctrine had nothing to do with the RAF and the use of air power. However, the connection was direct – the lessons of Bosnia analysed in the WPK also judged the use of air power, which was the main force used in the conflict. Therefore, the Army's peacekeeping doctrine shaped the future of PSO conceptualization and roles air power could play in this operational setting. Since the debate on consent and the distinction between peace enforcement and warfighting was quite fierce, the RAF had to consider a wide spectrum of air power use in the PSO environment. A clear distinction between the roles of air power in peacekeeping, peace support and peace enforcement was needed. Moreover, it had to be conceptualized in such a flexible way that it could adapt to any changes of the domestic environment, including shifts in the Army thinking on the nature of consent and distinction of the PSO roles each service could play.

Andrew Lambert argued that the experience of Bosnia showed that air power in peace enforcement can be used more effectively by improving synergy.[31] However, at the same time, Philip Sabin suggested that PSOs were not an entirely new phenomenon and that since they were 'shaped by complex and dynamic interaction of the strategies of the intervening states and the local combatants; in this, PSOs are analogous to limited wars'.[32] He concluded that since certain analogies can be applied to PSOs, they should be used as 'doctrinal considerations of PSOs proceeds, rather than treating PSOs as an entirely distinct form of activity in which the only way of improving our understanding is through hard school of trial and error in the operations themselves'.[33] This conclusion had a couple of further theoretical implications. First, if PSO was not entirely new and a certain analogy with limited wars could be made, then air power could be applied accordingly, without having to reinvent the wheel. Second, it meant that RAF's colonial experience of limited wars and insurgencies was another step towards a middle ground between peacekeeping and counterinsurgency (COIN). Finally, this implied that the conceptualization of air power in the PSO framework could evolve without waiting for finalization of the Army doctrine. This meant the development of independent thinking rather than the independent role of air power in PSO.

Even taking PSO doctrine as new guidance for future operations, air power was considered contributory to all four phases of the PSO environment: preventive diplomacy, peacemaking, peacekeeping and peace enforcement. The main benefit of air power was its remoteness from the place of conflict. Thus, it could be used according to the extent of political commitment. Air power could be used as a deterrent means in preventive diplomacy or to prepare the way for ground forces.[34] Its roles could be contributory in coalition activities (transportation of humanitarian supplies) or 'intermittent: activated and suspended in harmony with diplomatic and other actions or considerations in a peacebuilding process'.[35] In the reconnaissance role in PSO, air power had some essential advantages: air recce was less affected by consent constraints; it identified potential belligerents and discriminated them from the civilian population; it helped UN forces to gain escalation dominance; and it helped to identify intentions of belligerents.[36] Even in transport operations, air power was crucial for the movement of supply, equipment, airborne operations of insertion or redeployment of combat forces, aero-medical evacuation, insertion and recovery of Special Operations Forces (SOF) and combat recovery.[37]

In the conclusion, it was suggested that air power had the necessary attributes of multifunctionality and flexibility for both conventional interstate conflicts and the PSO environment. This multifaceted thinking on air power was also ready for the PSO doctrine of 1998, which was written under the direct supervision of Phillip Wilkinson. It demonstrated the first stages in the merging of PSO and COIN doctrines. Instead of achieving an absolute consent, the new doctrine conceptualized the use of coercion in a different way: to restore consent and achieve desired outcomes within international mandates.[38] A new doctrine was inspired by the experience of the late stages of Bosnia and replacement of

UNPROFOR by NATO forces – the Implementation Force (IFOR).[39] Although the new doctrine took a more modern direction, it still caused fierce debates. Conaughton argued for the necessity of a more practical operations-driven doctrine, and Wilkinson emphasized that 'doctrine should not reflect what happened but suggest appropriate responses'.[40]

The Army experience with PSO doctrine illustrated the complexity of conceptualizing the recent operational experience in a progressive way which often caused clashes with some traditional views. Moreover, this fierce struggle between different visions on peace enforcement suggested that independent RAF thinking on the role of airpower in PSO environment was well justified in the years preceding the third edition of AP 3000. Nevertheless, a new edition of AP 3000 heavily relied upon Wilkinson's doctrine, which became available at that time. The actual references to these elements should be traced through the text of the doctrine, in order to verify the extent to which the PSO environment and experiences of Bosnia had influenced and were reflected in the third edition of AP 3000.

The PSO reality was mentioned already in the first chapter, devoted to the nature of war and armed conflict. Different types of PSOs were identified in terms of the new types of conflict in which British Armed Forces might be deployed in the future. The doctrine addressed different types of conflict: general war, limited conflict, regional conflict, civil war, insurgency and terrorism.[41] Accordingly air power can be used in such operations as preventative diplomacy, conflict prevention and defence diplomacy, PSOs, peacekeeping, peace enforcement, post-conflict activity and peace-building and humanitarian operations.[42] Further description of each operation followed the same pattern: the explanation of the meaning of an operation for the conflict resolution, where it is on the ladder of conflict escalation and consent. A new edition of PSO doctrine *Peace Support Operations* (Joint Warfare Publication (JWP) 3–50)[43] was an authoritative source for the definition of each type of operation, while the UN Charter was used to explain the legal aspect.

This pattern can be explored with the reference to an example of peace enforcement. First, it showed where it fitted in other operations related to peace and security and conflict escalation: 'If a crisis deteriorates further or a humanitarian catastrophe develops, the mandate may be changed to authorize the use of force, typically via a UN Chapter VII mandatory Security Council Resolution.'[44] Further, the legal basis for operation within the UN mandate was explained thus: 'Such use of force is described as peace enforcement and requires compliance with a mandate to secure peace and restore international security.'[45]

Taking into consideration the Army's debate on the nature of consent and a gap between PSO and COIN, the doctrine emphasized its place in this argument and the importance of coercion applied in this context: 'Peace enforcement operations are undertaken to establish and maintain peace when consent may be lost or uncertain; peace enforcement operations are, thus, coercive.'[46] Because of the emphasis placed on the transitional role of peace enforcement before actual warfighting, it could be concluded that the doctrine was influenced by JWP 3–50. Moreover, AP 3000 recognized the authoritative status of the Army doctrine, using it as the source for definitions. In other words, this definition illustrated RAF thinking on the place of air power in multinational operations with a PSO component. It also showed the strengthening of interservice collaboration and vertical jointery.

Although a few years before the publication of the third edition, the RAF thinking was more single-service and air power oriented, the doctrine of 1999 was aimed at joint and interservice cooperation. This as shown by using JWP 3–50 as an authoritative source for description and characterization of operations with a PSO component. Although the experience of previous operations had influenced thinking on the roles of air power in the new environment, the doctrine was not case specific and did not adopt the experience of the last war alone, but illustrated the place of air power in the new strategic reality of multinational operations. To an extent, all three editions of AP 3000 were driven by personalities. However, in the first two cases, Andrew Vallance as DDefS inspired the revival of doctrine. In the case of the third edition, CAS initiated doctrine that reflected his vision of the RAF in multinational operations and joint discourse. Moreover, an active involvement of CAS did not undermine the role of DDefS, Stuart Peach. Thus, this doctrine illustrated the balance of their views.

Nevertheless, the joint route of doctrine also indicated a shift towards institutionalization of doctrine writing and strengthening of vertical jointery. In respect of the forces driving doctrine writing, operational experience was influential. It reflected substantial changes in the character of post–Cold War conflicts and the roles of air power. The doctrine was not written when the conflict ended and did not simply describe successful examples of air power. Instead, it stressed interservice connection both in terms of experience of Bosnia and doctrine writing. The time of publication and analysis of operational experience through synergy suggested the necessity of strengthening interservice collaboration or jointery. As a result, jointery as a means of reforming of the national defence became one of the defining factors of doctrine writing in the post–Cold War environment.

External contacts and foreign doctrines

The exchange of concepts and technologies between allies is another factor of the external environment influencing doctrine writing. The exchange of technologies is often classified. However, the exchange of ideas, conceptual frameworks and doctrinal experiences is traceable. Since the UK and the United States share a more profound bond in questions of defence and security, and had exchanged intelligence and technologies during the Cold War and continue to do so today, it could be expected for them to share a similar approach to developing their military doctrines. However, this was not the case. In all three editions, there were no systematic and officially institutionalized meetings on conceptual and doctrinal development. From the beginning of the 1990s, when the doctrine writing process was author driven and largely inspired by the personality of Air Vice-Marshal Andrew Vallance, there were no official meetings for the discussion of doctrinal matters on senior staff level. From 1977, when the first national symposium on *Air Power in the Next Generation* in cooperation with the British University Service Education Scheme and RAF Staff College in Bracknell, took place, it initiated a chain of non-official meetings, presentations and conferences to stimulate air power thinking both at the national and international levels.[47] In the course of preparing the first two editions of AP 3000, Andrew Vallance received assistance from American colleagues and air power specialists because of his personal contacts instead of official channels.[48] At that time, Dr Phillip Meilinger was among the primary contacts of Andrew Vallance. He served at the American doctrinal centre and visited Bracknell with lectures. John Warden, the father of 'parallel warfare', 'the system of systems approach' and 'the five circles' model was also one of close contacts.[49] However, despite the exchange of ideas and experience, American doctrine development procedures were not introduced into British practice. This was largely because new doctrinal ideas and Warden's concepts were even more opposed in the United States Air Force (USAF) than the introduction of doctrine in the RAF, in 1991:

> While stressing that by the eve of Desert Storm many in the Air Force had come to accept the wisdom of the Instant Thunder concept, in August 1990, all too many senior officers, having become prisoners during the 1980s of a tactical air power 'paradigm', opposed Warden's concept with a 'narrow-minded, anti-intellectual, and, at times, mean spirited' group think.[50]

Dr Meilinger, who served under Warden's supervision, at the Pentagon, claimed he 'was a lone voice, largely ridiculed and ignored; the serious thinking was going on in Bracknell/Shrivenham and Canberra'.[51] Therefore, although in the environment of personality-driven doctrine writing, connections with prominent American air power specialists did develop, the transition of doctrinal practices from the United States to the UK did not occur, mainly because the latter's American counterparts had to fight their own battle for creative thinking,[52] which was well ahead in the RAF. Dr Meilinger argued that, during the first post–Cold War decade, the RAF was more receptive to new ideas. The only institutionalized exchange of experience and ideas was through annual visits by DDefS to the Pentagon and then down to the School of Advanced Air Power Studies[53] at Air University, Maxwell.[54] Later, Dr Meilinger stated:

> I'm not sure it was as formal as it should have been. The RAF was the active courter in that relationship. Not a surprise to me ... The RAF also used to hold annual or biannual conferences and historical gatherings in London. I remember being so amazed at one of those when your CAS sat there for two days listening to every paper and then got up and gave the summary! Astounding. No chief of my air force would have even attended much less played such a key role.[55]

This statement illustrates that, although the exchange of interpersonal ideas existed in the 1990s, annual DDefS visits continued through the first post–Cold War decade, and major conferences took place in London, Cambridge, Washington and The Hague,[56] American doctrinal experience and practice were not transferred into the UK, in 1993 or in 1999. Thus, in the first post–Cold War decade, the interaction between the USAF and RAF was sporadic, mainly focusing on information exchange rather collaboration on doctrinal matters. Moreover, the first two Air Force Doctrine Centre Commanders (AFDC/CC) had close ties with their counterparts in the RAF and exchanged official visits. However, besides that and several visits of action officers that touched upon basic doctrinal considerations, no collaboration on doctrine development took place.

Since the RAF, together with DDefS, paid attention to the stimulation of creative thinking and created a more receptive environment for concept development, then there must have been other influential factors affecting doctrine writing rather than only the experience of American counterparts. It is worth noting that during this period, American thinking was influencing doctrine writers in the UK as well as senior RAF staff indirectly. In this context, Dr Peter Gray noted:

The interaction with Americans is conducted in the following way: Americans write doctrines, teach them, we take common courses or are exposed to the application in theatre. Visits that happen for experience exchange and not just about doctrine have the strongest influence on air power writers and their thinking. These visits are not institutionalised and happen mostly on the levels of staff, they might be US-eyes only courses or any other.[57]

Accordingly, it can be concluded that the impact of external contacts on the UK doctrine writing was rather indirectly influencing the general intellectual environment and interpreting lessons from previous operations. Writers and practitioners involved in doctrinal workshops were exposed to American conceptual framework and doctrine through exchange courses.

It can be concluded that in 1999 and further decades of doctrine writing, the exchange of ideas and concepts with allies had indirect impact on doctrine writing. Since the contacts between the RAF and the USAF were of an interpersonal and sporadic and thus indirect, and doctrine was not a primary topic for discussion, this factor was less predictable and not easily amenable to practical verification. Another consideration refers to the technical aspect: there is no paper evidence of meetings or workshops which demonstrate what was discussed or how it was applied by either side, if at all. Once again this finding corresponds to the classified nature of various materials of bilateral cooperation. However, the indirect impact of this factor suggests the existence of mediators who are more flexible in their contacts. This is the case of academics, particularly those who are former practitioners.

Foreign doctrines

Regarding the impact of NATO and foreign doctrines, NATO Allied Joint Publication (AJP) 1-A was referenced in the third edition of AP 3000: given the long-term ties with NATO, it is inevitable that the British approach to the use of air power in Allied operations should follow the principles outlined in NATO doctrine. Accordingly, NATO doctrine affected AP 3000 through the doctrine hierarchy. AJP 1-A was at the top of the doctrine hierarchy and identified the principles of Allied operations, which the national doctrines had to follow or at least not to contradict. Consequently, environmental doctrine like AP 3000 incorporated these principles. This was well demonstrated by the referencing of NATO doctrine and emphasizing the Allied context of the roles of air power. However, at that time, NATO doctrine was not at the heart of the national doctrinal practice as it is today. In the first post–Cold War decade, NATO doctrine was followed in terms of Allied operations, and not as a guide for the preparation of the national Armed Forces for the tasks outside the Allied context. It is worth mentioning that NATO doctrine was also changing. The Alliance also had to process the operational lessons of Bosnia, develop the Allied doctrine on PSO[58] and distinguish the role of air power in these operation.[59] Although the influence of NATO doctrines on AP 3000 can be traced, the main details of the use of air power in Allied operations were embodied in Allied doctrinal publications rather than in national environmental doctrine *per se*. The same is the case with the impact of foreign doctrines. Although it can be expected that the British, American, Australian, Canadian and New Zealand Air Forces would want to harmonize their doctrines in order to ease cooperation and Allied efforts, the practice shows that actual cooperation in doctrinal matters was minimal. Peter Gray, Tony Mason and Andrew Vallance argued that although the doctrines of Australia and New Zealand were and are read, they are not used as models for the doctrinal principles embodied within particular publications. On the other hand, it is not necessary, since there is always NATO Allied doctrine which is used by member states in Allied operations.

Overall, external factors were influential in the doctrine writing of 1999. However, the degree to which each factor had influence varied. The experience of previous operations and the wider context of threats and changes in security structures were more influential and thus better reflected in the text of the doctrine. However, external exchange of concepts and technologies and foreign doctrines had minimal influence and presence in this doctrine. Accordingly, a distinction should be made between the ways each factor could influence doctrine writing. Operational experience and changes in security threats were more influential since they posed the actual challenges that the RAF had to resolve and illustrate in its doctrine. Therefore, the external environment had a direct effect on doctrine, while conceptual exchange and foreign doctrines had indirect and circumstantial impact on the process, which is explained by the lack of an institutionalized framework for doctrinal cooperation. Concepts or foreign doctrines can influence networks or authors. The degree of influence depended on the authors' personal contacts and the purpose of each publication.

Domestic politics

External influences can be summarized as operational experience in the Balkans and PSO strategic realities. Domestic political factors can be narrowed down to the new Labour Foreign Policy, subsequent Defence Review of the Armed Forces and the introduction of jointery. The new government posed not only new objectives for the Armed Forces but also defined the way of reforming the Armed Forces in the post–Cold War era. In terms of foreign policy, the expeditionary approach demanded well-prepared and functional Armed Forces emphasizing the importance of quality and technological capacity rather than the size of the services.[60] In terms of budgetary cuts, the previous approach of reducing numbers was complemented with a holistic approach of cost-efficiency and interservice collaboration within jointery.[61]

The relationship between the Treasury and the military sector in the first post–Cold War years is worth discussing in order to understand the importance of this review and its influence on the Armed Forces. Despite the prevalence of conflicts in international relations and development of new threats in the 1990–1996, the domestic politics and decisions of the Treasury were driven by the so-called 'peace dividend' and the proto-defence review *Options for change*.[62] Following this narrative, it was suggested that the new environment would require smaller forces due to the diminishing conventional threats after the end of the Cold War. While from a political perspective, this trend made sense, the militaries called it 'options for cuts'.[63] The main implication of the Treasury-driven approach to reforming the Armed Forces was fragmentation. Thus, there was a lack of connection between capabilities and future operational roles.[64] On this topic, Prof Lawrence Freedman stated that 'over the 1990s defence spending was cut by over 20 percent, moving from over 4 per cent of GDP to under 3 … with the Gulf soon followed by an active role of Bosnia, at the same time as forces being cut, there were soon the familiar complaints about over-stretch'.[65] While the threat of total war ceased to exist with the end of the Soviet Union and the Warsaw Pact Treaty Organization, the necessity of reducing military budgets seemed justified in an environment lacking clarity and precision of both political and strategic objectives. Looking at that time retrospectively, the advantage of reforming the Armed Forces in the first five to seven years was lost. The financial cuts occurring during this time would define the limitations of the future reforms and spectrum of roles the Armed Forces could and actually had to play in different operational settings.

The SDR and jointery

The Strategic Defence Review (SDR) emphasized that the Armed Forces should be reformed along 'joint' lines. The main rationale for the introduction of the joint approach was the necessity of improving the capabilities of the Armed Forces through cost-efficiency and reduced numbers. A new approach corresponded to the global trend of shifting from human (number)-centric capabilities to technology-oriented composition of the Armed Forces. This tendency originated in the United States with the strengthening of the RMA debate and positive assessment of technological success in the Gulf War. The core of this approach was building smaller, more functional and technologically capable Armed Forces, emphasizing their capacities in the range of operations required by each government. In the case of the UK, the Secretary of State for Defence, George Robertson, argued that the joint approach was needed to improve the coordination of tri-service activities, in order to combine their unique experiences and thus maximize the strength of their strike, while avoiding duplication and waste of resources.[66] From strictly financial and political perspectives, the approach was sensible and easy to implement. However, for the three independent services, each with its own history, traditions and military ethos, the initiative was challenging. Addressing this issue, the SDR suggested:

> While single-Service skills and ethos will remain the essential foundation of all our military capability, most future operations will be conducted by joint forces composed of fighting units from individual Services. These will be under joint (tri-Service) command and control, drawing on joint intelligence capabilities and with joint logistics. We must therefore also build the joint approach into our doctrine and our preparation and training for operations.[67]

This paragraph is important for this book because it identified the place of doctrine in military practice and its utility in the joint environment. References to the joint approach within the AP 3000 third edition will be considered later, but this paragraph illustrates the general direction the doctrine followed. Moreover, in the AP 3000 third edition, when the Allied cooperation is characterized, a clear distinction was made between Allied and Joint Command and Control. The exact chain of subordination of C2 of Joint Forces was described as particularly important for the RAF and air power environment.[68]

Although the approach was maintained through the entire SDR paper, it also had its specific focal points and envisaged practical implications. First, the then existing Joint Rapid Deployment Forces were to be modernized in order to improve their capability and functionality in diverse operations, and renamed Joint Rapid Reaction Forces.[69] Subsequent changes in strategic transport, joint helicopter command, logistic enhancements and medical support were envisaged. Further, bilateral projects between the services were initiated. The

RAF and the Royal Navy (RN) were to cooperate in terms of Joint Force 2000, using both RN Sea Harrier FA2 and RAF Harrier GR7 aircraft as a combined force capable of operating from land or carriers.[70] Although this initiative illustrated the principles of synergy and jointery, it raised some concerns among the MOD Central Staff, who expected the usual friction between the RAF and RN, especially since SDR provided each service with a right to shape its own destiny, yet in a limited way.[71]

Although the paper identified the actual projects and suggested ways of cooperation between services, and acquisition of new platforms for the improvement and modernization of each service, the introduction of jointery into training schemes and doctrines was the most crucial tasks. Joint training was going to follow the RN/RAF Harrier initiative and Army/RAF training in the framework of ground-based air defence.[72] Moreover, the Chief of Joint Operations was given additional responsibilities and authority to intercede in terms of joint training and exercises. The further detailing of these enhanced duties was identified in the paragraph 174 of the SDR:

> The responsibilities of the Chief of Joint Operations will be enhanced. The post will have increased authority for enhancing the training and preparedness of the Joint Rapid Reaction Forces and will have a greater voice in stating joint warfare requirements. Budgetary authority and responsibility will also be increased and the post will become a Top Level Budget holder in its own right.[73]

The next step was to establish common joint principles of warfighting for the three services, bringing them together within a single conceptual framework. As a result, the Joint Defence Centre (JDC), aimed at spreading and institutionalization of 'a truly Joint Service vision',[74] was established.

Therefore, the SDR suggested the development of jointery as a way of reforming the Armed Forces, but what were the implications for the Armed Forces in general and the RAF in particular? First, unlike the previous proto-defence review of the Conservative government, *Options for Change*, the SDR was more constructive, systematic and detailed.[75] Second, the Labour Government was serious about reorganizing the Armed Forces within jointery. This was demonstrated in the authority of the Chief of Joint Operations, the introduction of the JDC, and immediate projects for services cooperation. Third, whether the services liked it or not, they had to consider this initiative and adapt accordingly. Finally, although defence policy was not in New Labour's Manifesto,[76] the SDR prepared under the Labour Government took into account the complexity of interservice cooperation. The general tone suggested that although the government supported the Armed Forces and their qualitative adaptation to the new environment, there was no alternative for services' development except jointery, emphasizing interservice cooperation across all levels. The rapid and meticulous presentation of jointery in SDR and immediate practical steps of its implementation illustrated seriousness of governmental intentions. For the Armed Forces, this meant that jointery the way to secure funding. This does not mean that the initiative was counterproductive in its nature or did not reflect the national and external strategic realities. Nevertheless, in terms of an interservice discourse, when justifying a certain purchase or sustainability of a platform, emphasizing a joint context could provide additional weight to the argument. Moreover, as CAS Richard Johns mentioned earlier, the SDR discussion illustrated limited understanding of air power potential in multinational operations. Thus, in order to navigate effectively in the overarching joint framework and have something to show for the next defence review, more attention should be paid to explaining the actual capabilities and characteristics of air power. Thus, besides initiating a new edition of AP 3000, CAS also ordered a more technical booklet on RAF capabilities:

> I also instructed the Air Warfare Centre to produce a booklet for wide distribution that catalogued all of the RAF's aircraft and weapons with their performance capabilities and characteristics ... I am confident that it was not a 'best seller' amongst the MOD's accountants more concerned with balancing budgets than understanding the cost competitive capabilities that gave best value for money – capabilities that relied on innovative technology to stay ahead of potential adversaries.[77]

The same was the case with conceptual framework and doctrines. The national doctrine hierarchy was evolving. The publication of a joint doctrine by the JDC would require incorporating the joint principles within the single-service doctrines. Although this might seem quite prescriptive and perhaps rather too early in the institutional culture, where doctrine was just beginning to gain its place; it was up to each service to determine the extent to which joint doctrine principles would be incorporated into single-service doctrines. For instance, a single-service doctrine could acknowledge the existence of joint publications and its subordination to joint principles. On the other hand, a doctrine could be written with jointery in mind, demonstrating not only doctrine hierarchy and adherence to joint principles, but emphasizing how the use of the described force could fit into joint requirements and how jointery oriented the service was.

The implications of the SDR for RAF doctrine

The SDR influenced the RAF not only in terms of the envisaged projects and prescribed cooperation with other services, but also in acquiring new technologies and their application to air power. The organizational changes the SDR triggered influenced every aspect of the service's existence – from teaching and training of new cadets in the joint framework, to the very process of conceptualization of air power and doctrine writing. In the prelude to the SDR, in 1997, three independent Staff Colleges merged into a Joint Services Command and Staff College, in order to provide joint teaching and preparation of personnel. The academy's staff was preoccupied with the development of a new teaching programme and curriculum suitable for all three services. As a result, library and academic staff lost the close connection to and involvement in preparation of materials for a new doctrine. During the preparation of the first two editions of AP 3000, librarians and academic staff were involved in data collection, analysis of case studies and preparation for further evaluation by the author, Andrew Vallance, and DDefS (although, in the case of the first publication, he was both the author and DDefS). The main data collected referred to the experiences of using air power in the past; and case studies, which would demonstrate the practical utility of the proposed theories.[78] However, after 1997, the connection between DDefS and academic staff weakened, mainly because the position of DDefS was not incorporated into the structure of academic personnel. While this instruction provided DDefS with greater independence, it undermined his ties with the academic staff. Therefore, after the SDR, doctrine writing was becoming more formalized, limiting the number of external participants. Although the initiation of a new edition was in the hands of CAS, DDefS was still responsible for writing it. This status quo demonstrated the service's independence in decision-making regarding doctrinal matters.

The SDR and jointery had another impact on the service – they threatened integrity and independence. As the history of the RAF demonstrated, the service has always had to fight for its independence, which inevitably affected the individual self-consciousness of airmen. The necessity of the RAF to distinguish itself from the other services induced a constant self-doubt, self-scrutiny and even under-estimation. As Dr Meilinger stated, 'Airmen in my country, and anecdotally in yours [the UK], Australia, etc., tend to be self-conscious and have an inferiority complex that is richly undeserved. We are reluctant to extol our virtues, which are many, and tend to defer to the senior services.'[79] However, the introduction of jointery as the primary way of reforming the Armed Forces did not establish two distinctive career paths in the RAF. The SDR did not change the way each service noted and promoted abilities of officers of all ranks, nor did it change the daily practices of collaborating with the other two services. By then, all three services had realized that single services were the best keepers of traditions and individual, organizational identity. However, from an operational perspective, each service was bringing different skills to support one another. Those who served in joint and Allied environments were naturally identified because they had a wider experience.

The tendency towards an Army-oriented approach was hardly conditioned by operational considerations of limited interference in the PSO environment. Neither the Gulf War nor Bosnia were particularly Army driven in their nature; synergetic in the case of the Gulf – yes, but not defined by land forces alone. According to Peter Gray, the main rationale for the Army prevalence was due to the following reasons:

> In 1997, in preparation of SDR, thinking was not threat-based, range of scenarios, studies were assessed. A number of scenarios on different scales were run through computer war games, evaluated a number of forces needed to conduct this or that task. The Army dominated, because it was able to say 'we need three times this in order to achieve that, because our doctrine said so'. So, they used doctrine to its full effect. The RAF could not say the same. That is where the 3rd edition of AP 3000 came from.[80]

In other words, it can also be assumed that the RAF had to follow the rules the SDR had introduced and institutionalized in order to remain in the game: 'This process of 1997–98 was embodied in establishment of Joint Doctrine Centre which is today known as DCDC. The idea was that all doctrines to be joint. Whether AP 3000 was a joint is another question. The 3rd edition was heavily supporting the Army. This was anomalous for RAF doctrine.'[81] Prima facie, there is nothing wrong with organizational change if it aims to produce greater ends. However, in the context of RAF strategic culture, any shift from the RAF-centred environmental doctrine towards an Army-oriented one could endanger the very purpose and understanding of the doctrine itself, potentially returning the RAF to a state of ignoring doctrine. Therefore, any controversy about which direction the doctrine should take could undermine the status of doctrine and simply return it to the point when personnel ignored it. It is also quite interesting whether the new direction in the third edition had any impact on doctrinal silence in the decade that followed. The next edition would see the light only in 2009. In any case, these ideas are discussed in detail when the fourth edition is analysed in the second case study. Now is the time to identify actual references to jointery and cooperation with the Army in the text of the doctrine.

Textual analysis of jointery and Army context in AP 3000 (1999)

The very introduction of this edition set the tone for the entire document, suggesting that its main aim was to adjust the service to the contemporary military context. The use of air power had to correspond to the existing strategic environment, which was shaped by the SDR, emphasizing the direction for expeditionary operations, the principles of flexibility and mobility of the UK Armed Forces. Moreover, the introduction acknowledged that the SDR initiated the development of joint doctrine.[82] This first paragraph of the introduction summarizes the drive to jointery and the need to fit the RAF into the joint environment and cooperation with other services. Later, this theme is reflected in how air power is described and applied. The actual examples in the document should be traced, in order to understand the extent to which this theme was sound and, thus, to evaluate its influence on perception of air power thinking and application.

The most revolutionary step was a discussion of the joint context in the chapter devoted to the theory of air power. In this respect, the main argument was that air power was no longer focused exclusively on air forces (a statement that was unacceptable for many). Air power was a matter of joint and combined business. It was argued that 'air warfare is now just as much a part of land and maritime warfare as it is a separate discipline'.[83] What we see here is an attempt to merge three distinct environments of the conduct of warfare into a single, joint one, and air power was meant to combine capabilities of all three. This idea was further justified through the following characteristics of air power: 'Is inherently joint, combined and multinational in nature. Encompasses forces drawn from all three Services. Is concerned with the effective exploitation of air power assets. Is supported by national civilian and commercial resources. Is influenced by, and in turn influences, the land, sea and space environments.'[84] From this description, the interconnectivity of three environments and three services is placed as a foundation stone for the provision of air power. This emphasis is entirely different from the one made in the previous editions. In the first two editions, air power was identified through the distinctiveness of the environment and the Air Force and wider military purposes.[85]

When considering implementation of jointery, cooperation with ground forces was highlighted. Although an equal amount of attention could have been paid to both sister services, the ground forces were particularly favoured. Tri-service cooperation was envisaged in terms of the manoeuvrist approach.[86] Accordingly, the enemy was to be defeated by destroying his cohesion and will to fight instead of his materiel, taking advantage of momentum and tempo to achieve shock action.[87] The core of this approach is 'an attitude of mind in which doing the unexpected and seeking originality is combined with ruthless determination to succeed'.[88] The doctrine declared that the application of air power was inherently manoeuvrist. It could be applied on its own or in support of a joint manoeuvre.[89] Furthermore, 'with careful, joint, planning the speed and precision provided by fixed and rotary-wing air systems can be linked with surface manoeuvre and indirect fire, increasing the available combat power which might be applied to an enemy's weak point'.[90] The description of the manoeuvrist approach in terms of the three services showed that the independent role of air power was not highlighted, although, the manoeuvrist approach allowed for it. Instead, obvious commitment to jointery and cooperation with the ground forces was noted. When referring to the utility of air power, the direct and indirect roles in Joint Force Employment were distinguished,[91] which was not simply a substitution for the terms 'decisive' and 'supportive' or 'secondary'. In both direct and indirect contributions, the role was complementary and supportive. Indirect air operations were envisioned for preparation of the battle space for further actions of the ground forces, while direct air operations 'can prove decisive in concentrating force and allowing manoeuvre from the air to complement rotary-air and surface force manoeuvre'.[92]

The very definition of direct operations and emphasis on 'can prove decisive' may seem hesitant and doubtful of the decisive potential of air power. The reluctance to be more supportive of the decisiveness of air power in direct air operations and the emphasis on its supportive role for ground forces manoeuvre can be explained in a few ways. First, the authors tried to downplay the independent role of air power in order to overcome the past shadow of the strategic bombing ethos and thus to make air power look more modern. Alternatively, it can be viewed as another step towards an Army-led approach of reforming the Armed Forces. The latter argument is quite relevant because in any instance of direct or indirect operation, the role of air power was to support the ground forces in their manoeuvre. The only difference would be the degree of its involvement and the close proximity of interaction between forces. The best examples are interdiction and close air support. Apart from distinguishing between Joint and Allied commands, AP 3000 explained the decision-making cycle involving the Joint Targeting Coordination Board (JTCB), its approval of the Joint Integrated

Prioritised Target List (JIPTL), Joint Estimate with further assignment of air power through Joint Force Air Component Commander (JFACC) air operation planning.[93] The main guidance for further actions was JWP 0–10 together with the RAF Air Operations Manual and AJP 1-(A): NATO Allied Joint Operations doctrine. The emphasis of jointery within future operations and the role of air power was illustrated not only by the description of the joint decision-making process and the subsequent steps in its implementation, but also by incorporating the joint publications of the JDC. Thus, this edition showed a connection to the national doctrinal process and a clear doctrine hierarchy.

The roles of air power

Another way to evaluate the extent the doctrine was joint and Army oriented is to explore which roles air power was ascribed in the text and how. The second part of the doctrine was devoted to the roles of air power. The positioning of roles had a particular purpose. The first two roles were information exploitation and control of the air. The chapter on information explained the use of air power in acquiring data and intelligence to provide support to planning, targeting and information for ground forces.[94] Here the intention was not simply to describe the information collecting role of air power or its contribution to the preparation of operations. The purpose was to show the central role of air power in data collection and timeliness of its attainment and distribution in strengthening what is today known as situational awareness. The doctrine stressed the significance of information in determining potential lines of operations and centres of gravity on both operational and strategic levels in order to achieve posed objectives: 'Air power platforms and systems play **a vital role** in gathering data and information; thus, the timely exploitation of information is a key core capability of air power.'[95]

The next chapter explained the utility of control of the air in different conflicts.[96] Control of the air was defined in one sentence with further interservice commitments in such a way: 'Friendly control of the air aims to restrict an opponent's ability to use air power against friendly forces.'[97] Consequently, this role was adjusted into the joint and Allied environment. Further emphasis on the vital function of this role across different types of conflict suggested the impact of the SDR and general strategic realities. However, it also demonstrated a vital need to promote air power in that new environment. The control of the air required a balance between offensive and defensive. Further, Offensive Counter-Air (OCA) operations were explained in detail, covering the following potential roles: airfield attack, suppression of enemy's air defences (SEAD), fighter sweep, escort and Command and Control Warfare (C2W).[98] Although attention was paid to the offensive role of counter-air operations, the main commitment was to joint actions, suggesting that other forces can substantially contribute to OCA in attacks on airfields and defence suppression, making these operations joint. The maximum effect could be achieved if joint capabilities of all services are taken into account.[99]

The next role, which was the most difficult to explain within a jointery-oriented doctrine was the strategic effects of air power. It was difficult to incorporate this role, owing to its association with the historically championed independence of the RAF. Promotion of this role could be counterproductive in the new joint environment.[100] However, it could not be ignored. The authors of the doctrine found another solution – they applied the same approach as to air power in general – adjustment of the strategic function of air power into joint discourse. The doctrine stated that since air power can reach and destroy adversary's centres of gravity, its actions inherently may result in strategic effect. However, it was acknowledged that this effect could be achieved in different ways through an independent or joint action within national or multinational frameworks.[101] Taking into consideration the history of the RAF and the association of strategic bombing with dogmatic thinking and interservice rivalry, much attention was paid to explanation that strategic effect did not equal strategic bombing or attack aircraft *per se*. It was emphasized that each combat air platform and related weapons were capable of achieving strategic effects.[102] Furthermore, the narrative followed the planning of the strategic effects of air power in joint campaigns in order to move away from even the slightest hints of associating air power for strategic effects with independent single-service action. The concept of centres of gravity, together with specific means and the importance of timing for achievement of the end-state were explored. It was also suggested that air power might be used together with two other forces, which, 'although aimed at the strategic centre of gravity, in support of the overall aim, may be mounted distinct from the joint campaign or from outside the theatre boundary; it is this distinction which sets air operations for strategic effect apart from other roles and missions'.[103]

This emphasis incorporated both the Allied nature of this role and its distinctiveness from other roles air power could play. In other words, it was a diplomatic attempt to placate both protagonists of jointery even in such matters as the strategic effect of air power and protagonists of the independent approach to air power. This example also shows that, at that time, it was difficult to 'sell' the strategic function of air power to the Army-oriented policymakers. On the other hand, this edition of doctrine did not try to do just that. It went to great lengths to detail the objectives of strategic effect and target selection and their correlation with political restraints and purposes. Importantly, it avoided grandiose claims that air power was a panacea to all problems; instead, it emphasized careful target choice to meet exact objectives.[104] Later, when levels of operations for strategic effect were explained, meaning concurrent (parallel actions with other forces), simultaneous (coordination with ground forces manoeuvre) and autonomous operations, directly dependent on aerospace; it was still emphasized that they 'may be distinct from theatre level operations but in support of the strategic aim or end-state'.[105]

Even in obviously autonomous air operation, the doctrine had to re-emphasize the commitment of the RAF to operational jointery, something which would have been quite obvious before and would never have been restated in the previous two editions of AP 3000. On the plus side, the importance of Precision-Guided Munition (PGMs) congruent to their level of success in Bosnia was stressed with further argument for the availability and potential of what was known then as unmanned combat air vehicle (UCAV). As the most technology-dependent force, the concepts and manoeuvrability were as good as the pilot in the cockpit and the technological characteristics of the aircraft compared to those of the adversary. Although the art of piloting and individual human skills had overcome various technological downfalls in the past, air power required cutting-edge or at least up-to-date technological innovations and investment in order to remain competitive in the battlespace and preserve multifaceted functionality. Reading between the lines, this aspect can be restated as follows: the air force was committed to the new trend of jointery and subsequent cost-efficiency, but for its better performance new technologies were essential.

This conclusion was particularly relevant to the next three chapters, which were devoted to joint force deployment and the role of air power in the joint operations, emphasizing direct and indirect operations, combat support air operations and force protection. The particular feature of the indirect air operations was a distinction between land/air synergy and air/maritime operations.[106] In those chapters, the synergy between services, and the importance of air power for jointery was re-emphasized through practical examples illustrating potential cooperation between the Armed Forces. In this context, it was restated that the inherent flexibility of air platforms allowed for a rapid switch from one mission and role to another.[107] Two conclusions can be drown from this statement. First, air power is an indispensable asset that can be used as a force multiplier, transport or enabler of situational awareness to strengthen the efficiency of the other forces used. Thus, by undermining the air force capabilities, the very essence of the cost-efficiency and interservice synergy of jointery would be undermined. Second, the inherent advantages of air power, such as flexibility, speed, reach and autonomy were still shown, arguing for its self-sufficiency and ability of taking different degrees of situational responsibilities. Overall, these numerous references to the multifunctionality of air power across different types of conflict looked like an attempt to secure a stable place for air power in the new strategic environment, no matter which operations dominated that environment. These measures also pre-empted any criticism of the RAF for being inflexible and reluctant to embrace cost-efficient reform of the Armed Forces.

There are a few more features of the text that are worth considering. Although the first two editions of AP 3000 outlined that the service had to change and adapt to the new realities, it did not include the SDR process and jointery, because they were introduced only in 1998. Therefore, the new doctrine was meant to explain a new path and promote the service's role in the implementation of jointery. However, there was also another purpose of the doctrine – to defend the service and air power in the face of the new financial cuts and restructuring of the service along joint lines. Unlike any other military force, air power is directly dependent on accurate and cutting-edge technologies. This doctrine, like any other, had to explain and secure understanding of this importance with policymakers. The importance of technology for air power was shown in two ways. First, it was demonstrated in the role of different technologies and air platforms in specific operational examples, like the benefits of UAVs. This approach was appealing to rational thinking, showing evidence of the significance of technologies for operational success. This feature also corresponded to the technology-centred approach manifested by jointery. Second, the role of technology was also illustrated in an indirect manner by using visual images. Readers' attention was attracted not only by textual examples of usefulness of technology for air power but also by its visual embodiment. Such a multichannel approach appealed to a more systematic realization of the connection between these technologies and specific roles of air power. Thus, the systematic perception of the unity between air power and its technological embodiment was achieved by incorporating various pictures of advanced aircraft and their association with particular roles of air power. The photo of Tornado GR4A was associated with armed reconnaissance,[108] Tornado GR1 with Air Launched Anti-Radiation Missile (ALARM) as an embodiment of the suppression of enemy air defences,[109] Harrier GR7 with Close Air Support[110] and even the long-awaited Eurofighter[111] were used as examples of multirole aircraft.[112] Forty-two photos were used in this edition, of which twenty-eight depicted contemporary aircraft associated with a particular role. Two pictures showed the same Eurofighter: the first picture immediately after the contents, which suggested the advanced technological dimension of the service. Eight pictures demonstrated historical examples of aircraft, and the other six depicted personnel and support facilities. These illustrations show one of a few trends in air power thinking and formal representation. Technology, particularly Eurofighter, were important for the RAF, which was the newest and most advanced at the time of doctrine publication. Nevertheless, the use of illustrations depicting Air Force personnel showed that despite being technology-centric, air power depends on airmen and their symbiosis with aircraft as a key to successful and effective use of air power. Among other illustrations, there were six charts explaining air operations directives (the planning process of assignment of air power),[113] the British doctrine hierarchy[114] and campaign planning tools for air operations with strategic effect.[115] Another aspect of the document is that although some practical examples of air power use or conceptualization were based on best practice or historical illustrations, the most commonly used contexts were those of the Gulf War and Bosnia. Accordingly, the document did not simply explain new theories and new context with reference to previous best practice, but actually incorporated both best practice and new experiences into the contemporary strategic context with further lessons and guiding principles for air power to adapt to the new challenges and develop responses accordingly. Thus, the document struck a balance between old and new.

Overall, unlike previous experiences of doctrine writing, which mainly reflected the new experiences gained in ongoing and previous operations, the new edition of AP 3000 was primarily influenced and subsequently driven by the internal political changes initiated by the SDR. While the previous two editions emphasized a single-service approach to air power, the third edition was inspired by the joint context. Another way to look at this transformation is in financial terms. Under the conditions of constant budgetary cuts, one way to secure a certain stability of funding and preservation of the service was the adoption of the Army-led joint approach. This does not mean that this decision was incorrect or did not fit into the existing strategic, political or financial realities; rather that it was different from the organizational culture within the service.

Although there were always protagonists of the synergetic approach, it had never been supported and applied at this level before. Despite its timely publication and subsequent provision of guidance for the service's adaptation to the SDR requirements, the doctrine had to overcome the reluctance of the service to adopt and follow what was an Army-led approach. This argument once again demonstrates the importance of domestic politics in the doctrine preparation process. In other words, with the introduction of jointery at national level, the process of institutionalization of doctrine writing started. At this initial stage, the joint publications were established as umbrella frameworks and no single-service or environmental doctrine could deviate from or contradict joint doctrine and further publications of the JDC. The analysis suggests that domestic politics and interservice relations were the crucial driving forces for doctrine writing, while the external environment and the experience of previous operations were the context or background for the internal changes. The cause–effect relation, in this case, is particularly important. Without changes in the external environment (the operational experience in the use of air power and the necessity for jointery), no crucial changes in the internal environment (the institutionalization of jointery and expeditionary warfare) would be possible. In fact, the internal environment offers responses to the threats and challenges posed by the external environment. The internal responses often take the form of White Papers or Defence Reviews. New defence policy objectives and each doctrine should correspond to them. In terms of this chapter, it can be concluded that, after 1998, the impact of the external strategic environment on the doctrine writing became more indirect than before. This impact is filtered through the systematic changes in domestic politics and interservice relations. Based on this conclusion it can be assumed that with each factor's proximity to the actual process of doctrine writing, the degree of that factor's influence should increase. The further analysis of the roles of academics and writers in doctrine preparation will verify or refute this statement.

4

Case Study of the Third Edition of AP 3000 (Part II)

This chapter continues the analysis of the first case study of the third edition of AP 3000 (1999). Unlike the previous chapter, this one concentrates on two other factors of doctrine writing: the roles of networks (academics and review boards) and authors in the process of doctrine preparation. This chapter illustrates that the involvement of academics in doctrinal workshops is secondary. However, collaboration with academics encourages critical, innovative and systematic thinking on air power. This collaboration also assists in the adaptation to a rapidly changing external environment. Moreover, academics and review boards influenced authors' decision-making in preparing first drafts. The impact of the authors' background on the intellectual nature of doctrine under consideration is also explained in this chapter.

Networks (academics)

While the first two factors influencing doctrine writing were easy to trace in the text, the other two are more difficult to pin down. This chapter addresses the role of academics and writers in the doctrine writing of 1999. Dr Oliver Daddow argued that authors of doctrine are inevitably in touch with the wider world and are influenced by the new tendencies in thinking on warfare, strategy and conflict. Consequently, academics can influence doctrine in two ways – directly through editing and revising doctrinal texts or 'informally in writing about conflict and strategy'.[1] However, academics can also link external and internal factors through their analytical thinking and knowledge. Academics process the existing data and transform into concepts which can be verified through best practice. Since this factor is quite difficult to trace, interviews and actual academic writing on the subject were the best sources for this exploration. Historically, a collaboration between academics and militaries proved to be fruitful, resulting in unconventional solutions to existing problems and development of creative thinking. The achievements of scientific intelligence during the Second World War are an excellent example of such collaboration. Nevertheless, as with any collaboration involving people coming from different backgrounds and disciplines, it was challenging to reach a consensus and drive progress. As a result, mixed perceptions among the Armed Forces of academic involvement in the process of establishing a conceptual component is far from surprising. Nevertheless, this collaboration often proved to be worth the efforts. During the interviews, not a single negative comment on academic involvement in doctrine writing was made. On the contrary, the active involvement of academics was viewed as of benefit for the development of the RAF and the future of air power.[2] Academic research on military topics is advantageous because academics are devoted to their specific area of interest and are likely to deepen their knowledge and gather information in detail within both a single discipline and the interdisciplinary framework. From one perspective, distance from the actual involvement in organizational processes, hierarchical interactions and unique squadron and service cultural identities allows academics to be more objective in the assessment of certain events and processes. Academics are driven by the necessity of collecting evidence to answer their research question. According to Andrew Vallance:

> In the 1990s, the weakness of the RAF was the lack of academics in its training machine. Nobody in the Staff College could be called a proper academic, in a sense of their activity. You are appointed for a certain position, then you move to another one ... rather like 'ships in the night'. On the other hand, academics are permanent; they bring continuity to their research and the topic they study.[3]

Subsequently, the cooperation between militaries and academics can be effective in the verification of developed concepts and processing of the existing totality of analytical materials accumulated by academics in the field of strategic and defence studies. Hence, the role of academics can be extended from an ordinary analysis of previous experiences and their potential improvement, to a more systematic role in the evaluation of a cause–effect relationship between the efficiency of military actions in the achievement of posed objectives and the impact on sociopolitical processes at home. It is not accidental that the last twenty years have witnessed the increased role of academics in preparation and informing of political decision-making. How active that involvement is and how eager institutions are to take into account academic suggestions is another matter. After the end of the Cold War, military actions and their implications became more accessible by the wider public through the media, with further increase of the accountability of the Armed Forces to the public at home.[4] These days, the best way to lose war is to lose it at home.[5] The best example of this is the initial reluctance of the British public to support military action in Syria.[6] Therefore, the role of academics can be in the adjustment of military objectives into a context and with a discourse understandable to a wider audience. Academics tend to be a link between militaries and civilians in mutual understanding of each other's motives. Placing this statement into the doctrinal discourse, the involvement of academics can help to clarify doctrines to a wider audience. This also includes policymakers, various branches of government and other potential stakeholders. Therefore, the doctrine might become more mainstream and understandable by the public. It should not be forgotten that the main function of doctrine is to guide the Armed Forces. However, it would not hurt if it was written in a public-friendly manner and incorporated in intellectual considerations.

With all the benefits of academic involvement in doctrine writing, there are also certain difficulties. Often academics have to overcome the scepticism and prejudice of some military practitioners in order to be heard and make a difference. In this context, another feature of RAF culture is a struggle between tactics-oriented and intellectual approaches. Each doctrine is scrutinized and criticized by protagonists of each group, making the favourable acceptance of each doctrine dependent on the balance between practical necessities and intellectualism. The main challenge for the RAF since the 1970s was to return intellectualism and broader thinking on air power into everyday organizational practice. In this context, the role of DDefS, as the main supporter of intellectuals, was in stimulating cooperation between academics and practitioners on both strategic and global thinking on air power. The intellectuals emphasized the necessity of comprehending the full picture of air power potential, thinking beyond the technological capabilities of that time.[7] Thus, a more developmental and insightful approach was suggested. The opposite group argued for a more holistic approach to presentation, thinking, teaching and application of air power. The entire air power discourse was meant to be tactics-oriented and look into what air power could practically achieve at that time instead of conceptualizing about unattainable future. So, this approach is oriented towards here and now. It argues for simplicity in air power thinking.[8] In terms of the doctrinal discourse, this dichotomy was of particular relevance because depending on who was responsible for its preparation and to which group he belonged, the doctrine had a different shape. If the doctrine was more practice oriented, the size of the document tended to be shorter, the language simpler and oriented to the military audience alone. In contrast, intellectual doctrine aimed to achieve the same objectives as practice-oriented doctrine, but with the adjustment of military doctrine into wider strategic and creative thinking on air power, or, as in the case of the third edition of AP 3000, into the context of jointery. The organizational, tactics-oriented culture originated in the historical danger and subsequent bravery in flying aircraft. That is why, until recently, those who did not fly were unlikely to go further than two stars.[9] Such an unspoken rule affected pilots' self-perception and positioning towards the rest of the service, other services and the wider public. Therefore, it is not surprising that intellectualism was and still is quite opposed by strict practitioners. As Andrew Vallance stressed earlier, pilots were likely to back their own units, while academics looked on the matter from analytical and objective perspectives. Therefore, certain clashes were unavoidable in justification of opposite or slightly different opinions.

The academic context of AP 3000 (1999)

Taking into account all the earlier-mentioned content, cooperation with academics in doctrine writing could have been active and direct. However, the situation was slightly different. The first way in which academics could influence RAF doctrine was the SDR itself. In this context, prominent specialists in strategic and conflict studies were consulted concerning their professional expertise on the subject matter. One of those academics was Lawrence Freedman.[10] Although this shows the participation of academics in the general reforming of the Armed Forces, their role was consultative, with no guarantee of further implementation. Another feature of the process was that academics were not involved in the discussions or shaping of the initial drafts of the SDR. Therefore, their contribution was limited and consultative as a second opinion or a fresh view on the discussed topic. The degree of the influence of their contribution was very limited, and often become a pro forma instead of a genuine inquiry on their vision to influence a behaviour or policy.

Despite this indirect influence of the prominent strategic thinkers on RAF doctrine, academics were involved in doctrine writing in a less official way. As was stated before, academics were contacted on an interpersonal level. However, there was also the institutionalized and continuous way of cooperation between air power specialists and academics – air power workshops. Air Chief Marshal Sir Michael Graydon, who was CAS in 1992–1997, in the foreword to a monograph on air power thinking wrote: 'Two years ago [meaning 1994] I established an Air Power Workshop, bringing together a team of Air Force Officers and senior academics to analyse the dynamics at work in Air Operations, not only in traditional conflicts, but also in highly topical area of Peace Support Operations. This book is the result of their deliberations.'[11] While the proceedings of these workshops were not available for the public, the outcome of these discussions was the publication of anthologies on air power. These publications mainly aimed to stimulate systematic and professional thinking on air power in terms of the post–Cold War environment. In this case study, two anthologies are of particular relevance. The first one was *The Dynamics of Air Power*[12] edited by Group Captain Andrew Lambert and Arthur C. Williamson. The second was *Perspectives on Air Power: Air Power in Its Wider Context*,[13] edited by the author of the third edition of AP 3000, Stuart Peach.

Each of these publications reflected specifics of air power thinking of its time. The first publication stressed the need to re-emphasize the roles of air power in the environment of both conventional and unconventional warfare. Both academics and practitioners had to explore lessons previous campaigns taught the RAF on the contemporary utility of air power and its future roles. The first part of the book addressed the 'Evolving Theory' of air power. Consequently, attention was paid to the clarification of features of air power as a key to its understanding and adaptation to new challenges[14]; evaluation of counter-air contest in terms of political and strategic implications[15]; practical considerations of synergy through the experience of previous operations[16]; contemporary evaluation of air power efficiency in terms of coercion[17]; and the relationship between air power, the changing sociopolitical reality and the image of militaries and warfare in public perception.[18]

These essays illustrated what the RAF elite and academics thought about changes of air power functions in the post–Cold War era. They demonstrated conceptual changes and ways of thinking on air power. These published essays are important physical evidence demonstrating cooperation between academics and RAF professionals towards systematic and interdisciplinary thinking and evaluation of air power functionality in a new strategic environment. In other words, academics suggested a conceptual framework of evaluation, while military practitioners assessed it against their experience and available resources. The military initiative of this symbiosis in the form of air power workshops argues for a greater orientation of this collaboration towards military needs rather than academia. Again, this suggests a more profound involvement of academics in strategic, intellectual thinking on air power and their active part in an evaluation of the lessons learned from previous operations. This feature was further reflected in the second part of the book, which was devoted to the evaluation of air power in conflict with PSO component. Accordingly, academics suggested concepts determined by the experiences of Bosnia and new characteristics of PSO. The strategic perspective of new operations,[19] the role of air power in them,[20] were followed by more practical considerations. For instance, attention was paid to support requirements,[21] reconnaissance and surveillance task,[22] air transport,[23] the counter-air mission,[24] air power and force in PSO.[25] Both academics and professionals did not aim only at simple recognition of lessons learned in the last campaign but at incorporating these lessons into the future application of air power. A military doctrine has the same aim – to adopt the lessons of past in order to fight the battles of today and tomorrow.

At first glance, no direct connection between this cooperation and doctrine preparation can be traced. In fact, from a doctrinal perspective, this accumulation of knowledge and the analysis of the use of air power in previous operations actually mattered and were taken into account. There was a direct connection between academics involved in these workshops and the doctrine writing of 1999. This link was DDefS, who was responsible for both accumulation of knowledge on global and contemporary use of air power and doctrine writing. In fact, each workshop involved senior RAF specialists, and was often attended by both CAS and DDefS. The latter would often be an editor of a final publication of a workshop. Overall, because introductions to these workshops were addressed by CAS, published by an authoritative institution and disseminated in the staff libraries, the importance of this material was formally acknowledged. Air power sceptics may argue that encouraging dissemination of this book did not mean that it was widely read and had the intended impact on air power thinking, and on the strengthening of intellectuality within the service and doctrine. Although this might be the case, the most important contribution of this book and air power workshops is that the future author of the third edition of AP 3000 was involved in them, edited the next publication and therefore was exposed to the intellectual discourse of that time. In the foreword to the second publication, a new CAS summarized the relation between two publications as follows:

> The result [of air power workshop] was 'The Dynamics of Air Power' first published in 1996, as a volume which broke a new ground in our thinking. This companion volume sets the foundation for describing air power within the wider context of contemporary warfare – conflicts that now embrace the development of new concepts involving matters such as space, coalition warfare and legal issues.[26]

The second publication is wider in its perspectives on air power. It was the result of various workshops held in the Centre for Defence Studies in London, during 1997. Like the military environment of that time, the new book paid attention to the increasing political role of air power. The first part, *Political Context*, evaluated new threats and challenges in the globalized and interdependant post–Cold War world, the relation between civil and military institutions and their impact on air power, coalition operations, the relationship between air power and international air law. The second part examined the technological context illustrating the prevailing RMA debate of that time: the meaning of technologies for air power, the implications of the information and space age and the air logistics of air operations. The third part referred to the military context and covered such topics as air power in joint warfare, coercion, the contemporary relevance of strategic bombing and the challenges of military power. Overall, the main aim of this volume was to stimulate thinking on air power in terms of a more complex reality – the multiple use of air power not only in the different types of conflict but also in the joint and Allied environments. In the general introduction to this volume, Stuart Peach wrote: 'Now we see air and space power in all their manifestations being employed with great utility around the spectrum of conflict. In addition to its independent application for strategic impact or effect, air and space power can be decisive in support and the key enabler for any joint or combined intervention campaign or expeditionary operation.'[27]

Thus, Stuart Peach re-emphasized the national strategic discourse of that time, but also proclaimed his vision of air power, which was further embodied in the doctrine he wrote. It is no coincidence that the volume he edited was titled *Wider Perspectives on Air Power*. As DDefS, he worked to stimulate more systematic and creative thinking on air power, which could contribute to diversity of its applications in the joint and Allied environment. This volume suggests a few considerations related to the third edition of AP 3000. First, Stuart Peach was not only exposed to the impact of academic and professional thinking on air power; he stimulated it as DDefS. He took an active part in its dissemination, which was the reason for his editing of the analysed volume. Second, the jointery-oriented discourse of air power reflected in doctrine was central to Stuart Peach's professional statements and subsequent thinking on air power. Third, his personal position on the air power dichotomy was definitely towards intellectualism and the systematization of thinking on air power. Finally, Stuart Peach's work with academics and professionals suggested his knowledge of the place of air power in the general defence discourse of that time, which again suggested that directly or indirectly, he was aware of academic knowledge on the subject and this was inevitably reflected in the doctrine he wrote. In fact, he was already working on the doctrine modernization at that time and mentioned it in the introduction, mainly referring to the necessity of its modification. He stated, 'and yet, theories and doctrines for air power remain largely in Cold War stasis.'[28]

The third edition was influenced by academics and had intellectual features in the narrative. Academic features can be traced through the entire document. First, the narration of the doctrine is very sophisticated and systematic in the explanation of a wider context of air power use and prevailing tendencies in strategy. This is particularly vivid in the first part devoted to the strategic context. Unlike the first two editions, the explanation of strategic environment is extensive and includes different perspectives of the same issue. Therefore, instead of bullet points, one would find lengthy book-style paragraphs aimed at the explaining the subject in a systematic and multifaceted way. Like academic works, this doctrine applied an inclusive approach instead of a simplistic one. For instance, the description of the dimensions of armed conflict took one and a half pages, tracing changes in armed conflict from the Cold War to the later years, emphasizing the changing character of the conflict in Bosnia.[29] The academic influence was evident not only in the number of details and systematic intention but also in the use of a sophisticated language. For instance:

> A conflict which is regarded as a war of national survival by one participant, may be viewed as an opportunistic border dispute by another. Level of interest in a conflict can vary from the extreme case where the very survival of the state is clearly threatened, to a situation where the interest at stake only marginally justifies the use of force.[30]

This paragraph demonstrates the existing academic thinking on the subject at that time. Unlike tactics-oriented doctrines, which use precise statements, without generalization or explanation of the situational nature of actions and conflicts, an intellectual doctrine aims at reflecting the contextual complexity of the discussed issues. Also, this paragraph illustrates an academically sophisticated language instead of a simplified military narrative. For instance, such terms as 'opportunistic' and 'marginal' are not terms in everyday military use. Another exclusively academic feature of the third edition was the inclusion of a separate chapter on further reading, which was entirely unconventional for a military doctrine. However, it is an ordinary practice for teaching manuals and textbooks. Looking at the selection of items for further reading, the general impression, once again, is that it aimed to build systematic understanding of air power through history. Therefore, instead of suggesting other doctrines, the list included academic books exploring the development of British and American air power through history.

So, what conclusion can be drawn on the role of academics in doctrine preparation process of AP 3000, third edition? First, the cooperation between academics and professionals took place before the doctrine was written. Second, two published volumes of air power and defence workshops suggest that thinking on air power was systematic and corresponded to doctrinal discourse, adjusting air power to the new strategic environment. Third, with the introduction of jointery as the way of reforming the Armed Forces, the shift from learning the lessons of previous operations to the systematic and multidimensional adjustment of air power into the joint and allied defence environment took place. Fourth, because the first volume was the result of air power workshops and the second of defence workshops suggests a shift of emphasis in administrative and technical terms. Stuart Peach was exposed to up-to-date thinking on air power due to his position as DDefS. In this case, day-to-day interactions, cooperation in workshops, conferences and meetings served as long-term consultations, shaping his overview. Finally, the impact of academic and professional discourse on the doctrine was present, but it was indirect. Thus, it can be concluded that Stuart Peach was aware of existing thinking on air power, as he was DDefS and it was his job to stimulate creative thinking. As he was a supporter of the intellectual approach to air power, academics partially shaped his wide overview on air power, which was reflected in the doctrine he wrote. On the other hand, there is also another consideration which should be taken into account – interpersonal relations.

Informal connections remain the dominant way of academic involvement in doctrine writing, and this was the case since the time of the first two editions of AP 3000. There are two reasons academics were involved through personal connections. First, looking at the defence studies field of research, one can notice that the majority of academics concentrate their attention on the Army and land warfare. In various discussions with practitioners of different generations, the conclusion is drawn that specialization in air power, particularly on the history of air power is rather non-stream. From personal experience, the author may say that there are few academics interested in air power doctrine or its conceptual component. Therefore, those few who actually specialized in this area are already known and in touch with the prominent military actors through conferences, various workshops, journal articles and interviews. The narrow circle of air power specialists and general narrow off-stream interest in air power make academics better known among air power people. Thus, contacts are more personal and direct in their nature. In fact, the main contributors to the two volumes on air power thinking discussed earlier were mostly the same few academics, including Dr Philip Towle, Dr Phillip Sabin, Professor Michael Clark, Dr K.A. Kyriakides and A.C. Williamson (a PhD candidate at that time).

Second, the traditional distinction between military personnel and academics is becoming blurred. Many retired practitioners, who combine both empirical military knowledge with creative thinking and are not opposed to intellectualism, after retirement, tend to get involved in academic activities. Although not all of them might be eager to teach courses, they tend to cooperate with various research centres and stay active in the promotion of air power and stimulation of more systematic and creative thinking on air power. The degree of involvement of those individuals, whose status technically is academic, is higher than those who are of no military background or from a different service. Although they might not have the same influence in decision-making and revising doctrines as those who are still in the service, they are directly involved in discussions and workshops. The best examples are Tony Mason and Peter Gray.

Doctrine authors and personalities

If RAF culture was doctrine friendly and viewed it as a core element of the adoption of the operational lessons and stimulation of thinking, then the role of authorship and personalities behind each publication would be functional rather than determinant in doctrine writing, dissemination and implementation. The experience of the first three editions of AP 3000, despite the difference in their emphases and purposes, was largely author driven. This corresponded to the need to reintroducing doctrine into RAF practice and attracting attention to it. The doctrine writing experience of the first two doctrines is of particular relevance, in order to realize the challenges of writing RAF doctrine and having it published.

The authorship of the first two editions

As already mentioned, Andrew Vallance was an enthusiast and inspirer of the reintroduction of doctrine into the service. Although succeeded by Group Captain Neil Taylor, Andrew Vallance was asked to assist in drafting of the second edition. He argued that there were a few challenges in preparation of the first two editions of AP 3000. First, there was the need to convince the RAF that doctrine was needed. As Andrew Vallance recollected, different levels within the RAF had different opinions and their own prejudices against doctrine: 'air crew did not support the idea. Senior officers argued: "I do not need it because I became Air Marshal without it." Middle-rank officers were the most perceptive'.[31] On the other hand, in order for the doctrine to be accepted and read, it was crucial to get the approval and the signature of the CAS under it. Once CAS wrote a foreword in the publication, it was recognized as an authoritative document. In the case of the first edition, the CAS was Air Chief Marshal Sir Peter Harding. The second was Air Chief Marshal Sir Michael Graydon. In terms of their attention to doctrine and its target audience, the main distinction between the two editions and the subsequent foreword by each CAS was in the widening of the target audience.[32] While the first foreword addressed mainly officers within the RAF,[33] the second edition aimed at all ranks and branches of the RAF.[34] In terms of doctrine, the role of CAS was to provide it with an authoritative nature and official recognition. The widening of the doctrine audience within the service and its continuous recognition by CAS suggest a few considerations. First, the very publication and the subsequent form of the doctrine largely depended on the personality and approach to air power adopted by a serving CAS and its consistency with doctrinal authors. Second, the widening of the audience within the RAF argued for the recognition of doctrinal application and the beginning of a gradual change in doctrine writing from an author-driven to an institutional approach, which is even more evident in the case of environmental doctrines written in the joint environment.

The second challenge for both editions was the incorporation of doctrine into training courses, which was quite complex due to the prevailing anti-doctrinal culture within the service. In regard to cadet training, it was essential for them to be ready to listen and then implement the gained knowledge. However, cadets were not opposed to the idea of doctrine *per se*, since their perception was yet to be shaped by the predominantly anti-doctrinal organizational culture. Unfortunately, 'the cultural problem of accepting the doctrine was deteriorating the higher you get'.[35] Andrew Vallance's devotion to the project was influenced not only by the prescribed position and duties but rather by a personal belief that the introduction of doctrine was good for the RAF. This explains why the initial doctrine writing was personality driven. It meant that Andrew Vallance, as the author and inspirer of the first edition of AP 3000, was the one to decide whom to involve in that process, with whom to discuss theoretical matters of warfare,[36] and what would actually go into the final draft.

For instance, Andrew Vallance involved Christopher Hobson, the chief librarian at the Defence Academy, and his team in the collection of data for case studies. He was not the only author and any feedback was welcomed from within the service: 'Some of the chapters were written by the Directing Staff. So, I edited them and sent them for consultation. Surprisingly, very little comments were received, little intellectual argument.'[37] Again, this situation demonstrates both personnel's reluctance to deal with the doctrine and the importance of Andrew Vallance's personality in its creation and further promotion within the service and the Staff College. The name of Andrew Vallance was so much associated with the first edition of RAF doctrine, that the then DDefS, Martin van der Veen, invited him to collaborate on the second edition of AP 3000. The authorship of the first two editions of AP 3000 is discussed here for a reason. It shows that the very existence of AP 3000 is due to personal beliefs of the people who initiated the process and wrote the doctrine. In terms of the doctrinal analysis, this experience demonstrates that the conceptual and purposeful discourse of a certain doctrine depended on who CAS and DDefS were at that time and how they interacted. From the personalities' perspective, it is relevant to look into the personal backgrounds of the people who wrote doctrine and who actually made it happen in the service.

The authorship of the third edition of AP 3000

In doctrine writing of the third edition, the main role was played by the Air Chief Marshal Sir Richard Johns. The exploration of the inside environment of doctrine writing was well covered in the article by Chris Finn, which was based on the personal correspondence with serving professionals of that time. As mentioned earlier, the new edition of AP 3000 was possible in 1996, as the doctrinal reflection of the air power lessons of Bosnia and the PSO environment. According to Air Commodore Steve Abbott, the intended edition was meant to be 'evolutionary, not revolutionary'.[38] At that volatile time of preparing defence review and introduction of jointery, for a doctrine writing process to be initiated, personal beliefs of DDefS would not be enough. The decision to start preparing doctrine had to be made by CAS. Initially, CAS Richard Johns was sceptical about a new edition. However, the rapid changes in the national defence, the introduction of jointery and subsequent doctrine hierarchy changed his position on doctrine.[39] Richard Johns became convinced 'that the final document needed to be endorsed by the other services, to recognize their contribution to the generation of national air power. Consequently, Edition 3 was the first to carry a joint imprimatur and was launched publicly at the RUSI by CAS and senior representatives of the RN and Army'.[40] Furthermore, Chris Finn noted that the main rationale for CAS's change of mind was due to his personal experience as the Director of Operations during the Gulf War, when he realized that the RAF's focus on tactical perspective and fixation with the Central Region were not efficient.[41] Moreover, CAS did not want doctrine to become dogma but rather be a means of boosting adaptation of the RAF to the changes that were already on the way:

> The eventual publication of AP3000 1999 provided an authoritative and up to date doctrinal statement to guide commanders at all levels, no matter the colour of their uniform, by shaping their thinking on the successful employment of air power in crisis of war. This came with a health warning that doctrine should not become dogma in a strategic environment that remained fraught with uncertainty. Doctrine needed to reflect a continuing process of review that examined definitions and concepts as well as the roles and missions of air power.[42]

While doctrine writing required formal commencement and authorization, which was provided by Richard Johns, its consistency depended on the consensus of views between its author and its inspirer. The then Group Captain, and now Air Chief Marshal, Sir Stuart Peach, perfectly fitted into the role. He had been commissioned to the RAF in 1977, and the first couple of decades of his career were characterized by practice-oriented experiences of photographic reconnaissance flights in Canberra, followed by three tours on Tornado GR1, both in the UK and abroad. In these tours, he was qualified as a weapons and electronic warfare instructor. In 1994–1996, he commanded IX Squadron (Bomber) at RAF Bruggen, in Germany.[43] The next stage of his career, which brought him to the doctrine authorship, started with an MPhil at Cambridge, received in 1996, followed by appointment as DDefS in 1997. There were several reasons why Stuart Peach fitted well into writing the doctrine under Richard Johns' supervision. First, he combined experience as a navigator with an academic approach to air power gained in Cambridge and as a part of his duties as DDefS. The position of DDefS inevitably required a creative, systematic and global view on air power and cooperation with academics. Second, from the beginning of the introduction of jointery into the national defence discourse, Stuart Peach showed support of jointery and considered it beneficial for the RAF. Apart from the general jointery and Army-friendly discourse of the third edition, this orientation was demonstrated in the already-mentioned introduction to *Perspectives on Air Power*.[44]

The consensus in conceptual discussions between CAS and DDefS was essential for reaching other services and making the doctrine jointery friendly. However, it does not mean that two practitioners had the same vision of the concepts and their layout in the new edition of AP 3000. In his memoire, Richard Johns recollected that they had numerous debates, with an equal number of victories on both sides: 'The drafting of the document to my satisfaction took longer than I anticipated as Stu Peach gamely confronted some of my prejudices and attitudes. As far as I can remember he won his fair share of our debates so it is no surprise that as I write he is Chief of the Defence Staff.'[45] Moreover, besides coming to a common ground within the service, a new edition had to pass the trial of the other two services. According to Chris Finn, in order to test practitioners' attitude to the ideas introduced in the third edition of AP 3000, the core themes were explained in the introductory article of the first publication of *Air Power Review*.[46] However, not all welcomed the shift of emphasis from three air campaigns to air capabilities:

> With attempts being made by some factions within the Air Warfare Centre and the dying embers of the RAF College to kill off AP3000 through the drafting of an 'Air Operations' chapter for the UK Operations Document. This was seen off by an alliance of CASD, ACAS, the Air Staff and the staff of the new Joint Services Command and Staff College, along with three heads of defence studies.[47]

The situation described earlier is of particular relevance for this book. It illustrates the role of individuals in securing official and systematic adoption of a certain theme within the RAF and in regard to other services. It also demonstrates new tendencies of doctrine writing in terms of jointery. Consequently, the difference in approaches between the preservation of doctrinal self-sufficiency and the correspondence to developing joint practices in accordance with the SDR was inevitable. In the joint framework, the role of authors was changing. The new tendency was towards decrease of their individual role and representation of collective thoughts. This process started with attribution of the joint feature to the third edition of AP 3000, but was finalized only with the change from a single-service to a joint authority.

In general, the doctrine-writing experience of the first two editions reflected a personality-driven approach, which to an extent secured its survival within both the service and interservice cultures. On the other hand, the third edition was different. With the introduction of jointery and its subsequent embodiment in organizational and structural changes, the process of institutionalization of doctrines began to take place. This would inevitably affect environmental and single-service doctrines, which was particularly evident with the establishment of the Joint Defence Centre (JDC) and the introduction of doctrine hierarchy. It meant that a doctrine was no longer simply a means of services' self-explanation to each other and a wider public. The lower level doctrines had to correspond to the general principles of joint publications. Consequently, the doctrine writing was politicized in interservice relations but this time within the framework of jointery.

In terms of the approach to doctrine writing, the shift was from 'the initiative from within' to 'authorisation from above'. In the first two editions, authorship was crucial and it was the driving force of doctrine development, while with the institutionalization of jointery the authors' vision was less important, since they represented collective ideas. In its turn, this meant a higher degree of subordination and control over the content. However, in the case of the third edition, personalities of CAS and DDefS were crucial. Moreover, the increased attention to doctrine as a means of implementing the RAF's way of cooperating with the other two services in the joint environment resulted in the declining flexibility of doctrine. From a long-term perspective, these were the first steps in the institutionalization of jointery and synchronization of doctrine writing across all three services. Consequently, this initial attempt to place the environmental doctrine prepared by a single service into the doctrinal/conceptual framework of two other services was the first stage of institutionalization of jointery.

Moreover, differences in authorship approaches to air power doctrine and the institutionalization of jointery showed two distinctive ways of writing environmental doctrines. In other words, in the post–Cold War era of the RAF's doctrine practice, two entirely different approaches were developed and embodied in the first three editions of AP 3000. Andrew Vallance emphasized this difference as follows:

> There are two possible approaches to writing an environmental doctrine at the strategic level. The first is to define the characteristics of the different environments in which mankind wages war (e.g. air, land or sea) and then elaborate on how those basic characteristics define what types of operations that are possible and practicable (and those that are not) within that environment. Once each of the environmental doctrines are established on a firm and realistic foundation, that then leads onto to the formulation of joint doctrine in which campaigns and operations in the component environments are brought together to define how best each type of warfare is integrated with the others to give the best strategic effect in any given set of circumstances.

The second option is to start with a 'joined up' doctrine setting out what is seen as the ideal approach to campaign planning and then try to dictate how operations in each environment should contribute to achieve that. I always favoured the first of these approaches as the most realistic, sensible and practical. I found that the second of these approaches tended to create formulaic approaches which could be unsound and started from the proposition that operations/campaigns in one of the 3 environments would always be the principal, and that operations in the other 2 would be obliged to conform and contribute as best they may, but not necessarily be used in the way that would maximise their own advantages. I felt that the 3rd edition essentially was based on that approach.[48]

This explanation is more than exhaustive, and it provides the context for the understanding of the environment in which the third edition was written. It also explains why this edition was not well received within the service and could not achieve its goals. Although the specifics of interservice dynamics would be an interesting topic for exploration, this is not the purpose of this book. The main conclusion concerning the role of authors in doctrine writing is that while previously authors could directly contribute to and affect the text of doctrine, starting from the third edition onwards, the degree of authors' impact and personal contribution declined in the joint environment. Authors become the tools for articulating common, systemized content, consistent with the prevailing doctrinal, joint network.

Conclusion

Overall, the third edition of AP 3000 was a continuation of the RAF post-Cold War doctrinal evolution. While the previous two editions were oriented towards the present, the new edition was the first air power doctrine of the decade to look into the future of the service and its reformation according to the posed objectives conditioned by the external and internal environments. It was evolutionary because it could look forward, because the first two editions analysed where the service was at that time and how the lessons of the Gulf influenced air power. It was intellectual and targeted a wider audience, because of the public attention to the military affairs and the increase of stakeholders in the military sphere. This doctrine entirely corresponded to its time and could not have been written in this form any earlier. Due to the rapid changes and the number of factors influencing doctrine writing, it was still a historical document of its time. Although it reflected the institutional ethos, it also demonstrated the strengthening of interservice cooperation, embodied in the joint approach of the publication.

In terms of the factors identified by Oliver Daddow, each of them had a different situational degree of influence on the doctrine writing of 1999. First, in terms of the external environment, the third edition was influenced by the lessons of the Gulf War and developing PSO realities after Bosnia. The doctrine illustrated operational experiences of both conflicts and the roles of air power, addressing the allied and joint environment of future operations. One of the reasons operational experience was well balanced and incorporated in detail was due to its harmonization with the Army PSO doctrine. However, the primary aim was the illustration of operational experience. The Army PSO doctrine was a means to this end.

Other factors of the external environment had a different degree of influence. The NATO doctrine was not yet in the heart of the national doctrine practice and affected the document only through the Allied publications in the doctrine hierarchy. Foreign doctrines of other Allied nations had little influence, if any, mainly due to the differences in national strategic cultures. The exchange of ideas and technologies with American allies had an indirect influence on practitioners through common training and joint courses and in Allied operations. Interpersonal contacts and visits of DDefS to Maxwell were still taking place and could indirectly shape certain ideas on air power and doctrine. However, they were not the forces shaping the form and contents of the doctrine. Therefore, although not all elements of the external environment were equally important, the most crucial one was operational experience. Operational experience identified the necessity of a new edition. However, the internal environment dictated its timing and the way it was written.

Second, in terms of the internal environment, the process of jointery and subsequent arrangements of reforming the Armed Forces directly influenced the new edition. Thus, the third edition of AP 3000 incorporated the lessons of previous operations into national joint discourse. The path of jointery required a closer cooperation with the other two services, particularly with the Army, and that was exactly what doctrine demonstrated. The significance of internal factor is that the new edition was published only when the jointery was initiated, which meant that the service had to adapt to the new rules of interservice collaboration, conceptualization of the use of force and doctrine writing. The introduction of jointery also defined the path the Armed Forces followed in the post–Cold War era. Doctrine was the guide to that adaptation. Thus, the internal factor defined the time of doctrine publication and shaped its content, roles and place in the doctrine hierarchy. This factor had a direct impact.

Third, in terms of networks, the influence of academics was important, although indirect. The main reason the document was highly intellectual and complex was due to the close cooperation between DDefS Stuart Peach and academic network of the time. Although academics were not directly involved in doctrine writing and drafting of the document, they provided substantial knowledge and analytical materials on changes in the strategic environment of that time. This was achieved through air power workshops and focus groups on security and defence studies conducted a few years prior to the publication of the third edition. The application of the intellectual approach reflected the importance of a wider audience for the service's positioning in the national defence. Although the assumption was made that with each level closer to doctrine authors the influence would be more direct, it was not the case for academics. Academic contribution was indirect, and it was systematically illustrated in doctrine because of Stuart Peach's favourable attitude to intellectualism and a wider academic discourse on air power.

Fourth, the influence of the author was direct and decisive to an extent. Although Stuart Peach was responsible for the new edition and made it academic and Army friendly, his judgements had to correspond to the vision of CAS. Since both CAS and DDefS were actively involved in the doctrine writing and managed to achieve consensus on the final look of the document, the author's contribution was not significantly constrained. However, if he had wanted to go a different way from CAS, then it would have been simply impossible, because doctrine was becoming more of an institutional document than an individual perspective on air power. Moreover, unlike the first edition, this doctrine as initiated by CAS and not DDefS. Therefore, the influence of the author was not the only defining factor. However, in contrast to the first two editions, the freedom of action diminished, because doctrine was becoming a recognized phenomenon of everyday military practice and strengthening of jointery.

The increased attention to doctrine *per se* and in the joint discourse resulted in the differentiation of approaches to writing environmental doctrine at the strategic level and the role of authors in it. In the case of the first two editions, the process was author driven and the tendency was to write environmental doctrines within the relevant services and only then to think about synergy and integration towards strategic effects. The third edition was characterized by the beginning of jointery and the establishment of a more institutionalized approach to doctrine writing. Gradually, the authors were beginning to be responsible for collective ideas rather than for their own. This was not entirely the case of the third edition, but the process was under way. The approach to writing environmental doctrine was hierarchical and 'joined-up'. This meant that joint doctrine would dictate subordinate doctrines in each environment, as to what strategic effects they had to achieve. Practically, the contemporary doctrine hierarchy was already in use.

Finally, in terms of the institutionalization of jointery, the third edition of AP 3000 demonstrated that the RAF had realized that the jointery was the formally accepted way of adaptation. Once again this was demonstrated through the application of a 'joined-up' approach to the writing of environmental doctrine. The initial stage of the development of jointery resulted in horizontal cooperation between different services. For instance, PSO doctrine was used for evaluation of the lessons of Bosnia. The use of PSO doctrine in the strategic air power doctrine was also a template for joint thinking on future operations and cooperation between the Army and the RAF. It was an important message demonstrating that the RAF was taking jointery-oriented direction seriously and was ready to follow it. Only a year after the SDR, the service managed to produce jointery-friendly environmental doctrine, which was an achievement. The next two editions of air power doctrine were to demonstrate that this orientation was far-reaching.

5

Case Study of the Fourth Edition of AP 3000

During the first post–Cold War decade, there were three editions of environmental doctrine which reflected the complexity of the strategic environment and its rapid change. Furthermore, the second decade was not lacking in events and factors reshaping the post–Cold War strategic environment. In terms of the international environment, Kosovo, 9/11, subsequent operations in Afghanistan and Iraq, the global economic crisis and change of various foreign governments took place over this time. In strictly military terms, jointery became the primary framework for reforming the Armed Forces and criterion for assessing military execution in ongoing operations. Its institutionalization was demonstrated in active development of the conceptual framework for tri-service cooperation, which was achieved through joint publications of the newly established Joint Doctrine and Concepts Centre (JDCC). Considering the timeliness of the previous edition, it would be logical to expect that new editions of air power doctrine would reflect each stage of this change. However, the RAF continued to operate without a new edition of its environmental doctrine until 2009, a decade after the publication of the previous one. This chapter explains why there was no new edition for ten years and the factors influencing writing of AP 3000, fourth edition, 2009.

The fourth edition of AP 3000 *British Air and Space Power Doctrine*[1] was initiated by the then CAS Air Chief Marshal Sir Stephen Dalton and prepared by the then DDefS Group Captain Alistair Byford. In the foreword to the fourth edition, Dalton stressed the necessity of a new conceptual framework for the employment of air and space power in the new operational environment.[2] This edition was distinctive, because it no longer concentrated exclusively on air power but also included another environment – space. Throughout, the air and space environments are addressed indivisibly. The consequent conceptualization of air and space power runs from chapter to chapter. The structure is simple, consisting of four chapters contained in a sixty-seven-page document. This was a significant simplification in contrast to the previous edition. Chapter 1, *The Nature of Air and Space Power*, explained the new definitions of air power and space power, the unique aspects of space power, the key enablers of both and the unique perspective of airmen. Chapter 2, *Air Power in the Contemporary Operating Environment*, looked into the current knowledge on the use of air power across different types of conflict and in the context of joint actions. Chapter 3, *The Four Fundamental Air and Space Roles*, analysed control of the air and space, air mobility, intelligence and situational awareness and attack, and their connection with joint action. Chapter 4, *Air and Space Command and Control*, looked into the Network-Enabled Capability (NEC) in terms of its incorporation into mission command and existing air command and control in the contemporary operating environment.

The context: The absence of doctrine

The absence of doctrine in the second post–Cold War decade after the publication of three editions in the first decade, not to mention the breakthrough of the third edition, was surprising. Although the core environmental doctrine was not reissued until 2009, the collection of Air Power Publications was replenished with other publications of the AP series – *AP 3002: Air and Space Warfare*[3] and *AP 3003: A Brief History of the Royal Air Force.*[4] AP 3002 explored the tactical details of the use of air power and answered the question 'how' it should be used, while AP 3000 answered 'what' and 'why' questions.[5] AP 3003 was written as a summary of RAF history for cadet courses at RAF College Cranwell, which was reflected in the foreword by the then CAS Air Chief Marshal Sir Jock Stirrup: 'This book is aimed primarily at those who have recently joined or are joining the Service, but we are distributing it to every serving member of the RAF and to the Cadet and Reserve organizations, including the University Air Squadrons. It is crucial that we all share a common understanding of our Service's history.'[6]

The diversification of the RAF air power publications and their direct connection to AP 3000, as an umbrella document, affecting lower level doctrines, argued not only for a return of doctrine into RAF practice but also for a more profound attention to its functionality. However, the renewed attention to doctrine and the increase in AP publications did not fit well with the absence of a new edition of an environmental doctrine as a framework document for the subordinate AP publications already released. Group Captain Chris Finn, who was DDefS from June 2002 until December 2004 and was involved in the doctrinal process of the time, explained this inconsistency. In fact, the need for a new edition of AP 3000 was one of the first matters Chris Finn addressed during his time as DDefS. The main rationale for the new edition was not the Kosovo campaign, or 9/11, or intervention into Afghanistan, but more trivial. Finn argued that the previous doctrine was not well understood and therefore was not taken into consideration within the service for the following reasons: 'AP 3000, third edition, was getting long in the tooth and it clearly needed rewriting. My feeling about that version was that Stuart have tried to put a lot of academic argument into it and it did not actually have a great utility for the Royal Air Force because of the way Stuart Peach had written it.'[7]

In his article on the subject, Chris Finn was even more specific on why this edition of the doctrine was not accepted by the service. It was suggested that the language of the manoeuvrist approach was more Army oriented and was of very little practical or guiding relevance for airmen.[8] The initial attempt to make air power doctrine Army friendly and therefore to introduce jointery into the service proved to be counterproductive due to the chosen form and narrative of the doctrine. From a practitioners' perspective, the doctrine looked too long, thus time consuming; too academic, thus requiring extra reading; and too Army (actually jointery) oriented, thus written for the Army to understand the RAF and air power. Therefore, the brilliant idea embodied in the third edition faced the cruel reality a few years later.

The new DDefS intended to address the issue in a more systematic way. He wanted to make two versions of doctrine, a detailed one and a thin one, the latter to be used by the cadets in the RAF College in Cranwell.[9] According to this plan, four publications were envisaged: a revised fourth edition of AP 3000, *AP 3001: Air Power Essentials, AP 3002: Air Operations* and AP 3003. The then CAS Air Chief Marshal Sir Jock Stirrup agreed to all four documents. While DDefS was working on the framework document, the Air Warfare Centre was charged with the writing of the operational manual AP 3002, which they prepared and later revised into the second edition in 2006. In terms of AP 3003, Peter Herbertson was asked to write a comprehensive summary of RAF history for cadets at Cranwell. It was by no means meant to be a critical history, because such a work would be too long.[10] Additionally, the document did not contain any references, since its main purpose was to inform newcomers and cadets rather than to make an academic contribution to RAF analytical history. Nevertheless, there are numerous books of references stored in the Cranwell library reflecting the tremendous work undertaken.[11] These features of the document illustrate a single-service practical necessity of teaching RAF history and not only Squadron history to cadets. This publication was produced in close cooperation with the Air Historical Branch (AHB). Although there were numerous contributors and writers, Chris Finn wrote a few chapters, while Mary Hudson from the AHB did all of the editing. The next stage was sending it for verification and intelligence clearance to the head of the AHB Sebastian Cox.

Eventually, two out of the four documents were published. However, AP 3000 was not one of them. According to Chris Finn, there were two reasons why this was the case. The first reason was that the operations in Afghanistan were not over yet and Operation Iraqi Freedom had begun. He stated: 'The AP 3000 did not happen because of the Afghan conflict. The Assistant Chief Air Staff of that time David Walker basically felt that there was no point of rewriting our doctrine until we'd go over the lessons of Afghanistan, plus of course the lessons of the second Gulf War. So, that took it out of my timeframe.'[12] The decision to interrupt the doctrine writing was well justified. It would be too time and resource consuming to write a new edition after each operation, especially when the gap between them was just a couple of years. Strictly from a practical perspective, if the doctrine preparation process had started immediately following the Kosovo campaign, taking an average time of eighteen months for its preparation, it could have been disseminated by the beginning of the war in Afghanistan. However, its relevance for the new operation would be doubtful, because a new conceptual framework would not be incorporated into existing practice. Second, except for a holistic consideration of evaluating the lessons of ongoing operations, the beginning of a new war had also affected the logistics of doctrine writing, taking away the people who could write it, including Chris Finn: 'At an early stage of drafting in 2003, Operation Iraqi Freedom intervened and the process was put on hold, both to enable the doctrinal lessons of the conflict to be identified and because many of the key players in the process were personally involved in the conflict.'[13]

The second reason was the ongoing institutionalization of jointery and the division of responsibilities between single services and joint institutions. The main issue was with the JDCC. With the expansion of jointery into various aspects of tri-service practice, the number of joint publications increased. However, each service still wrote its own environmental doctrine. Doctrines aligned with the joint discourse, but were under a single-service authorship. Their drafts were reviewed by the other services and the JDCC, in order to provide consistency in tri-service doctrinal publications. On the other hand, JDCC took a more centralized position and argued for the necessity of joint authorship. Chris Finn called it a 'discussion of who owns a single environmental doctrine'.[14] The main argument of tri-service practitioners was that doctrine should be written by people of that service under the authority of the head of the service in order for the doctrine to reflect the specifics of each service, concentrate on operational lessons particular to it, and therefore be accepted within the service. In the case of the RAF, the particular expertise and vision of aviators is known as air-mindedness. From the Army perspective, Alexander Alderson, the specialist in British COIN doctrine, noted: 'Any army needs soldiers with relevant and recent experience to write its doctrine and develop the concepts which should drive future tactics, organisation and equipment.'[15] This friction in views illustrates the two distinctive ways of writing an environmental doctrine explained in the previous chapter. The issue was not resolved in the time of Chris Finn. With the establishment of the Development Concept and Doctrine Centre (DCDC) in April 2006, service by service the responsibility of writing environmental doctrines was transferred to a joint authorship. Although this process influenced doctrine writing of the other two services, it caught up with the RAF after the publication of the fourth edition of AP 3000, which was still written under a single-service authorship.

Nevertheless, Chris Finn produced a draft of AP 3000. It was influenced by practical cooperation between the services in the operational environment of Iraq and by discussion of harmonization of approaches to doctrine. As a means of examining effects-based warfare 'with the aim of exploring what was becoming a common doctrinal language, despite having no basis in explanation or common understanding',[16] the three Heads of Defence Studies organized a joint conference. Its additional aim was to analyse the recent operational lessons:

> Additionally, the conference was held to capture the air power lessons of Operation Iraqi Freedom in May 2004, including the CAS (Air Chief Marshal Jock Stirrup), General 'Buzz' Moseley USAF (JFACC), Air Chief Marshall Brian Burridge (UK National Contingent Commander) and Air Marshal Glen Torpy (UK Air Component Commander). This established the facts of the air war and also addressed themes such as technology, legality and ethics and their doctrinal implications.[17]

This conference provided a practical and conceptual basis for the preparation of a new edition and some suggestions on how to place it into a joint context. Although Chris Finn's draft was never published, its distinctive feature was that 'it went through the review process of a tri-service environment'.[18] This fact meant that practical interservice cooperation and consultation was taking place, and this draft fulfilled the requirements of joint expectations to be accepted by all three services. It also meant that, technically, a new edition of AP 3000 would have been possible in 2005. However, it did not materialize. Since it was not possible to interview the next DDefS, Group Captain Neville Parton, it remains unclear as to why a new edition of doctrine was absent in his time frame. One of the reasons might be the change of campaigns in Iraq and Afghanistan from coercive to peace-building and stabilization.[19] Consequently, the evaluation of lessons and their adaptation in doctrine would require at least the completion of these campaigns in order to understand the role of air power in achieving the end state. Another reason could be internal. With the establishment of DCDC and the struggle for ownership over environmental doctrine, it could be wise for the service not to publish anything that might not be recognized by joint institutions and incorporated into training courses.

The earlier-mentioned discussion explains why a new edition of doctrine was not published in the first five years. It also describes the tendencies in doctrine writing. First, the publication of RAF doctrine depended on cooperation between CAS and DDefS. Any inconsistency between their views on doctrine could result in its absence. Second, the diversity of doctrinal publications reflected the differences in target audience each publication aimed to reach. Third, at that time, practically, environmental doctrine was still in the realm of single-service responsibilities. Consequently, synchronization of doctrinal changes within the tri-service environment was still far from reality. Any decisions on a new publication depended on single-service considerations and were not conditional on the other services' revisions of doctrines. Therefore, changes in doctrine in one service did not trigger subsequent changes in another, because there was no system to trigger them. Finally, in terms of the institutionalization of jointery, the process was painstaking and reflected the diversity of approaches from different stakeholders. Although JDCC did not succeed in achieving control over environmental doctrines, in practice tri-service/joint cooperation reviewed each other's doctrines. This does not mean that the process of tri-service reviewing was smooth, but because it took place, paying attention to the necessity of common doctrinal language in practical matters like effects-based warfare, jointery was progressing horizontally, while centralized and vertical jointery was still struggling.

Lessons of previous operations

The Kosovo campaign was the first post–Cold War NATO campaign conducted on its own without UN authorization. The air power contributed to Operation Allied Force forty-eight fixed-wing aircraft, 'of these, twenty-eight were strike aircraft (Tornado GR1s and Harrier GR7s), seven were air defence (Sea Harrier FA2 flown off HMS Invincible) and thirteen were support aircraft (air-to-air refuelling tankers, E3D early warning aircraft and one Nimrod); in addition some eighteen helicopters were deployed'.[20] This campaign had many lessons to teach. The Kosovo conflict showed that unlike the Gulf War, 'it was widely and mistakenly believed that coercive air attacks would quickly succeed'.[21] Another issue of the time was the difficulty of preserving the legitimacy of coercion and other military actions in the volatile environment of an ethno-culturally fragmented country.[22] The main problem for air power was not the precision in reaching targets, but getting target-by-target clearance. Both in American and British cases, approval for each target had to be obtained from political decision-makers in Washington and London, which added an extra pressure on the application of air power in a politically sensitive environment.[23] Another lesson was the crucial role of intelligence in enabling the precision and efficiency of air power. Target identification was essential for fulfilling the primary role of air power– reaching targets. According to Wesley Clark, air power was missing an effects-based approach due to its nature. General Clark commented on the insufficiency of destroying infrastructure in places that were not relevant to the war itself.[24] This misstep was to contribute to the complexity of the post–conflict recovery of the country.[25]

The core of the problem was not the choice of targets or preference to short-term achievements without considering long-term consequences. Nor was it strict ROEs, which aimed at the limitation of civilian casualties. However, strict ROEs resulted in repeated sorties towards the same target, while its relevance was time sensitive. The essence of the problem was a lack of understanding between policymakers, who were driven by the effects of the war on the international community, and consequent reluctance to deploy land forces; and military thinking in terms of tactics: reaching targets. Both parties needed to think more systematically about the exit strategy and subsequent implications after achieving the end state: the withdrawal of Serbian forces from Kosovo. As a result, the political assessment of the RAF performance was far from satisfactory: 'The number of munitions dropped by UK aircraft per strike sortie was significantly lower than the NATO average. The RAF flew 9.6 per cent of NATO strike sorties, but dropped only 4.2 per cent of the munitions.'[26] Apart from the strict ROEs, this inconsistency between sorties and targets was also due to bad weather and the technological inability of laser-guided Paveway I and Paveway II munitions to strike small and mobile targets.[27]

Overall, the following operational lessons can be derived from Kosovo. First, the campaign demonstrated that NATO as a defensive alliance had no experience in planning humanitarian interventions,[28] resulting in the 'lack of contingency plans for coercive actions'.[29] Second, although the use of air power in this campaign was often 'adjudged as a success',[30] it was less effective than in the Gulf War. High tempo and continuity of attacks in the Gulf were undermined by the complexity of the political situation in Kosovo.[31] Consequently, merging strategic, operational- and tactical-level targets under the same ROE and approval in London and Washington undermined the timeliness and efficiency of sorties. Other problems included flaws in the suppression of enemy air defences (SEAD), difficulty in finding and engaging enemy light infantry, civilian casualties,[32] and the need for logistics integration, particularly of a multinational component.[33] Third, a new conceptual approach to the use of air power together with political, diplomatic and other means was required. Finally, the operation demonstrated some tactical and technological concerns in the RAF performance: 'The campaign exposed RAF deficiencies in all-weather PGM's; battle damage assessment, secure communications; the ability to find, target, and engage mobile forces; and the ability to deploy units from main operating bases. Despite sustained resource constraints, all would be addressed before the next major commitment in 2003.'[34]

Unlike in Kosovo, RAF involvement in Afghanistan was supportive rather than decisive. During the first stage, it was mainly limited to provision of refuelling, surveillance and reconnaissance. RAF TriStars and VC-10s were deployed from the Brize Norton base in Oxfordshire, mainly due to their compatibility with the refuelling system of the US Navy and Marine Corps.[35] The Airborne Early Warning (AEW) E3-D Sentry and the Nimrod R1 provided surveillance while the Canberra PR9 conducted reconnaissance flights.[36] By January 2002, C17 and C130 Hercules were responsible for strategic and tactical airlift while Hercules and Chinook helicopters were used in support of Special Forces.[37] During the third stage of International Security Assistance Force (ISAF), starting in July 2006, the RAF played the same roles but in support of the new government and the ongoing process of reconstruction and stabilization of the country.[38]

Although the campaign became very unpopular due to its protracted character in securing stabilization and peace-building,[39] and the deaths of a Nimrod crew due to technological failure,[40] air power proved capable of performing supportive roles. However, one of the highlighted issues was the necessity of improving synergy of air and land cooperation because 'in Afghanistan we were finding that we were using close air support for strategic effect and in high manoeuvre, high tempo warfare, the relationship between air and land is now much, much more important',[41] which was further demonstrated in Iraq.

Air power proved effective in playing supportive roles in COIN environment. In the later years, before the publication of AP 3000, multitasking in the provision of ISTAR role and striking capabilities was required on a day-to-day basis. Moreover, these supporting roles proved the increased necessity of information for situational awareness and technological capabilities for its provision. The supportive role of ISTAR was becoming vital for precision of major strikes. In terms of supportive and decisive roles of air power, the distinction was blurring because what could be considered a secondary supportive role was actually vital for the provision of the so-called primary role for strategic effect. This was one of the reasons why air power capabilities were exchanged for air power roles in the fourth edition of AP 3000.[42]

For the RAF, the Second Gulf War was different from Kosovo and Afghanistan. It was characterized by the first full air–land integration with increase in precision of PGMs and operational tempo. The overall deployment of assets included '46,000 personnel, 19 warships, 14 Royal Fleet Auxiliary vessels, 15,000 vehicles, 115 fixed-wing aircraft and nearly 100 helicopters'.[43] Brian Burridge and Glen Torpy represented the British side. Apart from a rapid and complete integration with US forces, the key feature of the operation was a faster tempo in comparison to previous operations: 'Given the nature of the plan, which was designed to overwhelm the command and control of the Iraqi regime through high tempo and high manoeuvre, decision-making on targeting needed to move from what had been "sedate" to "fast and furious"'.[44] Associated with the high tempo, air–land integration shifted from linear to parallel warfare, meaning that instead of conducting an air campaign, preparing the way for ground forces to proceed on the second stage (linear), both air and land forces were attacking simultaneously (parallel warfare). Consequently, the complexity of the target set and the available time for its reach would determine whether it was approved on the spot or in London. Although strategic targets were mainly approved in London, targets of operational, tactical levels and rapidly mobile targets were approved on the spot.[45] Benjamin Lambeth wrote: 'Air Chief Marshal Burridge later summed up his role in this respect succinctly: if a target was to be attacked with a British platform, either he or someone in the British contingent to whom he had delegated authority had to approve it'.[46] A more relaxed targeting clearance is associated with the second feature of the campaign – the improved precision of PGMs. It was recognized that the choice of delivered munitions was towards PGMs instead of old-fashioned bombs. Out of 803 PGMs 679 were dropped, an 85 per cent rate, in contrast to 10 per cent in the First Gulf War.[47] In terms of conventional missiles, the main contribution of the RAF was in the introduction of the Storm Shadow[48] into operation, long before its anticipated entry date, which was provided through the Urgent Operational Requirements (UOR) scheme.[49] Its place in the operational arsenal was outlined as follows: 'Indeed, apart from the B-2 stealth bomber armed with GBU-37 hard-structure munitions, Storm Shadow provided General Moseley with the only significant deep-penetration target attack capability available to CENTAF. In all, 27 Storm Shadow munitions were fired throughout the campaign, mostly during the first few days against especially hardened enemy command and control facilities.'[50]

Another technological aspect of the campaign was the performance of UAVs. The British Army extensively used the Phoenix, a combat surveillance UAV, which was used in 138 sorties. The widespread use of UAVs and improved precision in Afghanistan and Iraq suggested a new era for air power, indicating that, finally, with new technologies, air power could achieve what it had always promised – surgical strikes. On the other hand, it also triggered a long-term argument about the costs of conventional and UAV technologies, which would be scrutinized under the policy of austerity. One of the most crucial lessons of the campaign was the necessity of improved cooperation with the land forces, particularly in terms of close air support. Glen Torpy stated: 'There is no doubt that we need to do more air-land integration. It is something that we knew about at least 18 months before we started this operation, and it was work that we had in hand: improving the procedure; looking at our equipment.'[51] In terms of strengthening jointery in the national Armed Forces, the experience of Iraq stimulated further development of jointery among the three services and air-land integration in particular. This was further reflected in the addition of a new chapter to the SDR and the publication of the fourth edition of AP 3000.

The reflection of operational experience in text

The influence of operational experience can be traced in two ways. First, it can be seen in the changes operational experience triggers in the strategic environment. Consequently, air power had to adapt to the new trends in strategic and operational environment taking into account all three services. In this way, incorporated experience is more systematic and usually highlights broader tendencies in the national defence and strategic discourse. The second way is to use examples from previous operations, exploring how air power was used and what it is capable of in the new strategic debate. The second way is more single service in its nature. In terms of a reflection of all three campaigns, the new doctrine gave equal attention to Iraq and Afghanistan, referring to each case nine times. In contrast, Kosovo was mentioned only once, in the introduction, mainly acknowledging that this conflict took place.[52] One of the reasons why this conflict was omitted was because the strategic environment of the time was more substantially shaped by the last two campaigns and the necessity of fighting insurgencies using the full spectrum of capabilities. The operational experience of Iraq and Afghanistan set the tone of the new edition, which argued for increased integration among all three services. Afghanistan and Iraq demonstrated the diversity of roles air power could play in different conflicts. In a sense, the general impact of operational experience was a practical demonstration of the improvement of jointery and air–land integration under the new technological and strategic conditions. As AP 3000 fourth edition stated: 'Other developments meriting consideration since the publication of AP 3000 Edition 3 include the renewed emphasis on air-land integration, the consequences of the fruition of joint theory and practice anticipated by the SDR, and the impact of Network Enabled Capability (NEC) on air command and control processes.'[53]

Operational experience notwithstanding, it is clear that NEC, which reflected the new stage of ISTAR development and information-driven approach to the Armed Forces integration and cooperation, was a vital addition. The essence of NEC is in integration of the Armed Forces into 'network of networks'[54] through coherent use of new technologies, information-processing software and training of personnel: 'Network Enabled Capabilities have particular utility, conferring decisive advantage through the timely provision and exploitation of information and intelligence allowing effective decision-making and the agile synchronization of activity.'[55] The inclusion of the concept of NEC in this edition leads to a number of conclusions. Although this concept had been introduced before Iraq and Afghanistan, operational experience and the need for air–land integration re-emphasized its importance for the Armed Forces. This is an example of how operational experience can affect the national defence and not just a single service. Since this concept referred to all three services; inevitably, it was going to be enforced through joint mechanisms like joint doctrine. For the RAF to adapt to the re-emphasized trend in national strategic discourse, the concept had to enter environmental doctrine. Accordingly, the incorporation of the NEC concept from higher to lower doctrine demonstrates the functioning of the doctrine hierarchy. Comparing the reflection of operational experience in the third and fourth editions, a few features can be identified. Although the third edition also explained general trends in the strategic environment, it used the same-level Army doctrine as its source and not a joint doctrine. This was the case for horizontal jointery. The fourth edition demonstrates vertical jointery established through hierarchical subordination between different levels of doctrinal documents. Since JDP 0–01 recognized the existence of NEC, its subsequent reflection in the fourth edition of AP 3000 (environmental doctrine) showed its subordination. Once again, this suggests a new stage in the institutionalization of jointery.

Concerning the second way of reflecting operational experience in doctrinal text, examples were used to highlight particular features of air power. Afghanistan was mentioned to demonstrate the flexibility of air power using the example of Harrier aircraft, which in May 2007 conducted an attack, then provided surveillance support for the land forces and ended with demonstrating presence in support of the land patrol.[56] Air attacks in 2008, when 'limited target sets within a well-controlled battlespace'[57] had a profound effect on the local population, were cited to show the distinctive character of irregular warfare. Other examples of Afghanistan included the air drop and transportation tasks of Hercules aircraft in terms of precision air drop[58] and force multiplying,[59] an argument in favour of 'the discrete insertion of small patrols in low-density battlespace',[60] and use of close air support in routine checks for improvised explosive device (IED) activity.[61]

The examples of long-term no-fly zone enforcement following the First Gulf War was used to illustrate that air power can overcome some of its limitations: 'The successful policing of the no-fly zones over Iraq on a twenty-four hours-a-day, seven-days-a-week basis for an eleven-year period from 1992 to 2003 demonstrates that the impermanence of air power is relative.'[62] Securing freedom of air and surface manoeuvre through the control of the air above Iraq,[63] and the flexibility of air sensors and their adaptation to irregular warfare, including the use of fast jet thermal imaging system in finding insurgents hiding in reed beds, were also discussed.[64] Iraq was referred to when explaining precision in Conventional Counter-Surface Force Operations. The improvement in precision made precision air attack the primarily means in force-on-force attacks.[65] Furthermore, the Iraq experience suggested complexity in the use of air power: 'Flexing high-value the United States Marine Corps (USMC) assets to service higher priority tasks elsewhere in theatre was very difficult, and the perception that organic capabilities were always available to the Marines sometimes inhibited a reciprocal flow of air support when it was urgently required.'[66]

Moreover, the new doctrine addressed one of the most substantial changes in air power of the time – the multifaceted employment of UAVs in both campaigns. UAVs are mentioned four times. First, it was argued that they increased ubiquity, covering a wider geographical area than surface systems could do.[67] Second, to refute the argument that air power lacked permanence or endurance, it was claimed that UAVs provided the extension of range and endurance of 'an unblinking eye'.[68] Finally, UAVs were used not only for kinetic purposes but also non-kinetic, since their mere presence had psychological impact.[69] Therefore, UAVs were shown to be a potent element of air power across different types of conflict. On the other hand, both conventional (Storm Shadow missiles) and UAV capabilities illustrated the core dependence of air power (manned and unmanned) on availability and further development of technologies.[70]

Overall, previous operations had a substantial impact on air power doctrine. While the third edition paid attention to the role of air power in peace support operations, the fourth edition stressed its place in COINs. However, in both cases, the emphasis was placed on the functionality of air power across different types of conflict and its inherently joint nature. Both editions reflected operational experience at both strategic and single-service levels. However, the third edition paid more attention to the explanation of strategic reality, which would be more suitable for joint rather than single-service environmental doctrine. With the introduction of strict doctrine hierarchy, the fourth edition sporadically referred to the main trends emphasized in joint doctrinal publications, stressing upon practical operational lessons relevant for air and space environments. Consequently, the two editions evaluated operational experience differently. The third edition explained general strategic discourse while the fourth edition was more practice oriented, paying more attention to the lessons particular for air power in COIN environment.

The internal environment

General defence policy discourse

The second post–Cold War decade can be characterized as turbulent and changeable in all aspects, and political life was no exception. Although the political dimension with all layers of its complexity could have been analysed here in depth in order to trace how it affected doctrinal development, it would require a book of its own. Accordingly, in this book, attention is paid only to political reflection on the Iraq and Afghanistan campaigns, how they shaped the national approach to fighting new wars and its reflection in the studied doctrine. The path of defence policy transition over the decade started with the introduction of a new chapter in the SDR.[71] It reflected the national response to the terrorist threat and thinking on the COIN means of fighting what became the Long War on Terror. This document was important for the doctrine of 2009 because it recognized the lessons of Afghanistan and argued for a systematic way of fighting wars. It also reaffirmed the expeditionary nature of future operations. Moreover, this document re-emphasized the vital importance of the concept of Network-Centric Capability (NCC) for the military discourse.[72]

This document also stressed that strengthening of tri-service cooperation within jointery was a precondition for the achievement of NCC. Consequently, if not for the Iraq war, a meticulous review of jointery could have been expected after the publication of *A New Chapter*. Both MOD and the Foreign Office argued that ongoing campaigns and future operations would be combined.[73] The asymmetric nature of COIN was becoming more dominant in the assessment of future requirements of the Armed Forces: 'We must be more prepared for "asymmetric" attacks (those avoiding direct conventional conflict with our military forces) by both state and non-state actors, including the employment of WMD delivered through a variety of means.'[74] Although *Delivering Security in a Changing World* mentioned jointery only in terms of the conclusion of the SDR 1998, it reaffirmed the crucial role of NCC in fighting COINs effectively and as a driving force for the interservice integration in diverse operational settings.[75] While the official defence papers evaluated the lessons for defence policy and their relevance for future wars, the Parliament was more interested in the reasons behind some issues of previous operational performance and subsequent implications for national policy. The issue of jointery was raised once again immediately after Iraq. The House of Commons Defence Committee (HCDC) stated:

> The future challenge of close air support, demonstrated by Afghanistan and repeated in Iraq, is how to supply timely and precise air support to small numbers of friendly forces in non-linear engagements, not how to destroy large enemy divisions such as Saddam's Republican Guards. It is a problem that does not appear to have been resolved by MOD. Given Repeated References to 'jointery' in official policy documents we are surprised that the operational practice of air-land integration has been so slow to change. We recommend that MOD addresses this question with much greater urgency than has been displayed to date.[76]

Mentioning of Afghanistan and Iraq, in this and the previous reports, was important for attracting attention to the practical implementation of jointery. No matter how unflattering and critical the recommendations of HCDC may seem, they still emphasized the existing gap between the conceptualization of jointery by JDCC, its organizational reflection by services and its operational application in the battlespace. As a result, this advice stimulated further strengthening of jointery embodied in the Comprehensive Approach: 'commonly understood principles and collaborative processes that enhance the likelihood of favourable and enduring outcomes within a particular situation'.[77] This approach originated in Joint Discussion Note 4/05, published in January 2006 by the JDCC. The main rationale for it was in combining capabilities to fit different types of potential conflicts, which required interdepartmental and interservice cooperation across various levels. The argument behind this approach was simple – provision of a cost-efficient reorganization of the Armed Forces and civil institutions in the harmonized and cohesive environment: 'Post-operational analysis of situations and crises at home and abroad has demonstrated the value and effectiveness of a joined-up and cross-discipline approach if lasting and desirable outcomes are to be identified and achieved.'[78]

For the military forces, the introduction of this approach required profound changes in how they cooperated with other governmental institutions and JDCC was to become the key coordinator of cross-governmental and interagency dialogue and subsequent cooperation.[79] The development of integration and cooperative tendencies among other agencies and the strengthening of JDCC resulted in a new wave of deepening jointery. At that time, acceptance of this approach by the Whitehall and its subsequent dominance in the upcoming defence review resulted in the renewal of jointery in a new institution of the DCDC, in 2006. Moreover, the struggle for the ownership over environmental doctrine was resolved in favour of joint authorship.

This defence policy discourse allows to draw some conclusions. The line between external and internal factors influencing doctrine was becoming more obscure. Operational experience was reflected in doctrine in two ways. First, lessons on the use of air power were incorporated. Second, in the political sphere, operational experience stimulated reforming of the Armed Forces, which had to be further shown in doctrine. The experiences of Iraq and Afghanistan drew attention to adaptability of the Armed Forces to the realities of COIN and asymmetric warfare. In its turn, the need for a more synchronized interservice cooperation brought back attention to NEC and jointery. Thus, government focused on the intensification of jointery. Comparing the two editions in terms of the institutionalization of jointery, a shift from horizontal to vertical cooperation took place. The third edition, influenced by the SDR and PSO, addressed their impact on air power through referencing the SDR and PSO doctrine, demonstrating the horizontal level of doctrinal jointery. The fourth edition reflected the vertical level embodied in the doctrine hierarchy. The general strategic trends and new concepts relevant for all three services would be introduced in joint doctrine, while in the environmental doctrine prepared by a single-service team these trends and concepts would be only briefly mentioned. Jointery had to obtain control over environmental doctrines in order to be fully synchronized within the services. Consequently, it may be suggested that this was the last attempt of the service to show that it could write joint environmental doctrine under its own RAF authorship.

Single-service joint environmental doctrine?

The aim of this section is to demonstrate the extent the fourth edition was joint or single service in its nature, and therefore the extent joint tendencies had influenced it. In the foreword to the fourth edition, CAS Air Chief Marshal Sir Stephen Dalton stressed upon the joint/single dichotomy of this edition: 'While the RAF is the prime custodian of the United Kingdom's air and space power capability and takes the conceptual lead in its delivery, AP 3000's title – British Air and Space Doctrine – reflects the inherently joint nature of air and space operations and the contribution of the other components.'[80] In the context of internal political discourse, this edition practically demonstrated that, despite its independent tendencies, the RAF was capable of writing a joint environmental doctrine under single-service authorship. It can be argued that this was the last attempt of the service to preserve its authorship of environmental doctrine. This was further demonstrated by distinguishing two aims and target audiences within the Comprehensive Approach. First, it had to send authoritative message to airmen how to employ air and space power. Second, it intended to inform sailors, soldiers and other actors of the Comprehensive Approach on the use of air and space power.[81]

Like all doctrines of the last decade, this edition included a paragraph identifying doctrine hierarchy and the place of that document in it. The rationale for this was twofold. First, this introduction helped in understanding the relationship between different levels of the doctrine hierarchy. Therefore, it assisted tracing the influence of main themes at different levels from joint, strategic and operational to environmental and tactical. Second, a clear hierarchy provided an understanding of what doctrine of each level was about, what information could be found and where. Reference was also made to the previous edition being 'generic to defence rather than being specific to the air and space domains … so AP 3000 Edition 4 has been précised to distil the essence of air and space power into a concise and digestive format, with the aim of complementing joint doctrine rather than replicating it'.[82]

These comparisons are important because they show a commitment to joint doctrine hierarchy of the time and subordination of the single-service environmental doctrine to it. The joint tone was demonstrated both in the introduction and throughout the document. The most crucial commitment was in emphasizing the joint nature of air power. There was a shift of emphasis in the definition of air power from means to ends. Consequently, the new definition of air and space power was 'the ability to project power from the air and space to influence the behaviour of people or the course of events',[83] whereas the previous definition reflected technological and means-oriented approach to air power: 'The ability to project military force in air or space by or from a platform or missile operating above the surface of the surface of the earth. Air platforms are defined as any aircraft, helicopter or unmanned aerial vehicle.'[84] This change of emphasis is crucial, since instead of the technological nature of air power and the necessity to appropriate cutting-age technological platforms, the functionality and orientation towards results were emphasized. Thus, it was easier to connect air power to the two other services and the joint environment, emphasizing common objectives and desired outcomes. It can be stated that a more strategy-oriented definition was applied. However, does this change illustrate an evolution in thinking on air power? In other words, is this definition a new one or a forgotten one? The new definition is in fact derived from the one Tony Mason established in the 1970s: 'Air power is the ability to project military force by or from a platform in the third dimension above the surface of the earth.'[85] This full circle of returning to the initial point illustrates both continuity of the conceptual framework and also the revival of strategic thinking on air power versus tactical considerations alone. Moreover, from an individual perspective, it also shows the far-reaching outlook of visionaries like Tony Mason.

Regarding characteristics of air and space power, a new edition re-emphasized the same attributes as the third edition: joint, combined and multinational nature; encompassing forces from all three services; use of existing air and space power assets effectively; incorporation of civilian and commercial resources;

and a reciprocal relationship with land and maritime environments.[86] The airmen's perspective or air-mindedness was described as inherently joint due to the necessity of thinking in terms of an entire theatre or Joint Operations Area (JOA) rather than individual geographical Areas of Operations (AOO).[87] It was argued that in the 'expeditionary and influence-based approach to future operations'[88] the inherent joint-mindedness of airmen would ease cooperation among different agencies, governmental institutions and non-governmental organizations (NGOs) in the context of the Comprehensive Approach. Once again, the RAF, as the custodian of the air and space environments, emphasized the importance of air-mindedness. The intention was to engage airmen who would understand and appreciate the full potential of air power.[89] In effect, it was a self-justifying doctrine, placing the RAF as the only custodian of the air and space environments and asserting the service's practical ability to create joint environmental doctrine. Instead of promoting an independent role, the doctrine advocated the inherent joint discourse of air power. The aforementioned HCDC criticism on the practical implementation of jointery was also addressed in the doctrine, suggesting improvement of air–land integration. It was stressed that in the multinational and intercomponent environment, integral planning was required. This could be achieved through joint design of the campaign from the outset, 'rather than air operations being added to a plan that has already been developed'.[90] This was to be accomplished by incorporating liaison officers into all three-service headquarters. The need for a more profound mutual sympathy and understanding of each environment was also addressed.

The core chapters devoted to *Air Power in the New Contemporary Environment* and *The Four Fundamental Air and Space Roles* detailed air power in joint context. They argued that in the contemporary battlespace, characterized by parallel rather than linear warfare, the full potential of air power largely depended on improvement of friendly force tracking techniques.[91] Although the potential of air power and its limitations in the new environment were shown, this argument was regress from the uniqueness and multitasking of air power to its supporting role of the ground forces at the tactical level. Although air power would provide ISTAR, it was concluded that 'close combat is likely to remain primarily the domain of the soldier'.[92] There were a few implications of this duality in explaining the contemporary operational environment. First, it re-emphasized the necessity of jointery. Second, it confirmed the significant role of the Army. Third, it acknowledged the enabling role of air power in COIN environment. This conclusion corresponded to the requirements of air–land integration in fighting insurgencies and recognition of strengthening jointery in the national defence. As in the previous edition, instead of the independent role of air power, which 'while highly responsive, is fixed and relatively inflexible',[93] deeper tri-service collaboration was emphasized. Moreover, the key to tri-service integration is not in purchasing new joint platforms, but in mutual understanding.[94] This entire discourse is reminiscent of the argument for the preservation of the service and prevention of its dissolution between other two services in the later Strategic Defence and Security Review (SDSR) process. This narrative is particularly interesting in the context technologies favoured by the SDSR.[95]

The air power core capabilities from the third edition were replaced by four air power roles, which recalled the traditional roles distinguished already in the post–World Wars' doctrines. Although all four roles described the multifunctional potential of air power, this potential was presented in the light of interservice cooperation. The most crucial feature of a cooperative approach to air power was the exclusion of its strategic role. It can be considered that the exclusion of what historically was the core of RAF independence was a sacrifice to jointery. Nevertheless, each of the roles could be performed at the strategic level. Once again, the service proved it could write an environmental doctrine of a joint discourse. Control of the air was a precondition and facilitating tool for securing freedom of manoeuvre in all three environments. Control of outer space was argued to be entirely joint and any counter-space operations would require joint force and cooperation across all three levels of warfare[96] through space situation awareness, defensive counter-space (DCS) operations, and offensive counter-space (OCS) operations.[97] Air mobility and airlift were explained in terms of their use in a wider global discourse of political objectives: transportation of military and civilian personnel and materials, provision of support of the local population in disaster relief or other humanitarian operations.[98] The success of the third role of intelligence and situational awareness depended on timeliness of the relevant information, which could be achieved by improving interservice integration. The challenge of air and space capabilities was not collection of the relevant and multidimensional data in order to establish awareness, but the development of situational understanding based on situational awareness.[99] Integration and synchronization of efforts were needed in order to achieve this:

> Effective surveillance demands both broad context and detailed information. Better understanding of situations and higher responsiveness are achieved when the two are balanced: too much time spent on context can lead to a late focus on necessary detail. While air (and to a lesser extent space) capabilities may provide a measure of both, all sources must be closely integrated – and the

direction, collection, processing and dissemination of products balances – to permit situational understanding to be developed from situational awareness.[100]

In terms of the offensive role of air power, it was argued that in the environment of overlapping levels of warfare, air power was a flexible and adaptable tool of coercion fitting even such complex campaigns as Afghanistan, where air power helped to reduce casualties among friendly forces and imposed pressure on the adversary.[101] Subsequently, air power served as force multiplier, decreasing the number of deployed troops, thereby mitigating casualties or the political implications of larger deployments.[102] Regarding coercion in irregular warfare, air power was argued to be useful because of precision weaponry and complementary capabilities. In terms of jointery, attention was paid to the three environments of attack delivery.[103] Attack delivery also acknowledged the fourth environment – information.[104] Among information operations, electronic warfare, influence operations and computer network operations were distinguished.[105] The last section of Chapter 3 addressed the four fundamental air and space power roles in the context of joint actions in order to emphasize the joint discourse of the doctrine and contemporary air power. In such a way, the entire chapter was summarized showing joint, integrating purpose.

Overall, the internal factors including joint structural changes and the development of new procedures in incorporating the external strategic environment into the national military discourse had a significant influence on the fourth edition of AP 3000. First, the general lessons and conceptual implications of previous operations were adopted in the doctrine not through the actual policymaking documents, but through a well-established doctrine hierarchy. However, awareness of general defence trends and their political context was present in this edition illustrated by references to NEC, the Comprehensive Approach and a new chapter of the SDR. Second, the new edition was influenced by the competition for ownership of environmental doctrine. It was an attempt to show that the RAF still could write joint environmental doctrine under single-service authorship. Third, in fact, the RAF wrote a joint environmental doctrine, which was illustrated in both its title and the narrative. Fourth, unlike the previous edition, this doctrine demonstrated jointery in its most practical aspect, in terms of both known experiences from previous operations and new ways of interservice cooperation and integration for future operations. Consequently, the previous edition (1999) was characterized by generic nature because it reflected the initial stage of jointery. The later edition was more practical, due to the implementation of jointery and the vital necessity of improving air–land integration in COIN environment. Both the reflection of operational experience and new joint realities were of equal relevance in driving the preparation of this publication. With the further development of jointery, the line between factors began to disappear. Operational experience being digested by the joint environment was then transferred into environmental doctrines. In other words, a more institutionalized approach was coming into practice, and it was not within a single service but from a centralized joint centre of DCDC.

The role of academics

Naturally, the constant involvement of the Armed Forces in diverse overseas campaigns attracted academic and specialist interest in the roles of air power in new conflicts. As in the previous decade, air power workshops continued to take place under the supervision of CAS and DDefS. The result of the next workshop was the publication of the *Air Power 21: Challenges for the New Century*.[106] It was edited by the then DDefS Group Captain Peter Gray. From the very title, the aim of the volume and preceding workshop was explicit – to examine the experience of the first post–Cold War decade of air power and identify trends in its development in a new century. Attention was paid to the political limits of air power in military intervention, with reference to the Balkan experiences; the flexibility of air power as first choice option; air power in the RMA discourse; and air strategy of recent operations from the perspective of the underdog and implications for the air power utility. This volume also covered European aspects of air power; dilemmas in commanding and controlling of air power; air power in expeditionary warfare, and thoughts on changes of its conceptual framework. An article by Brigadier Mungo Melvin looked into the historical aspect of the air–land interface,[107] 'which at this time was a neglected area'.[108] However, as the experience of Iraq demonstrated, although it was the most likely future of air power, it was the least predictable.

The next air power workshop volume was *British Air Power*,[109] also edited by Peter Gray. It addressed the functionality of air power in Afghanistan emphasizing the necessity of an effects-based approach to operation planning: 'inter alia, addressed evolving views on effects-based warfare, particularly with regards to strategic effect of air power and the challenges of the age of transformation'.[110] The continuation of these workshops and their multidimensional thinking on air power showed the endurance of cooperation between academics and professionals within the wider intellectual discourse of air power application.

More informal academic and professional discussions were taking place on the pages of an academic, peer-reviewed journal, *Air Power Review*. This journal served as means of stimulating wider thinking on air power and reflection of sometime unorthodox views on the subject. It usually published staff college papers, essays and views of practitioners. This journal provided an opportunity for British air power enthusiasts to come together and exchange their ideas on the past, present and future of air power. Like air power workshop publications, this journal demonstrated the continued cooperation between academics and professionals towards a more creative thinking on air power that could be used in doctrine writing. Moreover, DDefS would often chair an editorial board composed of both senior air power academics and practitioners. Thus, DDefS remained at the heart of creative thinking on air power and the most contemporary debates on the subject both within and national and international frameworks.

Another place where academics and practitioners cooperated was the Royal United Services Institute (RUSI). Various publications, discussion groups and official talks by senior practitioners from all three services and overseas allies assist in exchanging knowledge and disseminating findings of the most modern research projects. For instance, RUSI conducted Annual Chief of the Defence Staff Lectures, providing a platform for wider academic and professional audiences to communicate with the three chiefs. The CAS's Air Power Conference was of particular relevance, since it collected practitioners and academics from around the world and gave an opportunity to exchange the most recent practical and analytical materials on in the employment of air power in the changing world.

Through these forums, cooperation between academics and practitioners continued through the second decade, developing analytical materials of various views and degrees of creativity. It could have been expected that in the environment of such diverse cooperation and broader interest, academics would be actively involved in the preparation of the doctrine of 2009. However, that was not the case. According to the author of the fourth edition, academics were not involved in the process.[111] One explanation might be the influence of the experience of the previous edition. Since the third edition was considered too intellectual and was argued not to have the desired effect on personnel. Potentially, exclusion of academics could make the new edition more practice oriented and suitable for the purposes of a busy military service. On the other hand, this assumption is rather weak, because involvement of academics in doctrine writing does not necessarily mean that their suggestions would be decisive. The actual explanation is far more trivial. According to the author of this edition, the limited time frame for doctrine writing did not allow for discussion groups to take place. As a result, academics were not involved in the traditional doctrinal workshops.

The role of authors

Air Commodore Alistair Byford became DDefS after Neville Parton and Mike Hart. His career with the RAF started when he was a university cadet at St Catharine's College Cambridge. During the First Gulf War, he was qualified as Tornado Strike pilot, resulting in 4,000 fast jet flying hours. Later, he commanded No. 31 Squadron at RAF Marham and No. 904 Expeditionary Air Wing at Kandahar. In terms of staff tours, he had duties within NATO and European Policy Group. In terms of education, he took Higher Command and Staff Course at the Joint Services Command and Staff College, Shrivenham. There, he was awarded the British Aerospace and Sir Michael Howard trophies. In 2013, he was appointed Director Advanced Command and Staff Course and Assistant Commandant (Air). He retired from the RAF in 2017.

Looking into Alistair Byford's background, it becomes clear that if anyone could write a clear and comprehensible doctrine for both airmen and the Army, it would be him. He argued that the main rationale for the new edition of AP 3000 was in the numerous changes taking place over the decade. The main change was the country's involvement in COIN in both Iraq and Afghanistan, which demanded a concept of air and land integration. The effects-based approach was no longer popular. The new edition also had to reflect changes in the national doctrinal process, particularly the themes of the new edition of the joint doctrine. Additional pressure came from the upcoming SDSR and elections. In terms of internal considerations, a new edition was needed, which would be more comprehensible for the Army, since the previous edition was not understood even by all airmen.[112] Therefore, the new edition was timely. The impetus to write this edition originated with CAS, who argued it was needed and that DDefS was to look into its preparation. Alistair Byford argued that the time frame for its preparation was quite constrained and additional assistance was limited. It was written within a month and was not submitted for internal consultation and consideration due to the lack of staff at that time.[113] In the recent interview, Alistair Byford suggested that the new edition of AP 3000 was written according to the vision of the Assistant Chief of the Air Staff at that time, Air Vice-Marshal Sir Timothy Anderson: 'ACAS at that time, Timo Anderson would have more to say on the principles and the approach adopted in a new edition of AP 3000. He had a different vision than DCDC. He considered that to go into SDSR, a new doctrine had to be written and signed off by the RAF instead of a joint circulation.'[114] This consideration was largely conditioned by the ongoing fight between the RAF and the Navy over the carrier. The new doctrine aimed to set the value of independent air power.

Alistair Byford explained air power in terms of four roles in order to locate it within joint campaigning. The four roles corresponded to the historical roles of air power reflected in the early doctrines of the AP 1300 series (particularly the second edition of AP 1300). Concerning history, he said that despite its relevance for the understanding air power, this was not the place to elaborate on it. AP 3003 was the right book for studying history of the service.[115] However, the third edition also paid attention to the history of RAF doctrine, which was excluded from the fourth edition and was never looked into in the official history of the service. In the rapidly changing national doctrinal environment, knowledge of the historical stages of doctrine development might have been over-burdening. Comparing the third and fourth editions, Alistair Byford argued that the third edition was 'a great book but very comprehensive',[116] and, in terms of the air–land integration and mutual understanding as its preconditions, clarity and simplicity were the main requirements. He continued: 'Regarding my own ideas, I wanted to simplify it and provide distilled principles, not details. Being pragmatic, I wanted it to be concise; something cadets could look at before the seminar … to draw the essence and present it in a reasonably acceptable format.'[117] Moreover, both contributors to the doctrine came to a conclusion that historically airmen were not good at explaining air power and its potential to other people. So this edition was meant to provide some clear and easy-to-understand principles to explain what air power was and what it could do. Taking into account the author's perspective on doctrine writing and its conditionality, the final version of the document was once again influenced by operational experience and its embodiment in jointery. The necessity of making doctrine clear and understandable to the Army was a reflection of an ongoing process of language development and harmonization of terms in the joint discourse. The ongoing emphasis on the necessity of mutual understanding as a key to collaboration and subsequent integration suggests that, despite joint efforts and new stages of jointery institutionalization, the three services could not eradicate a century-long history of interservice rivalry and distinctiveness of organizational culture, especially in the context of the approaching SDSR.

In terms of the authors' general role in doctrine preparation process, it can be argued that, from one perspective, it was becoming less flexible in the joint environment. Although the doctrine was initiated by CAS, DDefS was the one to be responsible for it; he still had to think in advance what review boards from the two other services would accept and what they would challenge in the light of their organizational backgrounds. Accordingly, the challenge of writing a single-service environmental doctrine incorporating jointery was actually in having it approved and published. In other words, the main challenge for the service in producing environmental doctrine of a joint discourse was to write what was needed for the service, yet have it approved in a joint review. On the other hand, joint authorship provided an opportunity for a more smooth amending process, while restricting content.[118] This dichotomy would be emphasized in the doctrine preparation process of JDP 0-30. The experience of the fourth edition still does not demonstrate a completely instrumental approach to authors in doctrine writing. Probably, because Alistair Byford was the only person responsible for its preparation in a restricted time frame and with limited number of staff involved, the impact of his personality was still evident.

Conclusion

Overall, the absence of a new edition for a decade was dictated by practical considerations, institutionalization of jointery and consequent struggle for the ownership of environmental doctrines. Although a new edition was possible already in 2005, the ongoing campaigns in Iraq and Afghanistan could undermine operational lessons learned in 2003, producing a negative influence on the service and its framework document. Consequently, although operational experience stimulated thinking about the lessons of the previous/ongoing operations, it was not the major driving force of doctrine writing of 2009. Although the lessons of both Afghanistan and Iraq had been processed by 2005 on both single-service and joint levels, their inclusion in the RAF framework document was depended on the favourable internal environment rather than reflection of the new operational experience alone. The new edition was largely influenced by the most recent operations in Iraq and Afghanistan rather than Kosovo, of which there was little mention. This fact may have a twofold explanation. First, the Kosovo campaign aroused controversy as to its political and military assessment. Therefore, for political reasons, it was sensible to avoid controversy in a document written in a simple manner to bring clarity. Second, the last two operations were aimed at fighting COINs. A new edition had to explain the place of air power in COIN environment. Therefore, attention was paid to the up-to-date experiences of the two most recent operations.

As in the previous edition, internal factor had predominant impact on doctrine writing. However, this time the line between external and internal factors blurred even more. The experience of Afghanistan and Iraq reaffirmed the necessity of the institutionalization of jointery through the conceptual framework of NCC and the Comprehensive Approach. The increased attention to jointery in the political circles had direct implications for the doctrine writing of all three services, since in order to establish its complete authority and consequent synchronization, JDCC and later on DCDC, had to gain control over environmental doctrine. Inevitably, the new edition had to reflect jointery.

However, it also had to incorporate environmental doctrine into joint discourse rather than jointery into environmental doctrine. Thus, the approach still corresponded to the bottom–up principle of the first two editions of AP 3000. On the other hand, the fourth edition demonstrated that environmental doctrine can be joint, although written by a single service. It can be concluded that the last edition of AP 3000 demonstrated that even under single-service authorship, environmental doctrine can still be joint at its very core. The centralization of jointery and the struggle for ownership of environmental doctrine, as a means of promoting a single service and its preferred concepts drove doctrine writing of this edition and defined the time of its publication. The process was partly driven by the approaching SDSR, where effective self-explanation could be crucial for the service's survival.

The academic contribution was limited, not because of any reluctance to include academic opinion or because the new edition was simplified. The situational nature, restricted time and the number of staff available to produce doctrine meant that doctrinal workshops and discussion groups could not take place. The limited role of academics in this instance was determined by circumstance rather than an interservice tendency to limit academic involvement in the process. Nevertheless, the author was DDefS, and like his predecessors, he was on the frontline of academic research on air power. His awareness of the prevailing academic discourse of the time was beyond doubt.

The role of authors in the fourth edition was once again significant. Although it could have been expected to be more restrained with the development of jointery, the fact that authorship was still single service allowed considerable freedom of action. Greater autonomy in decision-making by the author once again influenced the nature of the fourth edition and its functionality, in terms of ownership of environmental doctrine, time constraints and limited members of staff involved. Inevitably, as with the previous edition, this one reflected the opinions of DDefS and CAS. However, as jointery became more institutionalized, the authors had to be mindful of what content would go through such review and what might be negotiable. However, ownership of environmental doctrine still provided the RAF and its authors with more freedom than joint authorship.

Although the fourth edition of AP 3000 was possible in 2005, it would not include the Comprehensive Approach, which was by then the salient point of joint doctrinal thinking. Consequently, there was no single driving force behind the publication of the fourth edition of AP 3000, but a complexity of external, national and interservice considerations. While operational experience provided the lessons to be used in the doctrine, national political evolution of these lessons and general operational trends of the global strategic environment defined their form. This absorption occurred through the process of jointery, which is different in each stage of its institutionalization. In its turn, the degree of joint progress defines the degree of freedom in reflection of single-service experience and the utility of doctrine in lobbying single-service interests.

Finally, when comparing the factors influencing preparation of the third and fourth editions, in both cases operational experience, although crucial for the employment of air power, was not an immediate reason for the revision of doctrine. Unlike the first two editions, the third and fourth were created for the joint environment, which required a certain degree of synchronization with other processes within the Armed Forces. Consequently, the changes in the internal environment were becoming more influential and definitive in doctrine development of the last two editions. While the third edition aimed to explain jointery *per se*, the fourth edition demonstrated that the RAF could create joint environmental doctrine before the SDSR. While the third edition reflected the prescriptions of the SDR, the fourth was preparing for it, sending a message to the SDSR review board.

Accordingly, doctrine development became closely connected with the defence review cycle and the reform of the Armed Forces. From a systematic perspective, it meant that, doctrine writing had not only been centrally initiated but also linked to the crucial review of the Armed Forces – the SDSR, in order to secure tri-service integration, and harmonization of their doctrines under a joint umbrella. The question was no longer about how well a single service could write a joint environmental doctrine, but about how to establish a unified national joint system, which could simultaneously reflect and adapt to any changes in the external strategic environment. The final stage of the institutionalization of jointery and its functionality in Allied cooperation is explored in the case study of joint environmental doctrine JDP 0–30, which is addressed in the next chapter.

6

Case Study of JDP 0–30

The next edition of air and space doctrine JDP 0–30, *UK Air and Space Doctrine*,[1] was published in July 2013. Unlike all previous editions, this one was the result of tri-service efforts under the joint umbrella of DCDC. However, the main author and organizer of its publication was the author of the fourth edition of AP 3000, Alistair Byford. In terms of timeliness, the doctrine was issued after another essential operational experience in Libya, the global economic crisis and the SDSR. It also reflected changes in the conceptualization of jointery and the development of a new doctrine writing cycle. In fact, it introduced a new chapter in RAF doctrinal history.

Like the fourth edition of AP 3000, this doctrine explained both air and space power but in a different way. While the previous doctrine traced the roles and functionality of air and space power as a unity, the new edition made a distinction between the two, emphasizing the difference in scale and distinctive attributes of each. Therefore, the document was divided into two parts, reflecting the specifics of each environment separately. Each part consists of four chapters explaining the nature, character, delivery and application of each type of power. A two-page conclusion is given in the end, followed by a Lexicon and Terms and Definitions. Subsequently, in contrast to the previous doctrine, the overall size of the document is twice as big, resulting in 130 pages. Like the fourth edition, the main emphasis was placed on clarity and simplicity in both the structure of chapters and language. It may also seem that the language is even simpler than in the previous edition. Each chapter had key points, summaries and different colour boxes identifying intersecting concepts and themes.[2]

From an organizational perspective, the replacement of AP 3000 with JDP 0–30 was explained as 'a part of the migration from single Service to joint theory and practice'.[3] It was also stated that the previous edition was largely influenced by the counterinsurgency (COIN) campaigning and subsequent air–land integration as an enabler of the comprehensive approach. The new doctrine followed the same approach but shifted the emphasis from campaigning to contingent operations. It suggested that since contingencies were unpredictable 'JDP 0–30 considers UK air and space power within a broader spectrum of conflict, where a cross-domain and integrated approach is more effective than bi-lateral air-land or air-sea cooperation'.[4] Changes included conflict prevention, homeland defence and the projection of influence and power; the return of air power strategic effects in all its roles; the significance of partnerships; the shift from a decentralized to a centralized approach to command and control and subsequent adaptive execution; and greater attention to space power in the national system of defence.[5]

This publication also showed new tendencies in doctrine hierarchy, which were not present in the previous edition. The document mentioned a variety of joint notes, which were mostly related to unmanned aircraft systems or other capstone doctrines at the operational/strategic level. The Joint Concept Note 3/12, *Future Air and Space Operating Concept*,[6] explained the future of UK's air and space power and project doctrinal trends of JDP 0–30 to 2035.[7] In this context, the doctrine explained the tenets, while the note extended them to the future. Apart from quite common reference to the equivalent NATO doctrine *Allied Joint Publication – 3.3 Air and Space Operations*,[8] a relationship to another nation's doctrine was outlined. US Joint Publication 3–14, Space Operations, was quoted as 'the primary source of space capability', further detailed by DCDC's *The UK Military Primer*.[9]

The entire shift from single-service to joint authorship of environmental doctrine after a long history of single-service organizational culture would inevitably result in a biased perception of a new publication. In the foreword to JDP 0–30, the CAS addressed the correlation between the single-service bias and joint realities:

> A joint approach to operations is almost always essential, using well-honed single-Service capabilities in approaching every scenario with an intuitive joint mindset. As airmen, we must develop a deep understanding of the environment in which we operate, and play that air-minded expertise back into joint, multinational and inter-agency discussions, from a knowledge and expertise point of view, but without undue single-Service bias.[10]

This foreword is crucial to the validity of the publication in the eyes of the RAF personnel, since it was authorized and supported by CAS, and suggested a holistic approach to the single-service/joint dichotomy.

The external environment/operational experience of Libya

One can try to see into the future and hope to apply experience and reform capabilities according to objectives. It can only be hoped for the next operational involvement to occur before all capabilities are reformed as planned. The Libyan War showed that this is often not the case. The unpredictability of threats demands constant readiness across different conflicts. This war was a test for the British Armed Forces, recovering from the results of the long-awaited SDSR with various policies and changes underway. While the internal implications of the Libyan War will be addressed in the section devoted to internal factors, this section addresses exclusively military considerations.

The Libyan civil war was another challenge for the Allied forces in terms of conducting military intervention after the negative experience of Iraq and Afghanistan. In this case, the main concern was the avoidance of a full-scale military presence on the ground, which characterized the two previous operations. In other words, the primary consideration was how to influence Gaddafi without making long-term commitment of NATO ground troops. As a result, instead of the ground forces, the preference was given to the other two services and associated types of military power. The British participation in US-planned Operation Odyssey Dawn, which aimed at the provision of a no-fly zone to support anti-Gaddafi forces, entered the history of the British Armed Forces as Operation Ellamy. According to MOD estimate in November 2011: 'At its peak, some 2,300 British servicemen and women were deployed on Operation ELLAMY. We deployed 32 aircraft including 16 Tornado GR4s, six Typhoons, five attack helicopters, refuelling tankers and specialist surveillance aircraft and helicopters. Over the course of operation we also deployed eight warships and attack submarines.'[11] During the Libyan War, air power was used in all four roles envisioned by the previous doctrine. In the early stage, the main tasks included cooperation with the Navy in the evacuation of UK citizens from the conflict zone and reconnaissance. Over a couple of days, over 800 UK citizens and over 1,000 citizens of 50 other countries were evacuated.[12] For this role, helicopters, Hercules aircraft and HMS Cumberland were used. In the long run, the projection of air power in Libya was intended to achieve three objectives: the suppression of the Libyan air defence, the provision of ISTAR and consequent protection of the ISTAR platform. In technological terms, the RAF Typhoons, which flew their first combat missions,[13] were initially intended for air-to-air combat in the support of no-fly zone task. They were further modified for the ground attacks, which Typhoons performed together with Tornados.[14]

The ISTAR for target detection was provided by the Sentinel platform. The Allied firepower was complemented with Storm Shadow and Brimstone air-launched missiles.[15]

The main targets were the pro-Gaddafi command and control sites. However, with the escalation of the conflict and the transferring of warfighting from the rural to urban area, the main concern in targeting and strikes was collateral damage, especially civilian casualties.[16] Prevention of non-combatant casualties is a part of the risk assessment and clearance of any target. However, in the Libyan War, it was extremely sensitive since the main rationale for the intervention was the prevention of civilian casualties.[17] Thus, media and public attention was drawn to the number of civilian casualties, scrutinizing every military action. Consequently, tactical actions could easily have tremendous strategic implications for the legitimacy of campaign and its success.[18] In this context, the process of target approval was stricter than in Iraq and 'many potential targets were rejected because of the risk of civilian casualties'.[19] However, the high level of precision was generally acknowledged.

Overall, UK Air Forces had flown around 3,000 sorties, 2,000 of which were strikes; of all NATO sorties as of 23 October 2011, an estimated 26,281 sorties and 9,646 strike sorties, the UK contribution is estimated at 11 per cent of the total and 20 per cent of strike sorties.[20] The Brimstone missiles were particularly useful command and control centres, ammunition sites and highly mobile targets.[21] Brimstone missiles allowed 'the UK a unique capability to strike difficult targets with little or no collateral damage because of the small size of the weapon and its warhead'.[22] However, since the majority of targets were mobile, the realization of the efficiency of the British missiles soon resulted in the stocks running low, 'down to single figures at one point'.[23]

One of the greatest paradoxes of Operation Ellamy was actually not the remarkably impressive performance of the service under conditions of austerity. Since some of the prescriptions of the SDSR did not take immediate effect and had not been implemented, ad hoc preservation of certain platforms provided extra capability and consequent efficiency of the RAF's performance. Of course, this refers to Sentinel and Nimrod, which were crucial in the provision of ISTAR in Libya. The deployed Nimrod R1 signals intelligence aircraft had to be decommissioned in 2011,[24] yet was extended in service for Libya. Sentinel had to be decommissioned once its role in Afghanistan ended.[25] Paradoxically, these two aircraft were essential in enabling situational awareness. Sir Stephen Dalton, CAS at that time, assessed Sentinel's performance as follows:

It [Sentinel] was fundamental. We were able to link up and securely pass information from the Sentinel aircraft providing the ground-mapping capability through the AWACS in E3 aeroplanes, through secure satellite comms, through data links to the Typhoon and form Typhoon to Tornado and onwards. All that was done … The technical capability is there, and it has proven itself to be combat-ready and combat-capable.[26]

Operational lessons and their reflection in doctrine

So what did Libya change in the air power discourse? What lessons can be derived and how were they reflected in the doctrine? First, once again air power proved capable of achieving objectives both on its own and in cooperation with other services. Consequently, the argument that air power was the tool of political 'the first choice' was sound. It could be also useful in strengthening the RAF position in the next SDR. The predominant and also successful use of air power in the Libyan War confirmed that air power was capable of conducting supportive roles, but also remained a key player in the direct provision of strategic effect of air strikes.[27] Although the previous doctrine explained four roles of air power, omitting the strategic effect, Libya demonstrated that it was premature to look at air power exclusively in terms of synergy and supportive roles.

Second, this war showed that 'air power' is not an abstract term and its achievement depends heavily on the unity of human potential and available technologies. The main emphasis is on the available technologies. In this context, the operation showed a high degree of the flexibility of air power in reaching targets in both rural and urban areas. It was also characterized by high precision even under the conditions of restraining ROEs. Consequently, despite the austerity, the technological core of air power should correspond to the strategic objectives and future operations. Thus, the need for a wider variety of UAVs was mentioned.[28] The technological consistency and timeliness crucial for contingent operations are considered dominant in the future.[29] According to Prof Christina Goulter, Operation Ellamy illustrated that manned platform proved essential since the availability of UAVs was limited due to the priority of the campaign in Afghanistan.[30] Moreover, she continued, 'although UAVs can provide valuable "pattern-of-life" intelligence once on station, the limited number of UAVs and the vast distances between areas of interest limited their ability to monitor what was a very fluid battlespace'.[31]

Third, Libya demonstrated another feature of contemporary warfare – 'a war amongst the people'.[32] This feature had already become evident in Vietnam,

Malaya, Bosnia and Kosovo, Afghanistan and Iraq. In Libya, this issue was raised once again because air forces were responsible for this campaign practically on their own. Functionality of air power and the number of tasks it could accomplish was restrained by the necessity of avoiding civilian casualties. The situation was even more complex since the operation in Libya aimed at the protection of civilians in urban areas.[33] Fourth, Libya reaffirmed that contemporary warfare was no longer only about physical manoeuvre and its coercive effects, but it was also about addressing public opinion both at home and abroad. One of the reasons why Gaddaffi supporters resisted for so long was due to the use of media broadcasting in support of his regime.[34] In terms of the use of air power, this lesson has two implications. First, air power should consider its secondary effects in terms of population in the battlespace in order to remain efficient in contemporary war. Once again, the psychological effect of air power had to be considered. However, this time it was no longer about the suppression of morale of the adversary's population but about public support and the legitimacy of actions. Thus, the success of air power is largely conditioned how it is perceived and if domestic and international support are preserved. Finally, although the operation was characterized by unprecedented precision and use of UAVs, the effective implementation of air power or any military force depended on implementation of a systematic approach to information and building situational awareness and desired outcomes.

Since Libya was mainly an air intervention campaign and had a different emphasis on the use of air power from previous operations, doctrine had to reflect it. The most substantial change in doctrinal discourse of the time was the return of strategic effect in JDP 0–30. Although the four roles were preserved from the previous edition, strategic attack was explored in terms of Role 3 Attack (Coerce).[35] Therefore, strategic attack was mentioned, but it was not given a separate role as in the first three editions of AP 3000. Instead, it was discussed in terms of two other types of targeting: counter-surface force operations and information activities. A page-long attention to strategic attack included its definition and an example of Israeli Operation Babylon 1981.[36] This suggests that although Libya demonstrated the independent performance of air power and the important role of strategic attack, it was not considered to outweigh all other roles. Thus, the inclusion of strategic attack was a step towards a systematic evaluation of the functionality of air power rather than an attempt to demonstrate its sovereign status in contemporary warfare. This description attempts to clear the audience's perception of air power strategic attack from its historical discourse and consequent misperception of the dogmatic nature of its utility. This feature can be attributed to joint authorship. Since JDP 0-30 was written with a tri-service audience in mind, the Army would be tempted to perceive air power for strategic effect as the dogma of strategic bombing. Thus, more clear and neutral wording was essential.

Furthermore, the experience of Libya and all the campaigns of the last two decades were addressed in the explanation of targeting. The success of air attack was argued to depend on reach, penetration of enemy defences, precision and matching effects correctly for targeting.[37] The emphasis was placed on the political will to use force and consequent necessity to use both kinetic and non-kinetic air power capabilities. This consideration was based on the previous experiences of air attacks that would achieve military/tactical purposes but have negative political or strategic implications. It was argued that traditional targeting was not suitable for different conflicts: 'This is because we are unlikely to delegate decision-making authority below the strategic level where there is the potential to create unforeseen or unwanted consequences.'[38] Apart from the strictness of ROE in the previous operation, this emphasis also argued for the need of winning wars at home and in the international arena, as well as in the battlespace. In such a way, the doctrine also reflected the need of addressing public perception and consideration of the aftermath of tactical decisions. In terms of national and international public support, the doctrine addressed the questions of legitimacy. It was suggested that the force had to be more pro-active in the explanation of what was done, and how and why to avoid the misperception of air power as 'a disproportionately violent, detached and indiscriminate form of force'.[39] This should be achieved through establishing a clear audit trail of decision-making and actions to prove legality.[40] From lawyers' perspective, although this approach to assessing performance might seem rational, from the perspective of practitioners it was a challenge. However, the paper trail of achievements could be a useful evidence/argument in the next defence review.

Derived from all previous operations, this edition introduced centralized execution in air command and control. Although the traditional approach of centralized control and decentralized execution remained predominant in the RAF practice,[41] centralized execution was desired or required in certain circumstances. They included small-scale missions with high stakes; when unfamiliar or less militarily capable allies are taking part in the operation, and when 'a lower-level decision-maker may not fully appreciate the link between tactical actions and strategic effects'.[42] Therefore, the new approach to execution is adaptive, meaning that centralized or decentralized approach is chosen depending on the situational requirements of a particular task. It can be argued that this change was conditioned by the combined experience of all previous operations, where the lines between levels of warfare became too vague and actions on the tactical level had undesired implications at the strategic.[43] Furthermore, this was also due to the magnified attention to civilian casualties in contemporary warfare and preservation of legitimacy of actions.[44]

The legal section of doctrine also addressed moral and ethical issues concerning UAVs and remotely piloted air systems. In this context, the main argument was that the use of new technologies in maximizing warfighting capability was not anything new, nor was the argument about fair and unfair means. It was also stated that UAVs do not lower the threshold for conflict because they still require political authorization, just as conventional means do. Furthermore, the morality of autonomous or robotic systems was argued to be controlled either by 'human oversight over all weapon-release decisions'[45] or by algorithms which determined their actions according to the imposed ROEs. Finally, the argument that control over UAVs was detached from reality was once again refuted, stating that strict ROEs were maintained along with advance observation of targets by conventional manned aircraft prior to the strike.[46]

The authors considered that they needed this justification of UAVs because of the contrasting views on the relevance of UAVs and their role in shaping contemporary warfare.[47] On the one hand, addressing this topic in doctrine suggests that the official military refutation of negative discussion was required. Consequently, in an attempt to reach a wider audience, this justification suggested that the performance and relevance of UAVs should be determined by military capabilities and warfighting requirements rather than simple public discussion. The justification of UAVs was a part of a more profound theme reflected in this doctrine – an even further step away from non-precision weaponry towards cutting-edge technologies and precision. It was argued that although non-PGMs are legally admissible and may achieve desired strategic effect, attention needs to be paid to perceptions that might undermine that effect.[48] In the light of this discourse, the justification of UAVs for a wider audience seems to be even more rational.

Consequently, the successful performance of Storm Shadow and Brimstone in Libya[49] demonstrated not only the importance of technologies in contemporary warfare and employment of air power. It also showed the vital need for sufficient technologies in power projection which should be assessed in terms of quality and precision rather than quantity and duration. Examples of this emphasis are present throughout the text. For instance, the main strengths of air power were identified in terms of quality and multitasking. The speed and reach characteristics of air power should concentrate air effects when and where they are needed. Moreover, PGMs allow creating psychological shock without using many aircraft.[50] In terms of operational experience, this holistic approach to technologies argues for the increased efficiency of PGMs over the last two decades and their consequent success in the last operation. However, this approach to technology was significantly influenced by the internal factor of the SDSR and the policy of austerity, which argued for the increased multitasking and complementarity of existing military capabilities.[51]

Although the crucial role of cutting-edge technologies for air power had been mentioned in all air power doctrines, the last publication emphasized it differently. Air power's high technological costs could be outweighed by its potential multifunctional application.[52] The next paragraph summarizes two decades of air power operational experience and suggests its future implementation: 'Air power is **cost-effective**, despite the high price of military aircraft and the sophisticated technology they use, because it multiplies effects. In some operational circumstances, this means we may avoid the need to commit surface forces altogether. Alternatively, we may create influence with economy of effort by using air capabilities to enhance the potency of other environmental capabilities.'[53]

Air power can play a decisive role in counter-land operations in conventional warfare or supportive and potential enhancing in irregular warfare, where attention is paid to stabilization operations and the security of people.[54] Regarding the supporting roles of air power, particularly non-lethal and non-kinetic aspect, the doctrine paid due attention to ISR. Once again, this can be an argument for the reflection of operational experience in the document or the recognition of the reality of the information age, which again is verified through operational experience and day-to-day security monitoring.[55] However, unlike the experience of Libya, which demonstrated the need for and availability of technologies, doctrine concentrated on the explanation of the relevance of ISR for the situational awareness. Consequently, the ISR discourse corresponded to the second role of air power – to inform. As in the previous edition, the emphasis was placed on the need for informational awareness as a precondition for campaign planning and evaluation of its effects. In terms of the five targeting functions, 'find, fix, finish, exploit and analyse',[56] the Cold War narrative had concentrated on fix and finish; the newly adopted approach shifted finding as a precondition of promoting understanding.[57] This understanding should facilitate preparation of an interdisciplinary and systematic profile, including such dimensions as human, cultural and social.

In terms of practical improvement of ISR, this edition followed the previous one in terms of NEC development. Although the language was more general and less concept oriented, it explained the same idea. The emphasis was placed upon the integration of cross-component capabilities into combat system to handle unforeseen and complex threats of the contingent environment.[58] From one perspective, this is an argument in favour of networking to improve the timeliness and accuracy of collected intelligence in the extremely versatile environment of contingency. From another perspective, this complementarity of capabilities corresponds to the conclusion of the SDSR and the consequent considerations of austerity – the ability to deploy small yet sophisticated and multifunctional military force in the shortest time, in any place in the world.

Overall, the operational experience of Libya was reflected in doctrine and thus influenced its preparation. In terms of the illustrative value of the recent experience, it was combined with diverse examples from the entire history of air warfare. Libya was used as a comparison to Kosovo in terms of lessons of air-led campaigns.[59] Then, it was mentioned in relation to the projection of power in Operation Odyssey Dawn,[60] the coercive role of air power,[61] sustaining expeditionary air operations,[62] the cross-domain interoperability in Operation Unified Protector[63] and offensive counter-space operations.[64] These examples once again suggest the relevance of the Libyan operational experience for the future of air power use and consequent impact on the recent edition of air power doctrine. However, it should be stressed that doctrine uses diverse operational examples of air power use over the last four decades. In its turn, this feature suggests not only the relevance of operational experience for air power and doctrine, but also the revived importance of history for both.

Internal factors

From the experience of the two previous editions of air power doctrine, it can be argued that defence reviews have a crucial impact on the Armed Forces and their self-perception and on explanation for the internal and external audiences. Doctrine facilitates incorporation of defence review into service's practice. While the third edition introduced jointery into air power discourse as the reflection of the SDR of 1998, the fourth edition explained further development of jointery at institutional-conceptual level in preparation to the new SDSR 2010. JDP 0–30 illustrated the concluding stage of jointery and the impact of SDSR on the service and doctrine writing. The main influence of the new defence review was not the introduction of a new core conceptual framework to reform the Armed Forces but the placement of budgetary restraints on their activities. The impact can be considered indirect, but this author would argue that it is sequential and hierarchical, affecting each level of defence hierarchy accordingly. First, this section addresses the general implications of the SDSR on the RAF. Then, the role of the SDSR in stimulating jointery in doctrine writing, which influenced JDP 0–30 is discussed.

The SDSR 2010

The new defence review was a document of its time and reflected situational factors effecting its preparation and motivation. The protracted commitments of the UK in Afghanistan were one of the features.[65] It is not surprising that the main theme of the review was cost-efficiency posed against unchanged defence objectives.[66] Once again, the main principle of restructuring of the Armed Forces was the development of high-quality, rigorously prioritized, balanced, efficient, well-supported, flexible and adaptable, expeditionary and connected capabilities.[67] Since the numerical approach was not an option for the achievement of these characteristics, the combination of multifunctionality and technological superiority was prioritized.

Consequently, the number of Armed Forces personnel was to be reduced. By 2015, the RAF personnel were to be reduced by around 5,000 to about 33,000, aiming at 31,500 by 2020.[68] However, this loss was to be compensated by the modernization of equipment. Future capabilities would include a fast jet fleet of Typhoon and new Joint Strike Fighter aircraft, which were chosen once again because of their multitasking potential. They were argued to be 'able to operate in the future high-threat airspace while providing air defence, precision ground attack and combat ISTAR capabilities'.[69] The Harrier fleet was to be removed from the service, while the Tornado fleet was reduced. In terms of strategic and tactical airlift fleet, the previous TriStar and VC10 were to be substituted with C-17, A400M Airbus A330. As mentioned earlier, Sentinel and Nimrod were to be substituted by 'the E3D Sentry AWACS to provide airborne command, control and surveillance. Rivet Joint signals intelligence aircraft to provide global independent strategic intelligence gathering, and a range of unmanned air systems to complement our strategic ISTAR assets and reduce the risk to our forces of operating over hostile territory'.[70]

The assessment of the SDSR in professional and academic literature is quite diverse and is not, in fact, the topic of this book.[71] The main relevance of the SDSR for this research is the changes it initiated and their reflection in JDP 0–30. First, the conclusion of the review emphasized technology-centred approach to cooperation in the joint, integrated environment. Although technology was always important for warfare, in this review its relevance was explained in terms of the vital need for sustainable capabilities rather than a traditional modernization. This tendency was further reflected in the MOD White Paper *National Security through Technology: Technology, Equipment, and Support for UK Defence and Security*, February 2012.[72] The entire document focused on how the MOD is planning to achieve 2020 targets through the open procurement principle[73] and value-for-money approach.[74]

Consequently, the concentration of both the SDSR and the MOD paper on the financial rather than conceptual aspect of defence suggests an inevitable atmosphere of economy and merging of functions. Accordingly, favouring of cooperation rather than independent actions was to be expected. The internal integration of the Armed Forces through jointery and in the external cooperation with the Alliance suggested this need of cooperation and synergy. In terms of these considerations, the shift from costly campaigning towards a cost-effective and mobile contingency looked more rational, especially if it reflected the same tendency within NATO.[75] At first glance, it may seem that the two ways of cost-effective integration within the Armed Forces and external cooperation with NATO are separate initiatives. This is not the case. The internal integration of the Armed Forces is a precondition for further intensification of cooperation with NATO. This trend in terms of the new doctrine preparation cycle and the institutionalization of jointery is described onwards.

The institutionalization of jointery

Unlike the previous doctrine, by the time of the new edition, DCDC had become responsible for the production of operational and strategic doctrines.[76] In other words, they produce capstone JDP, a variety of subordinate joint publications, joint concepts and notes. They also became responsible for the preparation of environmental doctrines in consultations with the specialists from the three services.[77] The ownership of environmental doctrines, no matter how controversial it is from the single-service perspective, gave DCDC an opportunity to institutionalize vertical jointery and reform doctrine writing process. As a result, no doctrine at the operational, strategic and environmental levels could be changed without profound changes in the national defence policy, joint doctrine, Allied doctrine or strategic trends developed by DCDC. Accordingly, the entire process of doctrine writing became centralized and hierarchical – changes at the upper-level doctrines would trigger consequent changes at the lower-level doctrines, introducing interdependence and complementarity. Consequently, unlike the previous two decades, doctrine initiation was no longer in the hands of service enthusiasts or CAS. Furthermore, the situational requirements, strict doctrine hierarchy and the centralized authorization of changes envisioned a more mechanical and institutionalized approach to doctrine writing.

Although previous doctrines were personalities driven and thus reflected the impact of personal background or overview on air power and its functionality, the new approach argued for the collective thinking and instrumental role of the doctrine writing team rather than an individual contribution. The new approach has a number of benefits. First, a strict prescription of content for each level of doctrine eliminates the potential of duplication and overstretching of its boundaries and functions. In terms of rational progression, ideally each level, lower doctrine should detail the ideas and themes of the previous level. Thus, knowledge is deepened according to the requirements of each level. Second, the interdependent hierarchy and the centralized production of doctrines at the operational and strategic levels contribute to the harmonization of changes. In other words, changes in doctrinal network can cause a domino effect, resulting in gradual adaptation on each level below the trigger. In the contemporary strategic environment of rapid changes and concentration on unpredictability of contingencies, such synchronization can be beneficial for the rapid adaptation of the Armed Forces to these changes.

In terms of the systematic approach to data collection, processing and analysis, DCDC has enough resources and staff to provide systematic and interdisciplinary analysis of case studies and operational examples relevant to a certain conceptual framework. Unlike the previous edition, more people could be involved in the doctrine preparation process and more time could be spent on its crystallization.[78] Another benefit is potentially increased understanding among the three services, which can be achieved through joint work on each environmental doctrine and the simplification of terminology and concepts. Regarding the doctrine hierarchy, it remained relatively the same within the levels of warfare, with a slight increase in joint publications, detailing existing doctrines or reflecting upon new issues not covered in the existing publications.

How does jointery lead to NATO?

The strengthening of jointery and consequent synchronization of the doctrine writing process contributes to a smoother and more centralized approach to reforming of the Armed Forces through the means of doctrine. The harmonization of changes also contributes to formalization of time frame for doctrine writing: eighteen months, on average. Of course, the ad hoc situations when doctrines were written in a month are exceptional, rather than a general rule. Therefore, in the synchronized doctrinal environment, incorporation of complex techniques of inter-Allied cooperation towards integrated and harmonized command and control could be effectively achieved through doctrine. The SDSR commitment to continue cooperation with NATO corresponded to NATO's new Strategic Concept adopted in November 2010 at the Lisbon summit,[79] which stressed the need for cooperation and cost-efficiency of efforts. The need for procedural improvement of bilateral and Allied cooperation, which was shown in previous operations, argued for a new approach to collaboration. The answer was in jointery as a promotion of a more profound cooperation with NATO in terms of a conceptual framework and consequent tactical synchronization.

In the previous two decades, the supremacy of the Allied joint doctrine was recognized and aimed at the provision of 'Allied Armed Forces with a framework of guidance to the conduct of operations'.[80] However, the new approach to national doctrines is to keep them as close to the NATO framework as possible. DCDC published a handbook on the development of joint doctrine, which explained this approach for the case of endorsed doctrines as follows: 'As the contemporary operating environment increases our likelihood to operate as part of a NATO-based coalition, doctrine should reflect common practices as far as possible. Therefore, it is policy to adopt NATO doctrine as our national doctrine except where there is a specific national doctrinal need.'[81] Consequently, it was suggested that except for the strategic- and operational-level doctrines, DCDC wrote national capstone joint doctrine and keystone publications. In preparation of all other doctrines the following advice was given: 'Adopt a NATO publication as a direct replacement for the JDP equivalent; add green elements to NATO publications to highlight national differences in approach; or produce national doctrine only when we are unable to use a NATO publication, or if there is no NATO equivalent.'[82]

For an unendorsed doctrine, both NATO and the UK make sure their publications are up to date and correspond to the existing/prevailing strategic environment and specific operational characteristics. In the event of a doctrinal gap or an immediate need to update existing doctrine, DCDC produced a Joint Doctrine Note (JDN).[83] This process could be initiated through the Joint Doctrine Steering Committee (JDSC). Consequently, due to the supplementary status of JDNs, they also favoured a greater degree of freedom and functional flexibility rather than doctrines. JDNs could be used to stimulate debates, collect and disseminate best practice to cover a gap when joint doctrine should be modified for operational requirements. JDN could also serve as means of stimulating a new doctrinal publication.[84] In terms of the levels of war, joint strategic- and operational-level doctrines were written by DCDC and the former NATO Standardized Agency (NSA). Now it is NATO Standardized Office (NSO). The previous leading role of DCDC in the preparation of the Allied Joint Doctrine was shared with NSA. However, DCDC still owned JDP series. Joint (Allied) tactical level was again shared by NSA and Joint Force Command Joint Warfare. Tactical (environmental)-level doctrines were in responsibility of the three services.[85]

The status of air power doctrine was explained in terms of doctrine subdivision into functional, thematic and environmental. Functional doctrine covered J1-J9 military branches,[86] while thematic ones placed functional doctrine into a specific context. On the other hand, environmental doctrine was meant to incorporate the other two into the specifics of each environment.[87] Having outlined this cross-level doctrinal typology, the document did not clearly state who would be responsible for the preparation of each type and how that would fit into the new doctrine preparation cycle. However, the new edition was authored by DCDC, and it remained the reasonability of DCDC nowadays, when it published the second edition of JDP 0–30 in December 2017.

Doctrine writing process was also reformed, introducing strict division of responsibilities and deadlines for their achievement. Since the process is multicomponent and well structured, there is no point in explaining each step. However, the importance of this prescription of duties should be explained. First, the exact division of duties and their clarity in the well-staffed environment contributed to timelier and better-organized doctrine writing, especially in times of austerity. Second, the centralized authorship of all JDP publications within one institution gave an opportunity of in-depth discussions. Consequently, numerous discussion groups consisting of academics and practitioners could contribute to the intellectualization and systematization of the process. The clarity of criteria for doctrinal drafts and their consequent relation to NATO standardization procedures allow for sufficient understanding of Allied practices and harmonization of national and Allied approaches. These criteria also serve as means for the effective implementation of Allied practices in the national discourse. In terms of national and Allied doctrinal harmonization, the newly introduced doctrine writing procedures aimed to bring Allied doctrine writing procedures and techniques closer to the national practice. They are also characteristic of the American doctrine writing apparatus, which is famous for its organization and strict subordination.[88]

The reflection of the new process in JDP 0-30

The aforementioned doctrine writing process was explained in the doctrine writing handbook only in November 2013. Although various procedural features were yet to be implemented, JDP 0-30 still had some elements of the new doctrine preparation process inspired by the institutionalization of jointery. Consequently, the impact of the new process in JDP 0-30 can be traced both in its content and in the procedures of its preparation. In terms of the content, the document illustrated the new doctrine hierarchy and the emphasis on NATO. In terms of procedural modifications, the roles of the authors and academics had changed. In the beginning of the document, the new doctrine hierarchy and the connection to other joint publications were outlined, as discussed earlier in this chapter. The explanation of hierarchy illustrated both the place of environmental doctrine in it and the interconnected nature of a new doctrinal environment. In this environment, JDP 0-30 is based on and complemented by the JDN3/10, *Unmanned Aircraft Systems: Terminology, Definition and Classification*[89] and JDN2/11, *The UK Approach to Unmanned Aircraft Systems*.[90] Joint doctrine notes reflect the technological dimension of JDP 0-30, detailing various notions which could not be fitted into an environmental doctrine. However, the importance of new technologies and the demonstration of the moral and ethical arguments together with technological efficiency were reflected in this edition. This suggests that the presence of the UAV argument in JDP 0-30 was influenced both by operational experience and by analytical thinking of JDNs.

Regarding the sequence of influence, first, operational experience and domestic political environment suggested the necessity of technological cost-efficiency. This trend was manifested in the corresponding JDNs and then the distillation of conclusions was put into the environmental doctrine. This statement is based on the preceding time of JDNs publication and its correspondence to the new doctrine writing process. Apart from JDNs, JDP 0-30 was also influenced by *Joint Concept Note 3/12*,[91] which looked into trends of air and space power use in the nearest future of 2035. In terms of the levels of warfare, JDP 0-30 guided the lower-level single-service doctrine, meaning tactical AP 3002. Because of the differences in authorship and approaches, certain publications of the AP series were rewritten. At that time, work was being conducted on the new editions of AP 3002 and AP 3003.[92] This shows a need for doctrinal synchronization within the service in order to fit into the joint hierarchy and further Allied system of doctrinal publications.

In terms of NATO orientation, all previous doctrines suggested that most likely future operations would be allied and under NATO's supervision. There is nothing new in emphasizing the Allied nature of future operations. However, although the previous two editions of AP 3000 outlined the Allied nature of future operations, they did not state any commitments to the Alliance and its consequent primarily role in operations. JDP 0–30 re-established this commitment at the environmental level, stating that NATO is 'the principal framework for UK operations'.[93] Such an emphasis in the environmental doctrine reflects not only the predominance of NATO in future operations, which is a usual direction, but also that the new doctrinal process was at work. In the previous doctrine writing process, such commitments were reflected mainly in Allied and joint doctrines at the strategic level, and not in an environmental doctrine. Thus, this suggests that the joint authorship followed the new NATO-led discourse of national doctrine writing. Further justification of the importance of the Alliance was explained in terms of US capabilities in command, control, communications, computers and intelligence (C4I), which are far more advanced than those of the European allies. However, the doctrine suggested that in the future countries like the UK and France might take the responsibility of framework nations in the cases when the United States did not fulfil this role. This duty could also encompass planning, executing and enabling air campaigns. Nevertheless, it was suggested that substantial support in providing specialized capabilities was expected from other allies.[94]

Once again, this discourse argued for profound cooperation with NATO, yet within a potentially different framework nation. In this instance, a more profound harmonization with the NATO conceptual/doctrinal framework would ease the planning process and consequent timely execution. This consideration of the new potential roles in the Allied operations also argues for NATO-oriented national doctrine writing. This orientation on NATO was further placed into the discourse of the UK dependence on the multinational cooperation and cross-government integration approach. This once again reflected the impact of the wider political framework of the time, meaning the conclusion of the SDSR and the consequent need of cooperation and integration for the sake of cost-efficiency. Thus, every opportunity of promoting interoperability and Allied cooperation should be used.[95] It was argued that although budgetary constraints could be felt, the integration in a conceptual framework was vital for alliances and partnerships in future operations. Consequently, the UK commitment to partnerships and alliances was in continued manning of NATO and EU air headquarters posts and 'by developing and implementing NATO doctrine and command and control as the basis for interoperability'.[96] In the footnote to this commitment, it was detailed as implementation of NATO C4I. However, it was essential to emphasize the role of doctrine as a means of incorporating this process in the national practice.

Apart from the general conceptual reference, the new NATO direction was illustrated in some structural and formational aspects. In terms of land-based deployment, the force was organized into expeditionary air groups and expeditionary air wings, each under the individual command of a senior UK airman. Expeditionary air wings were to replicate command and control structures characteristic of 'UK main operating bases in an expeditionary construct'.[97] However, the main guidance was NATO oriented, suggesting that RAF command and control structures had to interoperate with NATO structures, processes and doctrine where it was possible.[98] Consequently, the rationale was not political or conceptual justification but the practical concerns of efficiency in future Allied operations. The doctrine suggested that it was much easier to withdraw national Command and Control from a NATO framework and fulfil national operational tasks, than to force national C2 into the Allied framework when and how the situation required.[99]

This orientation on NATO structure was also conditioned by the previous experience of allied campaigns. Despite the usually successful cooperation between diverse forces of the Allied nations, one of the main difficulties in terms of structure and its consequent doctrinal reflection was command and control differences. For instance, one of the outcomes of the Second Gulf War was another discussion of different command and control approaches between the UK and US Armed Forces.[100] It was argued that the US approach was 'heavily dependent on the personalities of the most senior involved principals'.[101] Since future UK operations were unlikely to be outside an Allied framework and consequent cooperation with the United States, changes in the British approach to command and control within the joint context were suggested already in 2003.[102]

Other references to NATO included mostly practical illustrations from the Allied operations, which corresponded to the described tasks and performance of air power. The examples included a range of operations from the Gulf War to Libya. Another interesting feature of NATO influence illustrated in the document is the use of footnotes, which were often used to explain a particular aspect in terms of NATO discourse. For instance, in terms of ballistic missile defence, a NATO 2010 statement on the intention to develop a capability against missile attack was used.[103] The doctrine stated the need of ballistic missile defence and how it could be achieved at the national level and explained the place of this statement in NATO initiative. Another example was when carrier-enabled power projection of littoral manoeuvre was explained in terms of joint and Allied context. The description of a capability was entirely oriented at the joint context with a consequent incorporation of the Allied operational environment: 'Carrier-enabled power projection is an integrated and sustainable joint capability, interoperable with NATO that enables the projection of UK Carrier Strike and Littoral Manoeuvre power, as well as delivering Humanitarian Assistance and Defence Diplomacy. This in turn enables a joint effect across the maritime, land and air environments at a time and place of political choosing.'[104]

In this explanation, the complexity and interdependence of the new strategic environment and its conceptual reflection become evident. It reflected all the earlier-mentioned political and joint changes. First, it demonstrated the integration of all three services as a precondition of power projection. Second, such jointery was consistent with the Allied environment. Finally, it was multitasking and flexible because it could be applied in different scenarios and operations. Therefore, it was cost-effective and could be applied depending on the political situation. Regarding the general NATO discourse, the doctrine illustrated it through technical referencing to the NATO sources. For instance, *NATO Glossary of Terms and Definitions*[105] was used to identify certain terminological changes.[106] Other NATO documents were the Alliance's *Strategic Concept, Allied Joint Publication (AJP) 3.3 Air and Space Operations, NATO's Future Joint Air and Space Power*.[107] Again, in such a technical way a wider Allied framework was incorporated into national environmental doctrinal discourse in order 'to develop an effective conceptual framework for joint, multinational, intra-governmental and interagency air and space operations of the future'.[108] The new doctrine preparation process was also characterized by increased attention to the simplicity and accessibility of doctrinal texts. Although the entire simplicity discourse is nothing new for debates on doctrine, it was once again highlighted in the new doctrine writing process. The simplicity had to make doctrine more accessible for a wider audience, meaning beyond military personnel, but also make it understandable across services and in accordance with NATO terminology. Consequently, the key to mutual understanding was in the use of consistent, clear language and mutually recognized terminology. The doctrinal guidance suggested that authors should write at unclassified level, keeping a simple language and logical structure.[109] The use of plain English, limiting the number of abbreviations through the text and use of terminology either in generally accepted terms or in accordance with *NATO Glossary of*

Terms, were suggested: 'The ultimate source document for all terminology is the Concise Oxford English Dictionary. Where a definition already exists in the dictionary, you should use it without modifying or enhancing it. Before proposing a term, refer to AAP-06 and our national supplement to see if the term already exists.'[110]

This trend was evident in the text of JDP 0-30 on various occasions. Commonly used military terms were explained through their equivalents in the *Oxford Dictionary*. Accordingly, even the definition of air power was given in accordance with the dictionary.[111] Among other terms defined through the dictionary were 'secure', 'coerce', 'synergy' and 'influence'. AAP-06 was advised on such terms as the substitution of 'disembarkation' with 'debarkation', definitions of 'surveillance', 'air interdiction', 'close air support', 'collateral damage', 'counter-insurgency operation', 'deep attack', 'deterrence', 'situational awareness' and 'unmanned air(craft) system'. Other definitions were borrowed from various joint publications as advised by the handbook.[112]

This publication was distinctive because it included a lexicon at the end. While the fourth edition lacked a lexicon and the third edition included a list of general terms and bibliography, JDP 0-30 reflected the new doctrinal process even in the typology of terms and the sources from which they were taken. The lexicon included the abbreviations, terms and definitions used. The latter were subdivided into 'terms used for reference in this publication only',[113] 'new definitions' and 'endorsed definitions.'[114] The original source of each definition was given in brackets, linking diverse joint and allied documents and NATO-oriented discourse.

The role of academics

One of the relevant warnings in the doctrine writing handbook was against using excessively complicated language and leaning towards academic rather than military discourse.[115] Accordingly, the role of academics in the new institutionalized doctrine writing could have been quite modest, as in the case of the previous edition. However, the situation was slightly different. According to Alistair Byford, during the doctrine preparation process of JDP 0-30, academics were included in the discussion of drafts, and their opinions were 'fairly influential and largely accepted'.[116] In terms of continuity, this statement suggested that the role of academics in the doctrine writing remained the same throughout the studied period, and that the situational character of the fourth edition lacked their contribution due to time constraints and the lack of staff to be involved in the process. In the joint environment of DCDC, the provision of staff for doctrine development and drafting was not an issue. Consequently, involvement of academics was easier to arrange on a centralized basis.

Given the outlined role of academics, their suggestions were largely accepted, albeit not all of them. One of the longest academic discussions referred to the roles of air power, particularly control of the air and air supremacy. Practitioners argued for the inclusion of control of the air, while academics stated the necessity of air superiority. According to Alistair Byford, the latter was excluded because it was not relevant and 'the Taliban had no air power that could affect us'.[117] As the text showed, air superiority was omitted. Consequently, although not all academic suggestions were accepted, their participation was envisaged in the new doctrine writing process on a more systematic and regular basis; hence, their involvement in doctrinal workshops.

So, how does academic involvement fit into the new process? As before, the role of academics is advisory rather than decisive. This is logical, since military doctrine is an official and institutional document and should be prepared by practitioners. However, compared to previous editions, academics had less influence on the initial drafts. Consequently, they contributed through the doctrinal workshops but not the drafting process. The initial point of impact was a close cooperation with DDefS, who would then write a draft. This was the case of the first three editions. However, for a new doctrine, DDefS was no longer responsible for the preparation of environmental doctrine, and, like any other senior practitioner, was invited to take part in discussion groups as an advisory member.[118] In this context, the factor of critical and systematic awareness of air power tendencies embodied in DDefS shifted from the primary participation in drafting process to the advisory role in discussions. Although the general pool of opinions and perspectives would still remain the same, this shift once again confirmed jointery. The initial draft was prepared by the joint authorship and could not be influenced by academics and DDefS directly, as, for instance, in the case of the third edition, when Stuart Peach closely cooperated with academics.

In terms of the prescribed procedures of the new process, the role of academics on the initial stage of doctrine preparation is quite passive. It is in the provision of materials for widening the scope of the future draft. Among other main sources of information, project officers are advised to explore 'research papers from military education and/or academic institutions'.[119] Once again, it is up to the writing team to decide what resources they will consult and how thoroughly. In terms of further involvement of academics, the handbook suggested working with them in order to achieve objectivity and a systematic view on the prepared draft: 'You should also consider inviting outside organizations to assess your work. This will avoid bias as well as making sure that you have considered diverse perspectives, consulted the relevant subject matter experts and, therefore, have a better informed opinion.'[120] Consequently, the very statement of the need of unbiased and well-informed systematic opinions on the produced doctrine suggested the necessity of reaching a wider audience and consequently making the document simple and accessible. This conditionality of the unbiased nature of doctrine explains why academics are consulted together with the representatives of single-service and overseas practitioners: 'It is worth considering: interviewing all relevant joint and single-Service subject matter experts; enrolling academics and/or study groups at universities or research establishments; researching the experiences and lessons of foreign militaries, including NATO; and researching historical perspectives.'[121]

It can be concluded that the role of academics is recognized, although it is not very distinct from other potential sources of unbiased, systematic reflection of changes in the strategic environment. This process also shows that not every academic proficient in doctrinal studies will be invited to participate in discussions. Two factors would be relevant. First, the general background of an academic with regard to the Armed Forces, serving history or practical relation to the services tends to be relevant. In this context, a separate category of academics would be the teaching staff at the Defence Academy in Shrivenham. Their perspective is probably the most accurate, since apart from the academic and practical knowledge on the subject they can also apply their experience of teaching joint staff courses and the challenges of teaching a conceptual component including doctrine. Secondly, personal contacts still remain a crucial factor for an academic involvement.

Although compared to the fourth edition of AP 3000, JDP 0–30 was staffed more effectively and more academics were involved in discussions, Alistair Byford concluded, 'We could have involved more of academics. We involved those we had easy access to. I could have cast the net a bit further.'[122] He referred to academics who previously served in the RAF, and the AHB, and those teaching at the Defence Academy in Shrivenham. The Defence Academy is the first choice for academics due to logistics – it is situated literally a few minutes' walk from the DCDC. He argued that the involvement of academics was relevant as always, emphasizing the two functions of critical approach and historical accuracy. However, he suggested that 'there was not much thinking outside the box ... I would have preferred to be challenged more.'[123] This statement is of particular importance in the contemporary discourse of introducing innovation in the RAF and the necessity of critical perspective on certain decision-making. Constant involvement of the same academics in the discussions of a conceptual component might be beneficial in terms of their knowledge and expertise. However, the obvious limitation is the lack of unconventional and more innovative views from other areas of academic expertise. On the other hand, working with academics who understand the complexity of the military service proves to be more productive. Thus, the choice of academics involved largely depends on the purposes and vision of the author or authors of doctrine.

The role of authors

The main implication of the shift from single service to joint authorship was in the consequent change in the procedural and decision-making hierarchy of doctrine preparation. The previous symbiosis of CAS and DDefS in doctrine preparation was no more. The joint authorship of environmental doctrine resulted in the separation of DDefS from the decision-making and writing of the new doctrine. Although Alistair Byford was the author of the new joint edition, at that time he was involved in the process mainly because he had a new appointment within DCDC and not because he was DDefS. As already mentioned, DDefS at that time, Group Captain Peter Squires, was invited for the discussion of the working drafts. However, he was not involved in the drafting process.

Although the trend of moving from a single-service to joint authorship prevailed in the national doctrine writing, Alistair Byford argued that technically the RAF could make a case for a single-service authorship of JDP 0–30 equivalent. However, the problem was mainly a political constraint of SDSR 2010, which was disastrous for the RAF: 'There was a strong political imperative not to be seen making unnecessary moves towards a single-service direction.'[124] Thus, once again, it can be concluded that strengthening of jointery in the national practice and its attachment to the national defence reviews made it the primary force in shaping environmental doctrines after 2010. DCDC had more than a decade to build a well-structured doctrine preparation mechanism, where each element had its functional role, which was exact and prescriptive almost like tactical procedures. Consequently, a new NATO-oriented framework, the precise functionality and division of duties were crucial in the achievement of national and Allied jointery. Joint Doctrine and Concept Board (JDCB) provided general and systematic guidance of tendencies in doctrinal and conceptual development. In other words, it established the general conceptual framework for all doctrinal documents. It was chaired by the Vice Chief of the Defence Staff. At the time of publication of JDP 0–30, it was Stuart Peach. It can be suggested that having experienced the doctrinal reflection of jointery from single-service and environmental perspectives, Stuart Peach had the most systematic and well-founded perception of tendencies and challenges of doctrinal harmonization. While the JDCB identified the framework within which doctrine should develop, the Joint Doctrine Steering Committee (JDSC) provided procedural directions for writers on how to write doctrines. The chair was Director Concepts and Doctrine. However, the main duties were often delegated to the DCDC's Head of Doctrine, Air and Space. Below JDSC were writing teams formed for specific tasks.[125]

Regarding the distribution of duties, Director Concepts and Doctrine was responsible for strategic- and joint-level publications, the authorization of publishing and the distribution of doctrines. Assistant Head Doctrine, who represented the UK at the Allied Joint Operations Doctrine (AJOD) working group, through Head of Doctrine, Air and Space is 'the final judge on all doctrine layout, structure and content matters'.[126] While project managers were responsible for the project in general, project officers made it happen on time. Quite often, they were the authors of the project. However, in cases when there was no specialist in the target field within DCDC, lead agents from an external organization and contractors can be invited. When the adoption of NATO publication as a national doctrine occurred, external project officers could be invited. In terms of joint and single-service correlation, 'each service maintains a doctrine point of contact (ideally a SO1) within its warfare centre. Their function was to coordinate doctrine development within their Service. All single-Service doctrinal issues (including comments on draft publications) were staffed through these representatives'.[127]

The earlier-described structure of the doctrine preparation process corresponded to the final stage of the institutionalization of jointery, meaning the development of exact procedures and division of duties between structural elements. This formalization allowed to modify doctrines within eighteen months, which was the target time frame for the doctrine preparation process. Consequently, the instrumentalist approach to doctrine preparation was applied. From the perspective of covering gaps in the constantly changing strategic environment, and improving the Armed Forces' adaptation, such an approach could be considered holistic and purposeful. On the other hand, from the point of doctrine writing *per se*, the new approach made doctrine less personalized in terms of service and environmental orientation and authors' contribution. The transition from an author-driven doctrine towards an institution-conditioned one limited authors' vision and personal contribution. As mentioned previously, authors have begun to be responsible for the common ideas and existing organizational perception on the subject matter.

Regarding the administrative DCDC process of writing JDP 0-30, it went through four stages. First, internal air force consultancy took place. Alistair Byford recollected that being appointed at DCDC, it was different having consultations at the RAF. Since he had not been in the Air Force environment for some time, he was not aware of the recent internal trends and viewpoints within the service.[128] However, a certain detachment from the service could provide a new perspective on air power and its systematic articulation. Second, staffing of workshops involving all three services took place. Third, the initial draft was circulated for discussion. Finally, the document was signed off by the director of DCDC.[129]

Alistair Byford is the best person to ask about the changing role of authors in the new process. Having written the fourth edition practically on his own and contributed to the production of the latest joint one, he had a unique experience in this field. Comparing single-service and joint authorship from the writer's perspective, he argued that with the fourth edition he had more freedom in writing and shaping the initial draft, while the joint environment placed constraints on the writer's vision.[130] This means that writers were no longer decision-makers on what was in the draft. They also became more dependent on the decisions of review boards, discussion groups and workshops. From one perspective, it can be viewed as an instrumentalist approach to writers. From another, the importance of wider involvement of diverse specialists in order to achieve diversity became obvious. The commonality resulted in the adoption of systematic and interdisciplinary approach to the military tasks. In its turn, voluntarily or not, a wider discussion contributed to a more profound exploration and consequent knowledge of the issue in question.

As Alistair Byford stated, the fourth edition was written in haste and with minimum involvement of academics and limited discussions, while the preparation process of JDP 0-30 was 'staffed extensively, involving the Army and the Navy; lots of workshops and three or four drafts'.[131] Consequently, comparing single-service and joint authorship, although the joint environment limits the freedom of writers, it can contribute to profound exploration and understanding of the studied issues in the interservice and systematic framework. This is largely conditioned by the availability of resources, particularly human resources, which can be allocated to a doctrinal project within an institution that was created for the sake of doctrine preparation. Consequently, it is easier not only to get staff for doctrine preparation, but also to increase their experience and thus to speed up the harmonization of various doctrinal publications and their consequent acceptance within the Armed Forces. In terms of the service's self-explanation through environmental doctrine, naturally joint authorship was constraining. Alistair Byford stated that, in the new process the service lost actual control over environmental doctrine and could not promote certain suggestions of a technological or funding nature. However, 'you have a credibility of a joint doctrine',[132] meaning that this doctrine would be recognized by other services, while a single-service one could be still quite debatable in the interservice interpretation. To a certain extent, the functionality of doctrine *per se* had shifted from benefiting any particular service to functioning as a means of the Armed Forces' joint adaptation to the changes in the internal and external environments. The new cycle of doctrinal changes and its consequent connection to the defence reviews suggested that doctrine is a means of informing policymakers. It was envisaged that the JDP should be revised every five years. Consequently, this would trigger relevant reviews and changes in the entire hierarchy of doctrinal publications. A particular feature of the cycle is that it was to occur in the middle of the SDSR cycle. The doctrines were meant to influence policy in the middle of the SDSR cycle and thus provide a more up-to-date information on the conceptual framework of the Armed Forces. In fact, SDSR 2015 followed the first edition of JDP 0–30 (2013). Recently, the second edition of JDP 0–30 has been published in December 2017.

Conclusion

This chapter has described the most recent stage of the doctrine preparation process and consequent changes in air power doctrine writing. Irrespective of the previous RAF attempt to write single-service joint environmental doctrine embodied in AP 3000 fourth edition, it did not have the desired outcome. The demonstration of the RAF joint commitment failed to preserve ownership over its environmental doctrine. Therefore, ownership over air power doctrine was transferred to the joint institution of DCDC. This was largely conditioned by the need of synchronizing all environmental doctrines under joint authorship in order to create a national doctrinal system, which could adapt to new changes altogether and immediately, rather than when a single service decided to do so. In the global terms of Allied operations, this meant that the national conceptual framework and consequent practice could be easily adapted to the new trends within NATO. Thus, better cooperation and performance could be achieved.

In terms of the influential factors of doctrine preparation, as in the previous two editions, most recent operational experience had a profound influence on doctrine writing. However, this influence was not the primary force driving the initiation of doctrine preparation. Although the lessons of the Libyan conflict were processed and reflected in JDP 0–30, the operation itself did not trigger doctrine writing. Although it reflected the tendency towards contingency rather than COIN operations, the new doctrine analysed not only the lessons of Libya but also relevant experiences throughout the entire history of air power, paying slightly more attention to the post–Cold War era. In terms of the role of air power in contemporary warfare, it can be argued that Libya demonstrated that air power remained functional both on its own and in cooperation with other services, in that case, with the Royal Navy. While the second post–Cold War decade was characterized by the decline of air power optimism, the beginning of the third decade demonstrated that air power remained extremely functional and efficient tool.

In terms of the internal environment, once again the doctrine preparation process was related to a defence review. Unlike the first two case studies, the implications of the SDSR were not only in the reflection of the new conceptual framework or in the preparation to the next defence review. The SDSR emphasized austerity and its implications for the Armed Forces. Inevitably, it meant the importance of technological advantage as a means of multitasking and efficiency in contingent operations rather than the numerous deployments of the Armed Forces. It also meant the need for evolving cooperation in terms of jointery, which resulted in the process of synchronization of national doctrinal practices in harmonizing changes of the Allied environment.

Finally, with the process of the institutionalization of jointery and the formalized doctrine writing cycle with the NATO doctrine in the heart of the national practice, the line between factors of internal and external environments became blurrier. In this context, not only is doctrine influenced by the general trends of NATO doctrinal discourse or procedures of doctrine preparation, but also it gains new functionality. This functionality is in the accommodation of Allied trends into national military practice. This can be achieved in two ways. First, it can be done through a conceptual framework reflected in a series of doctrinal publications. Secondly, the exact hierarchical structure and interservice subordination in terms of doctrines give an opportunity to make adaptation to any changes systematic and fast, like a domino effect. However, although JDP

0–30 was prepared under a joint authorship and reflected the transition to the new doctrinal cycle and NATO-oriented doctrine, it also demonstrated that the new changes are still in the process of systematic introduction.

Concerning the role of academics in the new doctrine preparation process, their involvement is highly advisable and encouraged. Consequently, academics provide critical thinking on defence and strategy and advice on the evaluation of concepts and new paradigms. However, as in the previous editions, academics are involved not in the preparation of drafts but in their discussions and analysis. Therefore, the role of academics remains advisory and not decisive. Although the doctrine writing guide briefly mentioned the involvement of academics in discussion of drafts, the reality demonstrated that conceptual discussions were essential in the preparation of doctrine and that some of their advice were taken into account. In terms of the shift from single-service to joint authorship and the centralized production of doctrines in DCDC, the involvement of academics becomes easier. This is because the Defence Academy is right across the street and the involvement of teaching staff can be systematic. The centralized nature of joint authorship also contributes to a long-term relationship with academics from around the country. Thus, they can be consulted for a variety of doctrinal processes over a long period of time. Consequently, the centralization of jointery can contribute to a profound cooperation with academics, although the doctrinal guide does not emphasize it.

Concerning the authors, the first joint edition demonstrated the final stage of transition from a personalities-driven to an institutional approach. Although Alistair Byford, the author of the last single-service air power doctrine, was involved in the joint authorship, the degree of freedom he enjoyed with the previous edition had substantially decreased. Placing the process in the joint environment of tri-service review, authors' personal inspirations and the ability to make a creative and constructive contribution became limited. Consequently, doctrines become more and more institutional in their nature. Unlike the first post–Cold War doctrines, instead of reflecting institutional trends within a single service, nowadays, environmental doctrines project joint trends into a single service.

Overall, the new doctrine preparation process suggested several considerations. First, unlike before, the national Armed Forces were treated as an interdependant system, capable of rapid, synchronized changes. These changes could be caused by factors of the external environment. However, the response to them was conducted exclusively through internal, joint means. Secondly, treated as a joint system, the Armed Forces and consequent doctrines were inevitably connected with defence reviews. In this context, the functionality of doctrine in the newly introduced doctrinal cycle as in informing the Defence Review Board on how the Armed Forces were going about their business, emphasizing their wider functionality. In other words, doctrine continued to play a self-justifying role in SDR cycle. However, unlike before, it did so at the joint level rather than at a single-service and competitive one. The final part of this book seeks to illustrate the current place of doctrine in military practice, the role of a conceptual component, public perception and the initiative of Thinking to Win in organizational transformation of the RAF in the future.

7

Air Power Today and the Future

The previous chapters illustrated the change of approach to doctrine writing, from a single to joint authorship. These chapters also showed how articulation of single-service independent discourse was adapted to the joint environment of the DCDC. However, these chapters do not explain the current organizational use of environmental doctrine. This chapter seeks to re-emphasize the current utility of doctrine in RAF practice, touching upon some practical challenges in balancing doctrines. Hereafter, the role of doctrine in organizational transformation is discussed. The primary theme is the necessity of engaging the public and bridging the civil–military gap. It is suggested that a conceptual component and doctrine can act as a means of changing organizational culture towards a more public-oriented outlook. Finally, the revival of attention to the conceptual component of the RAF and the launch of the Thinking to Win (T2W) initiative are discussed.

Doctrine today

Considering the history of RAF doctrine and its post–Cold War development, it can be concluded that writing doctrine is a challenging task. It is often written not by career-makers but by people who are devoted to a more intellectual vision of air power and realize its systematic role in conjunction with other types of military forces. However, one man's vision is another man's nightmare. As a result, doctrine authors' intention to widen the personnel's vision clashes with the everyday challenges of military service. Serving personnel require a brief, digestible, comprehensible and useful document. For them, philosophical principles are often of little use in their daily tasks, training or missions. Consequently, the intended message of the doctrine falls on deaf ears, and it fails to achieve its primary purpose – reaching military personnel. Thus, to be useful for its primary audience, doctrine (more than any other document) should strike a balance between the breadth of the intellectual debates and the requirements of serving personnel. If this consideration is not fulfilled, the doctrine might be an excellent piece for an academic and wider audience, but military personnel might consider it 'long in the tooth', as in the case of the AP 3000, third edition. Thus, it is essential to realize what a good doctrine is, what it can achieve and what the pitfalls of writing a doctrine are to understand the role of doctrine in shaping the future of the RAF. This chapter is also intended to provide a more recent practical view on the use of doctrine.

Traditionally, three functions are attributed to doctrine: education, command and change.[1] In the conversation with various practitioners including Alistair Byford, there was a common theme: a doctrine is of greater use in an educational role than it is in training. Some would argue that doctrine is not very useful for training purposes mainly due to its abstract and philosophical nature. Many practitioners would agree. They acknowledge that a more philosophical narration of the principles of warfare and the overall conceptual component has a greater utility for officers and their further education in defence academies, rather than for cadets at air force colleges. One needs to distinguish between the different purposes of each type of institution. The primary purpose of RAF colleges like Cranwell is to bring people with different backgrounds to the common organizational mindset. Consequently, training courses and related teaching modules are directed towards this aim. In this setting, doctrines can be on the curriculum somewhere in the reading lists, but they are not taught as such. For instance, that is why AP 3003 was produced, aiming to provide cadets with a service history. On the other hand, defence or service academies provide an opportunity for serving officers to obtain knowledge in a joint and allied environment in order to proceed with their further careers. This is the right place to broaden one's knowledge. It is the place where a more intellectual approach is taken, and where doctrine has an educational role to play.[2]

One of the common questions anyone reading this book or any other academic piece on doctrine would ask is – what is a good doctrine? Since doctrine is aimed at military practitioners and should assist them in broadening their knowledge within a limited time, a good doctrine should be legible, easily understood, digestible and short, yet it should contain intellectual and philosophical strands. It should not be prescriptive on the strategic level, but should outline reoccurring themes that are further followed in operational plans and tactical manuals. A writer balancing the competing demands of good doctrine is confronted by a paradox: it should be intellectually inclined, but not critical, authoritative but not dogmatic, history inspired and forward looking. Thus it is not surprising that doctrines are often written by experienced practitioners exposed to academic influence and wider thinking on air power However, it also makes sense that they often write it in an academically inclined environment which allows them to achieve that intellectual cohesion of theory and practice without excessive criticism undermining the authoritative nature of the document.

Much has been discussed about authoritative versus dogmatic doctrine. However, from the contemporary perspective, the most important issue is the dichotomy between history-inspired and forward-looking aspect of doctrine. The primary importance of doctrine is to use the existing historical context as a background for the evaluation of the current situation of the service, with its goals and fighting strategies against future threats. Doctrine can serve as a tool of self-assessment and the establishment of long-term goal of organizational development. Also, in terms of defence reviews, doctrine can inform policymakers on the perspectives of the Armed Forces and their capabilities. However, does it mean that the contemporary utility of doctrine can be equated to a political memo? Following this argument, the informative role of doctrine in the new defence review cycle should not be the purpose in itself. Instead, it should be the outcome of an organizational self-assessment and a reflection of the vision of its future potential. Thus, in essence, the importance of doctrine lies in the evaluation of what the service can achieve right now, what it will be tasked to achieve in the future and what will be required to fulfil these tasks. Such an assessment of an organization could potentially allow for more realistic decision-making and policy-building. However, it should not be forgotten that 'doctrine has a role to play, but it has limited impact'.[3]

It is essential to redefine for whom today's doctrine is written in order to understand the contemporary utility of air power and its role in shaping the future of the air forces. The previous chapters illustrated that, in each case, the target audience was identified in the text of the doctrine. The overall post–Cold War tendency in target audiences can be summarized as follows. The first two editions of AP 3000 addressed military personnel of the RAF and other services. With the introduction of jointery, the third edition followed the pattern of joint doctrines aiming at multiple audiences. Starting with this edition, the distinction was made between the primary, military audience and a wider secondary audience of policymakers, agencies, allies, the public and even adversaries. However, in the final stages of the institutionalization of jointery, doctrines were aimed at the military personnel of the service, other services and policymakers.

Addressing the public as such was not prioritized in the last two doctrines. From a strictly practical perspective, this author agrees that doctrine should be written primarily for military personnel and doctrine should not become a political document. Regarding the wider audience, if doctrine is written with a general audience in mind, who among the public actually reads doctrine? However, the primary reason that doctrine keeps addressing a wider audience is that it needs to engage policymakers and articulate the service's position on various issues. Also, addressing the public is important because funding depends on public opinion.[4]

The author of the fourth edition of AP 3000 is more sceptical about the contemporary utility of addressing a wider audience. Moreover, the idea that doctrine is the primary means of informing the SDSR cycle does not show the full picture. Plenty of joint and Allied publications inform and influence SDSR. According to Alistair Byford, in the preparation for SDSR, all services are keener to use *Joint Concept Note 3/12: Future Air and Space Operating Concept (FASOC)*,[5] which provides the outlook on air and space forces capability development up to 2035. All three services find this document particularly useful in supporting their organizational agendas and making claims on platform acquisitions or number of forces required.[6] Consequently, doctrine is not the only framework document used to inform a defence review.

From a critical perspective, the rational question is, what is the current utility of doctrine? If it is not essential in training, but more likely to inform officers' further education, if it is not aimed at a wider audience, if it is not the primary means of informing SDR and winning relevant funding for the service, does this mean that doctrine is of little importance nowadays? In fact, despite not having a definitive impact in each of the earlier-mentioned roles, doctrine nevertheless has a partial influence in each of them, and its absence or lack of timely review would have a partial, but ongoing, negative impact on each of the roles discussed. Alistair Byford also agrees that doctrine is not redundant: 'No. It is relevant. Doctrine is important in shaping the cultural mindset. It subliminally sets the service's mindset. However, it does not have the same authority as it had 20 years ago. There used to be a fine line between strategy and doctrine.'[7]

Following this course of argument, it is seen that doctrinal functionality has come full circle: initially serving internal organizational purposes, coming to address interservice and wider audiences and now returning to an internal organizational function. Doctrine can be used as a means of organizational transformation and adaptation to the changes in the external environment. In a sense, its contemporary purpose has reverted to its initial role in the first editions of AP 3000. Just as Andrew Vallance intended to use doctrine to reform the RAF to meet the requirements of the post–Cold War era, so it may be used nowadays to reflect the RAF's organizational transformation. It may both contain the core transformative concept and serve as means of its dissemination and even implementation. The transformational role of doctrine brings us to the recent trend in the RAF for rethinking its conceptual component as a means of placing the service at 'the forefront of air power strategic leadership'.[8] Before discussing the RAF's innovative initiative, it is worth looking at the relationship between a conceptual component, public perception and organizational transformation.

A conceptual component, public perception and organizational transformation

The history of any organization is characterized by stages of growth and establishment, times of adaptation and transformation. It may seem that the necessity of modernization is inherent to military organizations, since the military field is oriented towards cutting-edge technologies and thus realizes the necessity of multifaceted modernization. In reality, the longer military organizations exist, the more complex, well established and rooted their organizational cultures become. Although debates about the impact of organizational cultures on military execution has existed for as long as military organizations themselves, one fact remains unchanged: a distinctive organizational culture is one inalienable feature of every air force in the world. Each organizational culture is shaped by the specifics of the environment in which a service operates. This helps to strengthen unity and improves the organization's performance in its field of military expertize.

The opponents of unique organizational cultures argue that this distinctiveness undermines collaboration between the services, hampering creativity and producing military thinking which is narrowly service- and tactics oriented instead of realizing any wider picture. On the other hand, instead of stigmatizing organizational culture, it can be used as a way of modernizing the Armed Forces to the requirements of the external environment. As Alistair Byford mentioned earlier, doctrine can shape organizational culture. In broader terms, a conceptual component that includes the principles of war, doctrine and conceptual innovation can define organizational culture. The transformational function of doctrine and the conceptual component is to shape organizational culture by influencing thinking process and modifying military execution. When we are talking about the Air Force, the phenomenon of 'airmindedness' must be considered. It may seem that this term names an unchanged approach to thinking and using air power. However, that is not the case. Traditionally, airmindedness was associated with lobbying single-service and independent air power. However, with the establishment of jointery came a shift towards emphasizing the inherently joint nature of air power, and, henceforth, airmindedness has encompassed that joint vision of air power. This shift in the meaning of this term, which is at the heart of RAF organizational culture, was introduced through doctrine, in its function as an authoritative means of sending a message to the service. This also meant that the RAF as an organization approved and initiated the change. Consequently, it can be seen that a conceptual component and doctrine provide the means of showing the way the organization wants to change, how it perceives where it stands at this point of time and in which direction it wants to go. The conceptual component helps defining the way airmen perceive themselves and how they adapt themselves and their culture to the challenges of the external environment. However, from a realistic perspective, unlike any other organization, military organizations are particularly difficult to reform. Due to the strict subordination and discipline embedded in military activities, creative thinking is not always stimulated or tolerated. Thus, the initiative to reform should come from above and include detailed directions for implementation and provisions for consequent outcomes for the affected personnel and the service in general.

When the subject of organizational transformation is explored, it is essential to discuss how organizations learn and thus change. There are plenty of approaches to organizational learning. However, there is one well-established theory, which was broadly discussed by military practitioners in the 1980s–1990s,[9] and has been recently revived in an article by Kronvall and Peterson.[10] According to Argyrys and Schon, the authors of the theory of single- and double-loop learning, organizations change and adapt differently depending on the way they learn. The single-loop learning refers to 'instrumental learning that changes strategies of action or assumptions underlying strategies in ways that leave the values of a theory of action unchanged'.[11] This type of learning envisages ephemeral or temporary changes based on a new experience. Certain insights and views might change, while the core and values of an organization remain unchanged.[12] Placing this learning into a military discourse, it may refer to the minor modifications of a predominant theory as a result of lessons learned from the previous operation, or from thinking in terms of the last war. This type of learning might be useful for the adaptation of the service to minor changes in the surrounding environment. In doctrinal terms, this learning would correspond to reviewing doctrines after major operations without changing the core of the conceptual framework. In other words, the traditional concepts remained unchanged, only refreshed by new operational examples.

The double-loop learning 'addresses the fundamental drivers of organizational behaviour and modifies, if necessary, the fundamentals of organisational culture, structure and organisation'.[13] This entails substantial changes in organizational mindset and adaptation of values and principles of military execution to the requirements of the time. This type of transformation is of a particular interest because it is aimed at systematic and in-depth adaptation of organizational culture and consequent behaviour. Placing this form of adaptation into doctrinal discourse, double-loop learning would be reflected in the establishment of a new conceptual framework, involving a different perspective on the conventional *modus operandi* which would result in a new mode of behaviour. This type of change requires not only a systematic approach to the establishment of a new conceptual framework for organizational development, but also attention to the ways of implementing it and subsequent monitoring of efficiency and long-term outcomes. Thus, for long-term transformation, the ways of modifying behaviour are crucial. This issue of organizational learning is relevant in the current RAF discourse due to the launching of a new conceptual framework, reforming the service for its centenary – T2W. The main aspects of this initiative and mechanism of implementation will be discussed later in this chapter.

Both types of organizational learning and consequent transformation have their place in organizational development. Since the second type of learning seeks to redefine the organization towards desired outcomes, the rational question is, what is needed for double-loop learning and consequent long-term structural changes in an organization? As in the case of any innovation, an inclusive environment, open to debates, discussions and thinking outside the box, is vital. In other words, both critical and creative thinking should be stimulated and given due attention. However, can critical thinking alone result in substantial changes to an organization? That is very unlikely. According to Tony Mason, there are multiple obstacles of innovating military organizations:

> To start with, such are the day-to-day pressures on the modern serviceman that he has little time either for reflection–the essential prerequisite for innovation– or even the time to develop the habits of reflection. If an innovation does come to mind and the service member proposes it as a change, the individual is then challenging the accepted wisdom, which, presumably, is either apparently

working successfully or has catastrophically failed. In the latter case, the time for innovation may be long gone. The former situation offers greater promise.[14]

Moreover the hierarchical nature of the military organizations and strict subordination make it particularly difficult to stimulate innovation from within, particularly from within the lower ranks of serving personnel. On the other hand, the higher ranks are likely to be more sceptical about innovations mainly because of greater responsibilities entrusted to their positions. This clash of approaches to innovation was once again covered in depth by Tony Mason in 1986:

> However, in our military hierarchies, the accumulation of experience and wisdom is associated with increasing seniority. Weight of opinion is usually accredited according to rank. One superior's appreciated innovator can be another superior's pain in the neck. Generally it takes a big man to accept that his subordinate's questioning of the status quo or his earlier decisions is well founded, unless perhaps he can be persuaded that the new ideas are in fact his own. The restless mind can make for an uncomfortable subordinate. Paradoxically, the more powerful, competent, and confident the air marshal, the more difficult it becomes to convince him that he may not be omniscient: it is the air marshal who must be prepared to fight with what he has available and who therefore is the most conscious of the costs in training time, of the possible reduction in readiness or fighting effectiveness, or the gamble involved in changing current proven operational practices under the threat of imminent enemy attack. It is not melodramatic to remember that the air marshal carries the responsibilities of not only the lives of his own men but possibly the fate of nations in his hands. It is scarcely surprising that he tends to approach innovation with caution.[15]

Thus, like any change, its theoretical necessity and practical implementation have to be realized and accepted by the organization.[16] The organization has to invest systematically in innovation, devoting budgets, human assets and time to the development of the innovative programme.[17] Furthermore, the final product should be given authority in the organization, stimulating its impact in shaping thinking and consequent behaviour, and thus redefining organizational culture. Also, there should be clear mechanisms for implementing new concepts through educational programmes, training courses and organizational procedures.[18]

However, would it be enough for a long-term transformation of an organization to have all of the earlier-mentioned processes and details in place? In theoretical terms, for generalization and classification, organizations may be considered as closed systems linked to each other in a hierarchy of a greater system. For instance, in a state (a large system), the MOD and military services are parts of a state hierarchy. In the case of a single service, interactions with the outer world are often either limited or viewed through the lens of the entire apparatus. Thus, communication between a single service and the outer world (e.g. the public) would be indirect and partial. Taking, for example, Clausewitz's trinity, despite the diversity of views on whether the concept is adequate today or not, the contemporary information age has resulted in a widening gap in understanding between the militaries and the civilian population they are sworn to protect.

Starting with the CNN effect in the First Gulf War, and continuing in media coverage of the Kosovo bombing, real-time footage of drone strikes and so on, the use of military force has become more exposed to the public criticism. Air power was under greater pressure than any other military force due to its mediagenic nature. With the introduction of the twenty-four-hour media cycle, the Armed Forces are becoming more accountable for their actions and processes of decision-making. Even situational, tactical decisions that could be justified a century ago are questioned today because they might have strategic implications and can undermine the legitimacy of a campaign. Moreover, in the case of air power, technological advancement and improvement of precision have made public expectations of bloodless warfare even more exaggerated. Although, at first glance, it may seem that these phenomena are not interrelated and should be resolved by each service, in reality they demonstrate a single problem – a widening gap between the public and the Armed Forces. Although it may seem that the division between civil and military domains is logical and prevails in all democratic societies, the reality is far from that. Irrespective of military achievements within a campaign, the way they are perceived by the public at home plays a crucial role in political decision-making, which often may not be counterbalanced by strategic considerations.

For example in Libya, after the traditional evaluation of campaign after 100-day threshold, the British media portrayed the campaign as irrelevant and of a little impact on the overall course of events in the country and the region. Thus, the media ignored the necessity of enabling the advancement of the rebels towards Tripoli, which in its turn enabled the success of the campaign. It was labelled as bombing for the sake of bombing. In its turn, this negative media discourse strengthened public antagonism towards this campaign. Consequently, more pressure was placed on the government, which in its turn demanded more results from the military. This cycle of winning wars at home is not new, but the widening gap of understanding between the public and the military makes it more damaging for the military sector. It creates a favourable ground for an adversary to target the will to fight (and to support fighting) by using information warfare to manipulate public opinion, particularly in liberal democracies. For instance, taking into consideration media coverage and consequent public perceptions of the last two air campaigns in Libya and Syria, the RAF's performance was viewed mainly through the lens of civilian casualties, drone strikes and the aftermath of both bombing campaigns. Media and public are very unlikely to enter into the debates on strategic planning, the technological characteristics of aerial platforms or budgetary restraints, not to mention the complexity of conducting war amongst people in an extremely hostile operational environment. This lack of understanding creates a functional soil for misinterpretation and use of information warfare to undermine the credibility and public trust in the Armed Forces.

There are also other reasons for the disconnection between the militaries and the public. First, the remoteness of conflicts from home and lack of existential threats to the population at home transform the images of war into TV screen experience. Although, initially, the CNN effect brought the atrocities of war to the home audience; in the long run it has resulted in people getting used to the images of war.[19] Thus, coexistence and disconnection between war and peacetimes occur. While militaries are at war abroad, and despite media coverage of this war, the general population lives in a time of peace and reduced alert to threats both direct and indirect. As a result, there is a miscommunication between militaries living through wartime and a civilian population experiencing the benefits of a peaceful life at home and the remoteness of war. Addressing this matter, Lieutenant Colonel Dan Brown concluded:

> In the absence of war or existential threat, a familiar and tired cycle is oft repeated: fleeting national euphoria (or relief) over the cessation of hostilities gives way to an underlying national fatigue, leading to decreased military budgets and menpower. Defence is then asked to prepare for a broad set of future contingencies with less resource, an imbalance that leaves the military unable to replicate the depth of thinking and pace of innovation it so recently enjoyed.[20]

A few words on the public perspective are needed in order to have a full picture of miscommunication. One of the primary causes of misperception and miscommunication is that both parties assume that they speak the same language. The militaries often assume that their actions and the successful achievement of posed objectives, under conditions of restrictive ROEs and limited budgetary funds, are understood and appreciated by a wider public.

Conversely, the public seldom has advanced knowledge of the atrocities of war and judges the complexity of war primarily through the lens of civilian casualties and the implications of a war for the region, rather than considering the actual achievement of posed objectives. Although the role of civilian casualties and the long-term implications of operations in contemporary warfare should never be ignored, greater public understanding of the nature of military force and its use in the achievement of political objectives would make the military's work easier, not to mention that military funding partially depends on the public opinion.

The readership of this book might assume that surely the public cannot be so poorly informed about the essence of military service and the use of force. The best way to illustrate the gap is to describe an experiment this author often does when presenting air power to a new audience. A group of third-year BA students were asked about their perception of air power. These students had no military background. Their acquaintance with the subject of defence came mainly through taking a few modules in International Security or Global Politics. They were not given a definition of air power nor of any other military force. They were asked to express their perception of air power in terms of an object, phrase and personality they associated with the term. Twenty-five years after the end of the Cold War, seventy years after the end of the Second World War and ninety-seven years after the establishment of the RAF, air power was perceived as bombs, civilian casualties and drones. The main personalities students associated with air power were not pilots, not Chiefs of Air Staff or Air Marshals, but political decision-makers, who authorized air strikes and initiated campaigns. The most common names were Tony Blair, George W. Bush and Barack Obama.

One of the most recent studies on the subject of public perception of air power is by Alan Vick from the RAND Corporation. His study of the American public perception of air power can be found in his book, *Proclaiming Airpower: Air Force Narratives and American Public Opinion from 1917 to 2014*.[21] One of the findings illustrates that public support for aviation and air power was exceptionally high in the first half of the twentieth century. However, the subsequent decades were characterized by a gradual decline, illustrating the loss of public enthusiasm for aviation. Nevertheless, he concludes: 'Shortcomings in Airpower Narratives Are Not to Blame for Changes in Public Opinion toward the USAF. When airmen come together to discuss the USAF's relative position among the services, its budget share, and its role in national military strategy, a common refrain is that the Air Force fails to "tell its story" in an effective manner.'[22]

What do these examples suggest about public perceptions of air power and the military in general? First, the assumption that the public understands in any depth the military profession, the hazards it faces or the way decisions are made and fulfilled is often far from reality. On the one hand, it may be argued that a younger generation is still in the process of gaining that education and by the time they are thirty their decision-making will be more informed and balanced. On the other hand, as active members of their society with voting rights, they can easily shape policy without reaching the full awareness. Moreover, in many cases, people simply choose not to explore the depth and breadth of military and defence issues. For instance, not everyone would be keen on taking a defence studies module in his or her Politics degree. Also, not everyone would be interested in joining the Armed Forces to have an insight into what the military service is about. Second, as mentioned earlier, disconnection between the military and the public is dangerous, because it may undermine the credibility of the national Armed Forces and be used to the advantage of adversaries in information warfare or even in an ordinary act of disinformation. Third, responsibility for informing the wider audience should not be placed on the media alone. A public engagement programme would benefit each service and the Armed Forces in general. However, a distinction should be made between recruiting campaigns and information initiatives.

Situating the organizational discourse within this narrative of the civil–military relationship provides certain insights into the processes of transformation and adaptation of air forces in the contemporary information age. Alan Vick offers three solutions. First, he suggests exploring 'means to increase the social currency of airpower. One possible path to increased social currency would compare civilian technologies that are getting the most buzz in tech circles (as well as the broader public) to USAF research and development programs'.[23] In other words, close alignment of technological development of both USAF and civilian sector could provide a common ground for communication, understanding and further promotion of the service and air advocacy. Second, Vick argues that it is crucial to 'anchor USAF narrative in big problems of concern to the American public. A strong airpower narrative (1) presents a difficult and important problem, (2) offers a big idea that describes how airpower can solve the problem, (3) has an emphasis on technology and innovation, and (4) ends with an aspirational vision for a better future'.[24] It can be argued that air power should answer a question of what air power can do for ordinary people. In other words, the assumption that everyone understands the utility of air power is misleading. It needs to be infiltrated into discourses easily understood by a wider audience. Finally, Vick suggests to:

use long-term public opinion trends to inform the USAF narrative. Whether simply divided in its preferences or moving toward an 'equally important' perspective, the American public is much less inclined to see one service as dominant ... The current direction of USAF outreach themes emphasising advanced technologies and innovation offers promise. It avoids the extremes of parochialism and bland jointness and is likely to resonate with a public that strongly associates the USAF with advanced technologies.[25]

Alan Vick's findings and suggestions are essential for building an effective communication strategy with a wider audience and transforming USAF's public profile. Placing his findings into the context of British public discourse, broadly speaking these suggestions can be applied to the RAF and could improve its public profile. However, complete replication of USAF approach might be counterproductive. First, the emphasis on the technological and innovative side of air power should definitely be made. However, unlike in the American case, more attention needs to be paid to explaining the relevance of certain technologies to the service and to British defence. For instance, although many taxpayers might be aware of the costs of F-35 for the national defence budgets, how many of them know of its actual operational advantages this aircraft provides for the service, and its role in the national defence? Moreover, often the first point of contact with any analytical data on defence spending is the mainstream media rather than, for example, official governmental or MOD websites. As a result, media coverage is already oriented towards a civilian evaluation of the situation instead of a military one. Thus, when emphasizing the technology-oriented nature of the RAF, it is important to raise public awareness of the role of these technologies by providing exact examples what these platforms can achieve compared to other services and other platforms. Moreover, one of the crucial messages that needs to be put across is that air power is one of many tools of military force used in order to achieve posed political objectives. A distinction needs to be made between the military's function, which is to follow exact orders in accordance with state policies, and public expectations of achieving long-term peace in a remote region with the minimum of financial, technological and human costs.

As well as identifying what can be done to explain air force to a wider audience, it is also essential to think about how it can be done and who can do it. One of the ways of bridging the gap can be the articulation of the RAF's conceptual component and operational performance to a wider audience. The transformative role of doctrine comes to mind. However, having discussed various occasions when an abundance of functions were ascribed to doctrine and doctrines were written for a wider audience instead of military personnel, there is a risk of overstretching the functions of doctrine undermining its utility for the primary audience – military personnel. If doctrine can be used as a means of indicating a certain conceptual framework that is linked to a wider policy of organizational change, then the wider policy of improving cooperation with a more general audience can be articulated through other means: memos, reports, briefings and pamphlets.

Another means of bridging the gap is by strengthening collaboration with academics, building networks and incorporating their experience into training courses and the development of a conceptual component. Although academics have a wider scope of public outreach than the militaries, their outreach is still very specialized. Academics mainly deal with the younger generation – students – and other academics. Occasionally, the public shows interest in their research. There should be a public interest in the first place, which can be stimulated or strengthened by research. It is very seldom that a single research project can create public interest in the blink of an eye. Moreover, the amount of knowledge they have and the level of clearance limit academic views. On the other hand, public talks and open discussions can make a difference. However, their sporadic nature would not have a tremendous impact on the public. The answer to bridging civil–military gap can be in all of the aforementioned and more.

For a transformation to have long-term instead of short-term implications, it has to be systematic and include treatment not of the symptoms but of causes of the problem. In this case, it would be a mindset. Thus, a conceptual component, as a thinking process, should be at the heart of the changes. One of the innovations should be to embed public-oriented and media-conscious thinking within the service. It can be included in teaching courses, doctrinal workshops, cooperation with academics and HR strategies aimed at hiring and keeping the most talented people.[26] The diverse backgrounds of military personnel and the addition of public and media-related discourse can each assist in recovering a connection between the Armed Forces and the public beyond the discussion of cutting military budgets in favour of social welfare.

Many serving men and women might consider this claim too managerial in nature, suggesting that a change in management approach cannot resolve the vital problems of the traditional civil–military gap. However, in this particular case, the use of managerialism is justified because the question is about improving communication with a wider audience that is more acquainted with the managerial approach than military subordination.[27] Moreover, by adopting Alan Vick's third principle of incorporating innovation into ongoing air force narratives, the source of innovation comes from unconventional and critical thinking. A better engagement with the public, improved communication and greater engagement with people's opinions and views of various aspects of air power could all stimulate different views on the subject.

Moreover, having conducted multiple interviews with serving and retired officers, many of them argued that at first they found talking to members of the public without military background very challenging. It was surprising that certain obvious military decisions were misunderstood or were seen as less obvious by the public. However, after a few experiences of public talks, they found the experience useful, because it helped them understand the gap and find ways of bridging it. One of the most useful outreach skills was finding the right language. On various occasions, they had to drop their military jargon and use simple, understandable notions to explain the more complex phenomena of their operational and serving experience. This type of interaction is a small example of how air advocacy can be improved.

In fact, various public events and initiates are in place and prove to be effective, considering the number of attendees. However, a more centralized and systematic approach would be needed to incorporate a century-old service into the information age of rapid changes and exaggerated expectations. On 20 May 1945, referring to a similar discussion on reforming the American Armed Forces after the Second World War, General George Arthur Lincoln wrote: 'I begin to think that what we need is a type of staff officer with at least three heads: one political, one economic, and one military.'[28] In the information age, a fourth head might be needed: a public relations head.

Thinking to Win

In 2015, three years before April 2018 – when it celebrates its centenary – the RAF launched a new initiative to reform the service as it enters the second century of its development. The T2W initiative took on board some of the ideas outlined earlier and argued for the necessity of building an innovative culture within the service as a way of reforming the entire force:

> T2W's key goal is to 'apply Air Power more effectively today and more imaginatively tomorrow' by clarifying our focus, inspiring innovation, and advocating the influence of Air Power. We will create a culture of innovation within the Whole Force, applaud the thinking power and opinions from all individuals. We must listen to and debate the issues of Air Power and ensure

that our leaders are well trained to sustain and develop innovation within the Whole Force.²⁹

Previous reforming initiatives were mainly reactive to the challenges of specific threats in the strategic environment: the end of the Cold War, the Gulf War and the PSO and COIN environments. However, in the case of this initiative, a more pre-emptive approach was taken. On 17 September 2015, in the speech introducing this framework, the Chief of the Air Staff, Air Chief Marshal Sir Andrew Pulford, stated that this initiative was intended to address the multiple threats in the present and predicted future strategic environments.³⁰ These threats were identified in three documents published by DCDC, *Global Strategic Trends 2040*, *Future Operating Environment 2035* and *Primer for the New Future Air and Space Operating Concept*. The themes of technologies crossing physical boundaries and the necessity of managing the electromagnetic environment, the blurring of national and overseas threats, and the proliferation of technologies boosted by globalization triggered the necessity of a broader thinking about air power use and its potential in various settings. He stated:

> So what can be done? Air power, by its very nature, has been at the forefront of technological development since its birth. And technology will inevitably have a part to play in our solutions but there is something much more fundamental that we can do first, think. To be more specific, that is to demonstrate 'thought leadership', our ability to think through new and difficult problem areas to identify innovative solutions.³¹

The RAF is following the same innovative strategy as the USAF, positioning itself at the vanguard of cutting-edge technologies and innovation. Furthermore, the RAF has placed a significant emphasis on improving its conceptual component as a key to the success of future air power. A significant step forward is the acknowledgement of the importance of innovative thinking together with cutting-edge technologies. It may seem rational to combine both. However, the history of RAF doctrine and the emergence of two distinctive schools of thought on air power illustrate that it is seldom the case. Such a multifaceted initiative also aims to bring both schools of thought together and work on effective solutions of the future of air power. Moreover, this approach is bridging an even more significant gap in the military field – a gap between the human and technological dimensions of warfare and the use of air power. By acknowledging the necessity of improving the human aspect of air power instead of its technological dimension alone, the initiative may, in fact, overcome certain limitations of tactics-oriented thinking in organizational culture and thereby stimulate creativity. In fact, the history of human civilization and warfare illustrates that innovations both technological and conceptual are driven by visionaries who exceed their time and available technologies. They are the ones to look into future and make it happen: 'Sometimes the vision of the innovators has outrun the capability of technology: the early submariners, the early aircraft carrier advocates, the first air power theorists, the proponents of surface-to-air missiles, and, just possibly, those enthusiasts who unreservedly espouse the cause of enhanced technology as the panacea for today's Western strategic dilemmas might be so categorized. Yet without such visionaries and without innovation, a nation's way of war becomes predictable; and predictable means vulnerable.'[32] Taking Tony Mason's warning on board, T2W initiate also highlights the role of people in various stages of decision-making and in the development of air power. On this subject, Howard Wheeldon FRAeS argues: 'Equally important is the realization that T2W should be as much about demonstrating the quality of the decision-making process, showing good leadership and recognising that it isn't just the quality of output and delivery that impacts but also the importance of how people are requested to do whatever it is that they are required to do.'[33]

The theme of human capital is predominant in T2W. Both military and civilian people are viewed as the source of creativity and shaping the conceptual component of air power. They are the ones who maintain existing technologies. Moreover, people are the ones who apply these technologies:

> Because success is defined by more than just availability of advanced technology, it is defined by its application, and that is determined by the quality of your human capital. History shows us time and again its value. Witness the contribution of Ashmore, Watson-Watt, Wilkins, Newall, Park and Dowding to the outcome of the Battle of Britain. They imagined and created an air defence system, perfected through multiple evolutions over time, which brought together new technologies for decisive effect. People thus 'won' the Battle, aided by technology.[34]

A curious feature of this initiative is that the drastic overreliance on technologies and the RMA which dominated military discourse after the First Gulf War is finally moving aside as the role of the human factor in the success or failure of the most cutting-edge technologies is acknowledged. This shift might be conditioned by a more realistic assessment of the nature of contemporary technologies and the necessity of real-time cross-verification of data, especially with the multiple cyberspace threats and technology glitches. However, it may also be due to the increasing dehumanization of the use of force in the Western society and the rise of the post-heroic warfare.³⁵ Moreover, this shift may also be attributed to the increasingly dominant public perception of air power through the lens of drones alone, which in the light of the recent operations was not very flattering. In any case, the revival of the human side of air power would contribute to a more balanced assessment of air power, its future conceptualization, application and public perception.

The core of T2W includes eight initiatives aimed at developing a creative, inclusive and innovative environment: a common vision, training to win, driving innovation and change, supporting ideas, recognizing our talent, develop diverse thinking, new ways of applying air power and promoting air power.³⁶ At first glance, these initiates are intended to stimulate and establish the culture of innovation in a systematic manner. Moreover, according to this document, multiple procedures and criteria for assessing the progress of this initiative are envisaged. The implications of this initiative would only be seen in the years to come. However, some activities were already in place once the initiative was launched. First, Group Captain Paul Wilkins, who held the position of DDefS in 2015–2017, did much work related to T2W. Various workshops, academic debates and conferences were devoted to the discussion of the conceptual component and the future of air power. For instance, the air power conference organized by the RAF Museum and the Royal Aeronautical Society, *Air Power: Now and the Future*, London, 29–30 September 2016,³⁷ primarily explored creative and unconventional thinking on air power. One of the distinctive features of the conference, acknowledged by the organizers in their closing remarks, was that speakers' and discussants' visions were primarily qualitative and interdisciplinary in their nature rather than technology- and tactics oriented. The conference illustrated a diversity of visions and perspectives on air power, which would seldom be expressed by representatives of a single organizational environment. Moreover, both professional and academic discussion of the conceptual component was conducted on the pages of *Air Power Review*, primarily the first issue of 2015.

Besides the earlier-mentioned activities, there were multiple roundtables and discussions behind closed doors across various locations of the RAF, in the Defence Academy and DCDC. Once again, at this point, it would be difficult to evaluate the efficiency of this initiative and its impact on a new air power doctrine, which was published in December 2017. Thus, due to the nearness in time of the writing of this book to the publication of a new edition, a full evaluation of it cannot be included. In a follow-up to this book, assessment of T2W, its impact on a new doctrine and their respective roles in reshaping the organizational culture of the RAF will be conducted.

Nevertheless, there are still a few considerations regarding T2W worth mentioning here. First, no matter which concepts T2W comes up with, or how they will be expressed in the doctrine and in other organizational documents, the primary concern will be the practical value and how the proposed transformation is put into practice. To achieve the desired outcome, an interim stage of dissemination of the document (presumably the doctrine) should be addressed with the due attention. In other words, having a conceptual framework is great, but making sure that it is read is an entirely different task. There are many tricks that can be used for dissemination purposes. For instance, people tend to read paper copies better than digital format. Follow-up seminars and discussion workshops assist in spreading the ideas contained in doctrines. On the other hand, the RAF is taking full advantage of digital technologies by streaming annual air power conferences to a number of RAF bases. Moreover, social media provides an immediate dissemination of doctrines and exchange of ideas between various stakeholders. It can also be used as a means of improving communication and bridging civil–military gap. In order to engage a wider military audience, a systematic, multifaceted outreach programme for T2W and the consequent doctrine would be beneficial.

Instead of conclusion

Another important consideration of this initiative is that although T2W proclaimed a multifaceted reformation of the service, as with many other initiatives the public dimension was not addressed in full. The initiative called for the involvement of both military and civilian experts, but it does not address the role of public and its evaluation of air power performance. This feature is a distinctive difference between the British and American approaches to positioning air power in the contemporary strategic environment. While USAF realizes the necessity of engaging and taking the public on board in promoting air power, the RAF remains more conservative in its vision. In other words, despite the proclamations of innovation and boosted creativity, the necessity of overcoming the civil–military gap and reintegrating air power into social dimensions is not emphasized. Once again, adding the public engagement to this initiative would make it even more systematic and could provide an understanding of the social implications of air interventions and drone warfare. One useful practice could be to send various serving officers to give open public lectures on T2W at higher education institutions across the UK. First, this activity would help to inform both the younger generation and academics about the RAF perspective. Second, it would help strengthen inter-institutional contacts. Such initiatives do exist already due to personal contacts. However, the centralization of such practice could widen services' outreach capacity and improve communication with the wider audience. Finally, the costs of such an initiative would be minimal, but the benefits are enormous. In any case, time will show how T2W will shape the RAF organizational culture and the role of doctrine in it. However, such an innovative initiative was supported at the highest level in the service illustrates that the organization has realized the necessity of substantial reforms in order for the service to face and match future requirements in a turbulent and uncertain world.

Conclusion

From 1999 to 2013, the development of RAF air power doctrine was characterized by a change in approach to writing environmental doctrine influenced by the process of the institutionalization of jointery. The approach that characterized the first two post–Cold War editions was personality driven, but this was later substituted with an institutional approach. The defining factor of this change was the process of jointery as a centralized process of reforming the national Armed Forces. Therefore, at each stage of the institutionalization of jointery, environmental doctrine had a different shape and purpose. In the most recent stage of the development of jointery, authorship of environmental doctrine has changed from single service to joint.

The introduction of doctrine into RAF post–Cold War practice was defined by the history of the RAF. Chapter 2 showed how single-service authorship may contribute to the misuse of doctrine for political purposes and turn it into dogma. With the establishment of the RAF as an independent service, the main function of the doctrine was to embody the service's primary concept – strategic bombing. Although various revisions of AP 1300 took place, the concept remained the same. Inevitably, this contributed to the perception of doctrine, as the vessel of this concept, being dogma and the source of narrow-mindedness. Historically, the RAF's misuse of doctrine was influenced by political considerations and the need of the service to survive. To an extent, such conceptual self-sufficiency had contributed to a unique role of the service in the national defence in 1918–1957. It also resulted in complete redundancy of RAF doctrine, when it could not secure the strategic nuclear function for the RAF.

Thus, from the 1970s, the RAF existed without a conceptual framework of its own and only used the NATO tactical-level doctrine. Furthermore, the political use of doctrine through RAF history and the dogmatic character of the first doctrines resulted in the complete rejection of doctrine within the service.

The main outcome of such a history was the development of a distinctive anti-intellectual culture within the service. Since doctrine was viewed as dogma and the service's attempts to promote its interests, everything written on a strategic level, stimulating creative thinking, was treated with suspicion and immediate rejection. Nevertheless, Neil Cameron's initiative to stimulate intellectual thinking within the RAF by establishing the post of DDefS created favourable ground for Andrew Vallance's initiative of reviving doctrine in the post-Cold War era. Because not everyone supported intellectualism, the process of bringing doctrine back into RAF practice was painstaking. However, after the end of the Cold War, the service needed a precise conceptual framework in order to know where it was at that time and how it had to change to adapt to uncertain strategic environment.

The history of RAF doctrine illustrated that over-stretching of doctrinal functionality can turn doctrine into dogma. A continuous misuse of doctrine for political purposes can undermine the credibility of doctrine *per se*, resulting in service's scepticism of any intellectual practice and conceptual component in general. The history of RAF doctrine also explained and put into perspective the establishment of personalities-driven approach to doctrine writing in the first two editions of post–Cold War doctrine. Andrew Vallance's initiative was conditioned by the necessity of service's adaptation to the post–Cold War environment. The first edition explained where the service was at the end of the Cold War. The second edition evaluated the experience of the Gulf War and lessons for the RAF. Those two editions were the basis for the development of the RAF's doctrinal practice, because they summarized the Cold War and the first post–Cold War operational experience. Although they were still Cold War oriented, they paved the way for the post–Cold War doctrines looking towards the future and the place of the RAF in the joint environment. This historical discourse answers two questions. First, it demonstrates the organizational culture concerning the place of doctrine in RAF practice before the studied period. Second, it shows that the first two doctrines were transitional in their nature, due to the unclear strategic environment of that time. However, only with the centralized initiative of reforming the Armed Forces within the joint lines could crucial changes in the process of doctrine writing become possible.

The introduction of jointery created the necessity of more profound commitments to tri-service cooperation demonstrated in Chapters 3 and 4, which were devoted to the case study of AP 3000 third edition. At the time of preparation of this edition, jointery was in its proto-stage of institutionalization and required services to establish their commitment to the joint environment.

Consequently, the third edition of AP 3000 interpreted the operational experience in terms of joint discourse with a consequent commitment to a close cooperation with the Army. Although vertical jointery and precise doctrinal hierarchy were yet to be developed, the doctrine showed commitment to horizontal jointery. Accordingly, PSO doctrine was used in order to harmonize the lessons of Bosnia and joint thinking on the role of the Armed Forces in future operations. The third edition demonstrated the RAF's jointery-oriented stance and ability of producing a jointery-friendly doctrine.

Consequently, from this edition RAF environmental doctrine was jointery inclined rather than personalities driven like in the first two editions of AP 3000. Regarding the relationship between the factors influencing doctrine, the degree of influence was different. In terms of the external environment, the operational experience of the Gulf War and PSO realities of Bosnia had a dominant impact on the rethinking of the roles of air power in a new strategic environment, while other factors of the external environment were indirect in their influence. First, NATO doctrine was in transition as well and it had no direct influence on AP 3000. It could only have an indirect impact through the Allied publications. Second, the limited influence of foreign doctrines of Allied nations was shaped by differences in strategic cultures. Third, the exchange of ideas and technologies with the service's American counterparts was indirect, conducted through joint courses, common training and in the battlespace. The DDefS visits to Maxwell AFB took place at that time and could shape thinking. However, no evidence was found that these visits were the forces shaping the content of the third edition of AP 3000. Therefore, although the factors of the external environment triggered the necessity of doctrinal reflection of the new trends, it was the internal environment of jointery that dictated the tone and shape of the new edition. In the joint discourse of the third edition of AP 3000, the shift from a personalities-driven to an institutional approach was still not finalized. This was demonstrated in the roles of academics and authors. As DDefS, Stuart Peach was exposed to the most advanced academic thinking on air power at that time. He wanted to write a more academically inclined doctrine. The influential role of academics and reflection of academic discourse in the text and structure of the third edition demonstrated that personalities still mattered, albeit to a lesser extent than before.

Chapter 5 illustrated that the experience of subsequent campaigns and their reflection in the national political discourse only stimulated further stages of the institutionalization of jointery. In the environment of interservice rivalry and established doctrine hierarchy, the fight for the authorship of environmental doctrine became crucial for the further institutionalization of jointery. In terms of the ownership of environmental doctrine, the fourth edition of AP 3000 demonstrated that the RAF was capable of writing joint environmental doctrine under single-service authorship. Accordingly, such an attempt could provide the service with extra leverage in the environment of strengthened jointery and its centralization in DCDC. Regarding the factors influencing the process of doctrine preparation, continuous operational involvement, the protracted and changing character of campaigns resulted in the lack of a new edition for almost a decade. Although the fourth edition was aimed at the analysis of British experience in COIN operations, the document practically emphasized the diversity of air power roles in the joint environment of COIN.

However, operational experience was significant in stimulating domestic debate on jointery and the Network Centric Capability and the Comprehensive Approach. Furthermore, it resulted in the renewal of a discussion of air–land integration and the necessity of the synchronization of environmental doctrines under a joint umbrella. Since the aim of the fourth edition was to demonstrate how joint a single-service environmental doctrine could be and since it was written after the SDSR, the role of academics was limited, and the role of the author was decisive. However, unlike the first two editions of AP 3000, although the doctrine was written by a single author, his influence was limited by the joint discourse of that edition and its political purposes in the preparation for the SDSR. Consequently, the process of doctrine writing was one step closer to an entirely institutional approach. The time of doctrine publication and its content were defined by the process of centralization of jointery and the struggle for ownership over environmental doctrine, which was the means of protecting a single-service vision of air power. This was partly conditioned by the approaching SDSR, where an extra means of self-explanation could be crucial for the service's survival.

Chapter 6 addressed the last stage of the institutionalization of jointery. At this stage, jointery was characterized by the centralization and strict division of duties and responsibilities between the NATO Standardization Agency, DCDC and the three services. The doctrine hierarchy, interim procedures and the process of doctrine preparation were harmonized in relation to the national defence reviews. Consequently, the last studied edition of air power doctrine, JDP 0–30, demonstrated the joint authorship of environmental doctrine and the new procedural elements envisioned by the new joint doctrine writing process. It also reflected the most recent trends in the institutionalization of jointery placing NATO at the heart of the national doctrinal practice. Accordingly, this doctrine emphasized the increased number of joint publications and the place of JDP 0–30 in a more complex doctrinal hierarchy. The text also corresponded to the requirements of joint publications.

Concerning NATO discourse, unlike previous editions, this one stated direct commitments to NATO practice and its incorporation into the national doctrinal practice. In terms of the last stage of the institutionalization of jointery, doctrine gained new functionality. In the new five-year doctrine cycle, revision of doctrine directly related to the national defence reviews. In this context, doctrine served as a mean of influencing policy. If environmental doctrine was in single-service ownership, it would give the service extra power. Therefore, centralized ownership contributed to a common direction and consequent influence on policy. However, the extent to which it was mutually beneficial for the three services remained controversial.

Regarding the correlation of factors influencing the process of doctrine preparation under joint authorship, once again operational experience was not the driving force. Accordingly, although the lessons of Libya were reflected in JDP 0–30, the operation itself did not trigger doctrine preparation. Furthermore, although the doctrine reflected the tendency towards contingency rather than COIN operations, it used diverse operational examples through the entire history of air power, paying attention to the post–Cold War era. Regarding the role of air power in contemporary warfare, Libya demonstrated that air power remained functional both independently and in cooperation with other services. In the case of Libya, the RAF closely cooperated with the Royal Navy. Therefore, while the second post–Cold War decade was characterized by air power pessimism, the beginning of the third decade showed that air power was still extremely functional.

The recent stage of the institutionalization of jointery and consequent institutional approach to environmental doctrine was also demonstrated in the change of roles of academics and writers. First, as before, the role of academics remained advisory and not decisive. They took part in the discussion of drafts and advise in their fields of expertise. However, they have less direct impact on the overview of the writers of doctrine, because the role of writers has changed. DDefS was no longer the primary author of air power doctrine. A group of writers is responsible for collective ideas representing the joint institution's perspective on environmental doctrine. Although it can be argued that the doctrinal process suggested an instrumental approach to academic involvement, the centralized joint environment provided a wider range of opportunities for academic participation. This was demonstrated in numerous discussions taking place in the preparation of JDP 0–30.

In terms of the aforementioned shift in the approach to writing environmental doctrine, the change of the role of writers in the joint environment was a crucial culmination of this change. Hence, although the third and fourth editions of AP 3000 reflected joint tendencies, they were still written by DDefS. Although, in both cases, doctrine preparation processes were under the scrutiny and authorization of CAS and still reflected certain institutional restraints on content, authorship was personalized, and each doctrine reflected the distinctive approach of its author. Only with the transition of authorship from the RAF to DCDC did authorship become truly institutional, joint and less personal. Overall, the development of the RAF air power doctrine in 1999–2013 was shaped by the process of the institutionalization of jointery. Although new campaigns were the source of operational lessons, air power doctrine development differed according to the stages of institutionalization of jointery. With each edition, doctrine was becoming closer to cooperation with the other two services and the joint environment.

Chapter 7 illustrated that despite ambivalent attitudes towards doctrine and its multiple functionalities, it remains relevant nowadays, and may serve as the means of organizational transformation of the RAF and of the Armed Forces in general. Faced with intensifying public scrutiny of air power, air forces need to pay more attention to their public profiles, investing in personnel with more diverse backgrounds, stimulating public engagement and air advocacy in a more systematic way. The revival of attention to a conceptual component was recently illustrated in RAF initiative of Thinking to Win. This initiative illustrates the necessity for the service to evolve together with the society it aims to protect, taking on board diverse practices from different disciplines and professional experiences. It is still too early to judge the outcomes of this initiative in terms of the practical reorganization of the RAF. However, it is a step towards embracing a multifaceted future that requires innovative and creative thinking, flexibility and adaptability more than ever before. One way or another, air power doctrine and a conceptual component in general will be a part of this process of organizational transformation and adaptation to the requirements of the second century in RAF history.

Notes

Introduction

1 Oliver Daddow, 'British Military Doctrine in the 1980s and 1990s', *Defence Studies* 3, no. 3 (Autumn 2003): 105.
2 Ibid., 107.
3 Ibid.
4 Ibid., 108.
5 Ibid., 110.
6 See Markus Mäder, *In Pursuit of Conceptual Excellence. The Evolution of British Military-Strategic Doctrine in the Post-Cold War Era, 1989–2002* (New York: Peter Lang Publishing, 2004) and Alexander Alderson, 'The Validity of British Army Counterinsurgency Doctrine after the War in Iraq 2003–2009' (PhD thesis, the Cranfield University, 2009).

Chapter 1

1 Angus Stevenson, *Oxford Dictionary of English*, 3rd Edition (Oxford: Oxford University Press, 2010), 516.
2 Ibid., 517.
3 *British Defence Doctrine* (Joint Warfare Publication 0-01), 2nd Edition. Prepared under the direction of the Director General Joint Doctrine and Concepts on behalf of the Chiefs of Staff (Shrivenham: JDCC/MOD, 2001), 1–1.
4 Neville Parton, 'The Development of Early RAF Doctrine', *The Journal of Military History* 72, no. 4 (October 2008): 1158.
5 Harald Høiback, 'The Anatomy of Doctrine and Ways to Keep It Fit', *Journal of Strategic Studies* 39, no. 2 (2016): 190.
6 Ibid.
7 JWP 0-01 (2001), 1–1.
8 Ibid.
9 Ibid.
10 JWP 0-01 (2001), 6–1.
11 *Operations Manual, Royal Air Force* (Confidential Document 22). Prepared by Command of the Air Council for Air Ministry (London: Air Ministry, July 1922), 1.

12 Colin Gray, *The Strategy Bridge: Theory for Practice* (Oxford: Oxford University Press, 2010), 77–78.
13 JWP 0-01 (2001), 1-1.
14 Colin McInnes, 'The British Army's New Way in Warfare: A Doctrinal Misstep?', *Defense & Security Analysis* 23, no. 2 (June 2007): 136.
15 Ibid.
16 Charles Grant, 'The Use of History in the Development of Contemporary Doctrine', in *The Origins of Contemporary Doctrine*, ed. J. Gooch (Camberley: TSO for the Strategic and Combat Studies Institute, 1997), 7–17.
17 Eliot A. Cohen, 'The Historical Mind and Military Strategy', *Orbis* 49, no. 4 (Fall 2005): 575–588.
18 Ibid., 576.
19 Douglas Porch, 'Writing History in the "End of History" Era – Reflections on Historians and the GWOT', *The Journal of Military History* 70, no. 4 (October 2006): 1067.
20 Carl Von Clausewitz, *On War* (Princeton, NJ: Princeton University Press, 1989), 140.
21 Ibid., 141.
22 JWP 0-01 (2001), 1-1.
23 In 2007, this department was replaced by two separate ones: The Department for Business, Enterprise and Regulatory Reform and the Department for Innovation, Universities and Skills.
24 JWP 0-01 (2001), 1-1.
25 Ibid.
26 *Allied Joint Doctrine*, AJP - 01 (D). Promulgated by the Director of NATO Standardization Agency (Brussels: NATO Standardization Agency, December 2010), 1–1.
27 *Operations* (Army Doctrine Publication). Prepared under the direction of the Chief of the General Staff (Shrivenham: DCDC, November 2010).
28 JWP 0-01 (2001), 1-1.
29 Ibid., 1-2.
30 *UK Defence Doctrine* (Joint Doctrine Publication 0–01), 5th edition. Promulgated by the Chiefs of Staff (Shrivenham: DCDC/MOD, 2014), 25.
31 Ibid.
32 Paul Wilkins, 'Conceptualising the Conceptual Component: One Airman's Perspective', *Air Power Review* 18, no. 1 (2015): 16.
33 Gray, *The Strategy Bridge*, 77.
34 Andrew Methven, 'It Is Not High Time the Doctrine Industry Published Its Doctrine on the Limits of the Utility of Written Doctrine', *Defence Studies* 3, no. 3 (Autumn 2003): 146.
35 McInnes, 'The British Army's New Way in Warfare', 134.

36 JWP 0–01 (2001), 1–5.
37 Ibid.
38 *Joint Doctrine Development System* (Chairman of the Joint Chiefs of Staff Instruction 5120.02C). Promulgated by the Director of Joint Staff (Washington, DC: JCS/DOD, 13 January 2012), A–3.
39 *Allied Joint Doctrine Development AAP-47 (A). Supplement to AAP-3(J)*. Promulgated by the Director of NATO Standardization Agency (Brussels: NATO Standardization Agency, September 2011), 1–3.
40 JWP 0–01 (2001), 1–5.
41 *British Defence Doctrine* (Joint Doctrine Publication 0–01), 3rd Edition. Promulgated by the Chief of the Defence Staff (Shrivenham: DCDC/MOD, 2008), 1–3.
42 Ibid.
43 Gray, *The Strategy Bridge*, 25.
44 JDP 0–01 (2008), 1–4.
45 AJP - 01 (D), 1–1.
46 Roger Thomas, 'Doctrine and Technology: Engaged, To Be Married?' *The Naval Review* 86, no. 3 (July 1998): 217.
47 Tony Mason, 'The Technology Interaction', in *Perspectives on Air Power: Airpower in Its Wider Context*, ed. S. Peach (London: HMSO, 1998), 132.
48 John Glock, 'The Evolution of Air Force Targeting', *Air & Space Power Journal* 20, no. 2 (Summer 2006): 22.
49 Thomas, 'Doctrine and Technology', 218.
50 Roger Thomas, 'Doctrine and Technology: Engaged, To Be Married? – II', *The Naval Review* 86, no. 4 (October 1998): 344.
51 Barry Watts, 'Doctrine, Technology and Air Warfare', in *Air Power Confronts an Unstable World*, ed. R. Hallion (London: Brassey, 1997), 28.
52 Tony Milton, 'My Job: Director General Joint Doctrine and Concepts', *The RUSI Journal* 145, no. 2 (April 2000): 17.
53 ADP *Operations*, 2–5.
54 Ibid.
55 Ibid.
56 AP 3000 (1999), 2.6.1.
57 *British Defence Doctrine*, 2nd Edition.
58 ADP *Operations*, 2–6.
59 *Campaigning* (Joint Doctrine Publication 01), 2nd Edition. Promulgated as directed by the Chiefs of Staff (Shrivenham: DCDC, December 2008).
60 Ibid., v.
61 *Understanding and Intelligence Support to Joint Operations* (Joint Doctrine Publication 2–00), 3rd Edition. Prepared under the direction of the Chiefs of Staff (Shrivenham: DCDC, August 2011).

62 *Campaign Execution* (Joint Doctrine Publication 3–00), 3rd Edition. Prepared under the direction of the Chiefs of Staff (Shrivenham: DCDC, October 2009).
63 *Logistics for Joint Operations* (Joint Doctrine Publication 4–00), 3rd Edition. Prepared under the direction of the Chiefs of Staff (Shrivenham: DCDC, April 2007).
64 *Campaign Planning* (Joint Doctrine Publication 5–00), 2nd Edition. Prepared under the direction of the Joint Forces Commander and Chiefs of Staff (Shrivenham: DCDC, July 2013).
65 *Communications and Information Systems Support to Joint Operations* (Joint Doctrine Publication 6–00), 3rd Edition. Prepared under the direction of the Chiefs of Staff (Shrivenham: DCDC, January 2008).
66 *Security and Stabilisation: The Military Contribution* (Joint Doctrine Publication 3–40), 3rd Edition. Prepared under the direction of the Chiefs of Staff (Shrivenham: DCDC, November 2009).
67 JDP 3–40.
68 *Military Contribution to Peace Support Operations* (Joint Doctrine Publication 3–50), 2nd Edition. Prepared under the direction of the Chiefs of Staff (Shrivenham: DCDC, June 2004).
69 ADP *Operations*, 2–8.
70 *The Fundamentals of British Maritime Doctrine: BR 1806*. Prepared by Command of the Defence Council (London: H.M.S.O., 1995).
71 *British Air Power Doctrine (Air Publication 3000)*, 3rd Edition. Prepared under the direction of the Chief of the Air Staff (London: TSO, 1999).
72 ADP *Operations*, 2–8.
73 *Countering Insurgency. British Army Filed Manual Volume 1 Part10* (Army Code 71876). Prepared under the direction of the Chief of the General Staff (London: MOD, October 2009).
74 ADP *Operations*, 2–8.
75 *UK Air and Space Doctrine* (Joint Doctrine Publication 0–30). Prepared under the direction of the Joint Forces Commander and Chiefs of Staff (Shrivenham: DCDC, July 2013).
76 Alistair Byford, interview with the author, Shrivenham, 11 September 2013.
77 Chris Finn, interview with the author, RAF College Cranwell, 7 November 2013.
78 AJP - 01(D), 1–1.
79 Ibid., vii.
80 ADP *Operations*, 2–6.
81 McInnes, 'The British Army's New Way in Warfare', 127–141.
82 Ibid., 131.
83 Methven, 'It Is Not High Time', 130–148.
84 Colin S. Gray, *Modern Strategy* (Oxford: Oxford University Press, 1999), 36.
85 Ibid.

86 JDP 0-01 (2011), 5-4.
87 Oxford dictionary online; see https://en.oxforddictionaries.com
88 Gray, *Modern Strategy*, 36.
89 Neville Parton, 'In defence of Doctrine… But Not Dogma', *Defense & Security Analysis* 24, no. 1 (March 2008): 84.
90 Watts, 'Doctrine, Technology and Air Warfare', 21.
91 Yehoshavet Harkabi, quoted in Colin Gray, *The Strategy Bridge*, 79.
92 Colin Gray, *The Strategy Bridge*, 79.
93 Ibid.
94 Ibid.
95 Markus Mäder, *In Pursuit of Conceptual Excellence. The Evolution of British Military-Strategic Doctrine in the Post-Cold War Era, 1989-2002* (New York: Peter Lang Publishing, 2004), 108.
96 James Tritten, 'Navy Doctrine: Lessons for Today', *The Naval Review* 84, no. 1 (January 1996): 18.
97 Mäder, *In Pursuit of Conceptual Excellence*, 162.
98 Ibid.
99 Eric Grove, 'Themes in Navy Doctrine' (paper presented at the 1st Meeting at the British Military Doctrine Group, Shrivenham, 3 February 2002).
100 Thompson Redvers, 'Post-Cold War Development of United Kingdom Joint Air Command and Control Capability', *Air & Space Power Journal* 18, no. 4 (Winter 2004): 76.
101 John Ferris, 'Achieving Air Ascendancy: Challenge and Response in British Strategic Air Defence, 1915-1940', in *Air Power History: Turning Points from Kitty Hawk to Kosovo*, eds. S. Cox and P. Gray (Oxon: Routledge, 2002), 30.
102 Andrew Vallance, interview with the author, London, 11 July 2013.
103 Tony Mason, interview with the author, Cheltenham, 19 June 2013.
104 Barry, Watts, *The Foundations of US Air Doctrine - The Problem of Friction in War* (Maxwell AFB: Air University Press, 1984), 56.
105 Milton, 'My Job', 15-19.
106 Alexander Alderson, 'The Army Brain: A Historical Perspective on Doctrine, Development and the Challenges of Future Conflict', *The RUSI Journal* 155, no. 3 (June 2010): 10-15.
107 Peter Gray, 'Air Power or Aerospace Doctrine 2010?' *Air Power Review* 3, no. 2 (Summer 2000): 7-21; 'Air Power & Joint Doctrine: A RAF Perspective', *Air Power Review* 3, no. 4 (Autumn 2000): 1-15.
108 Philip Sabin, 'Perspectives from within the Profession', *Air Power Review* 8, no. 4 (Winter 2005): 23.
109 AP 3000 (1999), introduction.
110 Chris Finn, interview with the author, RAF College Cranwell, 7 November 2013.
111 Alistair Byford, interview with the author, Shrivenham, 11 September 2013.

112 Robert Cassidy, *Peacekeeping in the Abyss: British and American Peacekeeping Doctrine and Practice after the Cold War* (Westport: Praeger, 2004), 110.
113 Paul Strickland, 'USAF Aerospace-Power Doctrine Decisive or Coercive?' *Air Power Review* 4, no.1 (Spring 2001): 21.
114 Resulting in rigidity of mind and overreliance on traditional ways in a new environment.
115 Richard Overy, 'Doctrine Not Dogma: Lessons from the Past', *Air Power Review* 3, no. 1 (Spring 2000): 33.
116 Ibid., 34.
117 Ibid.
118 Ibid., 46.
119 Mäder, *In Pursuit of Conceptual Excellence*, 71.
120 Andrew Hoskins and Ben O'Louqhlin, *War and Media* (Cambridge: Polity Press, 2010), 41.
121 Mäder, *In Pursuit of Conceptual Excellence*, 74.
122 Tony Mason, interview with the author, Cheltenham, 19 June 2013.
123 Ibid.

Chapter 2

1 Richard Langworth, *Winston Churchill, Myth and Reality: What He Actually Did and Said* (Jefferson: McFarland & Company, 2017), 214.
2 AP 3003 (2004), 1.
3 Ibid., 4–5.
4 Ibid.
5 Eric Grove, 'The Case for The RAF', in *The Question of Security*, eds. M. Codner and M. Clarke (London: RUSI, 2011), 212.
6 AP 3003, 9.
7 Tami Biddle, 'Learning in Real Time: The Development and Implementation of Air Power in the First World War', in *Air Power History: Turning Points from Kitty Hawk to Kosovo*, eds. S. Cox and P. Gray (Oxon: Routledge), 5.
8 E.R. Hooton, *War over the Trenches: Air Power and the Western Front Campaigns 1916–1918* (Birmingham: Midland Publishing), 29.
9 AP 3003, 10.
10 Biddle, 'Learning in Real Time', 8.
11 Peter Hart, *Somme Success: The Royal Flying Corps and the Battle of the Somme 1916* (Barnsley: Pen & Sword Military, 2012), 32.
12 Christina Goulter, 'The Royal Naval Air Service: A Very Modern Service', in *Air Power History: Turning Points from Kitty Hawk to Kosovo*, eds. S. Cox and P. Gray (London: Frank Cass, 2002), 58.

13 Ibid.
14 Hooton, *War over the Trenches*, 45.
15 Hart, *Somme Success*, 73.
16 Richard Hallion, 'Battlefield Air Support: A Retrospective Assessment', *Air Power Journal* 4 (Spring 1990): 8.
17 Phil Carradice, *First World War in the Air* (Stroud: Amberley Publishing, 2012), 56.
18 AP 3003, 35.
19 J.R. Ferris, 'Catching the Wave: The RAF Pursues an RMA, 1918–1945', in *The Fog of Peace: Military and Strategic Planning under Uncertainty*, eds. M. Tufts and I. Talbot (Oxon: Routledge, 2006), 78.
20 James Cate, 'Development of Air Doctrine 1917–41', *Air & Space Power Journal* 26, no. 2 (March/April 2012): 135.
21 General Han Christian Smuts was ordered by Prime Minister Lloyd George 'to solve the air defence problems of Britain – quickly' (AP 3003, p. 24).
22 Biddle, 'Learning in Real Time', 11.
23 AP 3003, 54.
24 Ibid., 55.
25 *Operations Manual, Royal Air Force* (Confidential Document 22). Prepared by Command of the Air Council for Air Ministry (London: Air Ministry, July 1922).
26 Neville Parton, 'The Development of Early RAF Doctrine', *The Journal of Military History* 72, no. 4 (October 2008): 1163.
27 Ibid.
28 Parton, 'The Development of Early RAF Doctrine', 1164.
29 Ibid.
30 CD 22, 128–133.
31 Ibid., 1.
32 Parton, 'The Development of Early RAF Doctrine', 1165.
33 CD 22, 126.
34 AP 3003, 25.
35 Philip Meilinger, 'Trenchard and "morale bombing": The Evolution of Royal Air Force Doctrine before World War II', *Journal of Military History* 60, no. 2 (April 1996): 245.
36 Ibid., 256.
37 J.R. Ferris, 'Achieving Air Ascendancy': Challenge and Response in British Air Defence, 1915–1940', in *Air Power History, Turning Points from Kitty Hawk to Kosovo*, eds. Sebastian Cox and Peter Grey (London: Frank Cass, 2002), 26; Allan English, 'The RAF Staff College and the Evolution of British Strategic Bombing Policy, 1922–1929', *Journal of Strategic Studies* 16, no. 3 (1993): 408–412.
38 Ferris, 'Achieving Air Ascendancy', 28.
39 CD-22, 2.
40 Ibid., 54–67.

41 Ibid., 54–55.
42 Ferris, 'Achieving Air Ascendancy', 27.
43 Quoted in ibid.
44 John Ferris, 'Fighter Defence before Fighter Command: The Evolution of Strategic Air Defence in Great Britain, 1917–1934', *The Journal of Military History* 63 (October 1999): 847.
45 AP 3000 (1999), 3.12.5.
46 Ibid.
47 English, 'The RAF Staff College', 412.
48 Ibid., 413–416.
49 Parton, 'The Development of Early RAF Doctrine', 1173.
50 Ibid., 1174.
51 Ibid., 1161.
52 AP 3003, 56.
53 David Omissi, *Air Power and Colonial Control: The Royal Air Force 1919–1939* (Manchester: Manchester University Press, 1990), 29.
54 AP 3003, 61.
55 *The War Aim of the Royal Air Force* (CD 64. Air Staff Memorandum No. 43. S. 28279) (London: the Imperial Defence College, October 1928).
56 CD 64, 3.
57 Ibid.
58 Air Ministry, *Royal Air Force War Manual. Part I – Operations* (Air Publication 1300). Prepared by the direction of Command of the Air Council (London: Air Ministry, July 1928).
59 AP 1300 (1928), Chapter I, para 3.
60 Ibid., Chapter I, para 4.
61 Ibid., Chapter I, para 5.
62 Ibid., Chapter I, para 6.
63 This chapter was in the course of preparation at the time of doctrine publication.
64 AP 1300 (1928), Chapter VII, para 5.
65 Omissi, *Air Power and Colonial Control*, 58.
66 AP 1300 (1928), Chapter XIV.
67 Tami Biddle, 'British and American Approaches to Strategic Bombing: The Origins and Implementation in the World War II Combined Bomber Offensive', in *Airpower: Theory and Practice*, ed. John Gooch (London: Frank Cass, 1995), 101.
68 Scott Robertson, 'The Development of Royal Air Force Strategic Bombing Doctrine between the Wars: A Revolution in Military Affairs?' *Airpower Journal* 12, no. 1 (Spring 1998): 43.
69 Scot Robertson, *The Development of RAF Strategic Bombing Doctrine 1919–1939* (Westport: Praeger Publishers, 1995), xxiv.
70 Robertson, 'The Development of Royal Air Force', 44.

71 James Corum, 'The Luftwaffe and the Coalition Air War in Spain, 1936–1939', in *Airpower: Theory and Practice*, ed. John Gooch (London: Frank Cass, 1995), 80.
72 James Corum, 'The Luftwaffe and Lessons Learned in the Spanish Civil War', in *Air Power History*, eds. S. Cox and P. Gray (Oxon: Routledge, 2002), 66–93.
73 On the other hand, as the experience of the Second World War proved, they did not realize that without fighters' coverage, their bombers were quite vulnerable to attack.
74 James Corum, *The Luftwaffe: Creating the Operational Air Power, 1918–1940* (Westbrooke: University Press of Kanzas, 1997), 6.
75 Murray Williamson, *Strategy for Defeat: Luftwaffe 1933–1945* (Honolulu: University Press of the Pacific, 2002).
76 Murray Williamson, *Luftwaffe* (Baltimore: Nautical & Aviation Publishing Company of America, 1985).
77 Air Ministry, *Royal Air Force War Manual. Part I – Operations* (Air Publication 1300), 2nd Edition. Prepared by the direction of Command of the Air Council (London: Air Ministry, February 1940).
78 Chris Finn, 'British Thinking on Air Power – The Evolution of AP3000', *Air Power Review* 12, no. 1 (Spring 2009): 57.
79 AP 1300 (1940), Chapter IX, para 1.
80 Ibid., Chapter IX, para 3–21.
81 Ibid., Chapter IX, para 6.
82 Ibid., Chapter XII, para 1.
83 Tony Mason, 'British Air Power', in *Global Air Power*, ed. J.A. Olsen (Washington, DC: Potomac Books, 2011), 25.
84 One of the prominent experts on this subject is Sebastian Cox, who is the head of the Air Historical Branch (AHB) of the RAF.
85 Sebastian Cox, 'The Organisation and Sources of RAF Intelligence', *Air Intelligence Symposium: Bracknell Paper* 7 (1997): 6–7.
86 Ibid., 7.
87 Ibid.
88 *Understanding (Joint Doctrine Publication 04)*. Prepared under the direction of the Chiefs of Staff (Shrivenham: DCDC, December 2010), 2–13.
89 Ibid., 2A-1.
90 Cox, 'The Organisation and Sources of RAF Intelligence', 6–7.
91 JDP 04, 2–12.
92 Andrew Brown, *J.D. Bernal: The Sage of Science* (Oxford: Oxford University Press, 2005), 188.
93 For further reading, please see Reginal Victor Jones, *Most Secret War* (London: Hamilton, 1978); Roy Conyers Nesbit, *Eyes of the RAF: A History of Photo Reconnaissance* (Stroud: Sutton Publishing, 2003).
94 Biddle, 'British and American Approaches', 97.

95 Robin Higham, *Unflinching Zeal: The Air Battle over France Britain, May-October 1940* (Naval Institute Press, 2012), 202.
96 Ian Gooderson, *Air Power at the Battlefront: Allied Close Air Support in Europe 1943–45* (Oxon: Routledge, 1998), 87.
97 Ibid., 89.
98 Richard Hallion, 'The Second World War as a Turning Point in Air Power', in *Air Power History, Turning Points from Kitty Hawk to Kosovo*, eds. Sebastian Cox and Peter Grey (London: Frank Cass, 2002), 98.
99 Tony Mason, 'British Air Power', in *Global Air Power*, ed. J.A. Olsen (Washington, DC: Potomac Books, 2011), 32.
100 John McManus, 'The Sword of St. Michael: The 82nd Airborne in World War II', *Journal of Military History* 76, no. 1 (January 2012): 289; Sebastian Ritchie, 'Learning the Hard Way: A Comparative Perspective on Airborne Operations in the Second World War', *Air Power Review* 14, no. 3 (Autumn/Winter 2011): 11–35.
101 Richard Overy, *The Bombing War: Europe 1939–1945* (London: Allen Lane, 2013), 443.
102 Richard Overy, 'Allied Bombing and the Destruction of German Cities', in *A World at Total War: Global Conflict and the Politics of Destruction 1937–1945*, eds. R. Chickering and S. Forster (Cambridge: Cambridge University Press, 2005), 279.
103 Sebastian Cox, 'The Dresden Raids: Why and How', in *Firestorm: The Bombing of Dresden 1945*, eds. Jeremy Crang and Paul Addison (London: Pimlico, 2006), 45.
104 Walter Boyne, *The Influence of Air Power upon History* (Barnsley: Pen & Sword Aviation, 2005), 217.
105 S. Richards, 'The Decisive Role of Air Power in the Pacific Campaign of WWII', *Air Power Review* 6, no. 2 (Summer 2003): 62.
106 Air Ministry, *Royal Air Force War Manual. Part I – Operations* (Air Publication 1300), 3rd Edition. Prepared by Command of the Air Council (London: Air Ministry, January 1950).
107 AP 1300 (1950), 19.
108 Ibid.
109 Ibid.
110 Ibid.
111 Ibid.
112 AP 3003, 191.
113 Robert Self, *British Foreign &Defence Policy since 1945: Challenges & Dilemmas in a Changing World* (Basingstoke: Palgrave Macmillan, 2010), 42.
114 AP 3003, 191.
115 Ibid., 235.
116 Ibid.
117 Ibid., 237.
118 Frank Barnaby and Douglas Holdstock, eds., *The British Nuclear Weapons Programmes, 1952–2002* (London: Frank Cass, 2005), 60.

119   AP 3003, 237.
120   Kristan Stoddart, *Losing an Empire and Finding a Role: Britain, the USA, NATO and Nuclear Weapons, 1964–1970* (London: Palgrave Macmillan, 2012), 101.
121   Grove, 'The Case for the RAF', 214.
122   Air Ministry, *The Royal Air Force Manual. Part I – Operations* (Air Publication 1300), 4th Edition. Promulgated by Command of the Air Council (London: Air Ministry, March 1957).
123   AP 1300 (1957), viii.
124   AP 1300 (1957), Chapter XII, 87–97.
125   Ibid., 28.
126   Thomas Redvers, 'Post-Cold War Development of United Kingdom Joint Air Command and Control Capability', *Air & Space Power Journal* 18, no. 4 (Winter 2004): 74.
127   Chris Finn, '"British Thinking on Air Power" – The Evolution of AP3000', *Air Power Review* 12, no. 1 (Spring 2009): 58.
128   Markus Mäder, *In Pursuit of Conceptual Excellence. The Evolution of British Military-Strategic Doctrine in the Post-Cold War Era, 1989–2002* (New York: Peter Lang Publishing, 2004), 109.
129   AP 3003, 239.
130   Ibid., 241.
131   Mason, 'British Air Power', 49.
132   Tony Mason, *British Air Power in the 1980s* (London: Guild Publishing, 1984), 20.
133   Quoted in Mason, 'British Air Power', 50.
134   AP 3000 (1999), 3.12.9.
135   Grove, 'The Case for the RAF', 214.
136   Tony Mason, interview with the author, Cheltenham, 19 June 2013.
137   Finn, 'British Thinking on Air Power', 58.
138   Tony Mason, interview with the author, Cheltenham, 19 June 2013.
139   Tony Mason and E.J. Feuchtwanger, eds., *Air Power in the Next Generation* (London: Macmillan Press, 1979), ix.
140   Neil Cameron, 'Air Power: Thinking about the Future', in *Air Power in the Next generation*, eds. Tony Mason and E.J. Feuchtwanger (London: Macmillan Press, 1979), 1.
141   Mason, 'British Air Power', 22.
142   *Design for Military Operations – The British Military Doctrine*. Prepared under the direction of the Chief of the General Staff (London: HMSO, 1989).
143   Mäder, *In Pursuit of Conceptual Excellence*, 86.
144   Ibid.
145   Ibid., 88–89.
146   Ibid., 161.
147   Ibid.

148 Ibid., 162.
149 Ibid., 154.
150 Redvers, 'Post-Cold War Development', 78.
151 Sebastian Cox and Sebastian Ritchie, 'The Gulf War and UK Air Power Doctrine and Practice', in *Air Power History: Turning Points from Kitty Hawk to Kosovo*, eds. S. Cox and P. Gray (Oxon: Frank Cass, 2002), 288.
152 Andrew Vallance, interview with the author, London, 11 July 2013.
153 Andrew Vallance, '*The Evolution of Air Power Doctrine within the RAF 1957–1987*' (MPhil thesis, the University of Cambridge, 1988).
154 Ibid., 5.
155 Hobkirk Michael, 'The Heseltine Reorganisation of Defence: Kill or Cure?', *The RUSI Journal* 130, no. 1 (1985): 45.
156 Andrew Vallance, 'Air Power Doctrine', *Air Clues* 42, no. 5 (May 1988): 166.
157 Mäder, *In Pursuit of Conceptual Excellence*, 115–116.
158 Andrew Vallance, interview with the author, London, 11 July 2013.
159 *Royal Air Force Air Power Doctrine* (AP 3000). Prepared under the direction of the Chief of the Air Staff (London: HMSO, 1991).
160 Andrew Vallance, interview with the author, London, 11 July 2013.
161 Ibid.
162 AP 3000(1991), foreword.
163 Ibid.
164 Ibid., 5.
165 Ibid., appendix B.
166 Finn, 'British Thinking on Air Power', 62.
167 *Royal Air Force Air Power Doctrine* (AP 3000), 2nd Edition. Prepared under the direction of the Chief of the Air Staff (London: HMSO, 1993).
168 Richard Shultz and Robert Pfaltzgraff, eds., *The Future of Air Power in the Aftermath of the Gulf War* (Alabama: Air University Press, 1992), 10.
169 Mäder, *In Pursuit of Conceptual Excellence,* 117.
170 Thomas Keaney, 'The Linkage of Air and Ground Power in the Future of Conflict', *International Security* 22, no. 2 (Fall 1997): 148.
171 David Callahan, 'Air Power Comes of Age', *Technology Review* 97, no. 6 (August/September 1994): 65.
172 Deptula David and Charles Link, 'Modern Warfare: Desert Strom, Operation Iraqi Freedom and Operation Freedom', *Air Power History* 54, no. 4 (Winter 2007): 39.
173 William Head, 'The Battle for Ra's Al-Khafji and the Effects of Air Power January 29-February 1 Part 1, 1991', *Air Power History* 60, no. 1 (Spring 2013): 5.
174 Bingham Price, 'Air Power in Desert Storm and the Need for Doctrinal Change', *Airpower Journal* 5, no. 4 (Winter 1991): 35.
175 AP 3000 (1993), 71.

176 Sebastian Cox and Sebastian Ritchie, 'The Gulf War and UK Air Power Doctrine and Practice', in *Air Power History: Turning Points from Kitty Hawk to Kosovo*, eds. S. Cox and P. Gray (Oxon: Frank Cass, 2002), 290.
177 Lawrence Freedman and Ephraim Karsh, *The Gulf Conflict, 1990–1991: Diplomacy and War in the New World Order* (Princeton, NJ: Princeton University Press, 1993), 68.
178 Norman Schwarzkopf and Peter Petre, *It Does Not Take a Hero: The Autobiography of General H. Norman Schwarzkopf* (New York: Bantam Books, 1992), 268.
179 AP 3000 (1993), 71.
180 John Olsen, *Strategic Air Power in Desert Storm* (London: Frank Cass, 2003), 129.
181 AP 3000 (1993), 71.
182 Olsen, *Strategic Air Power in Desert Storm*, 155.
183 AP 3000 (1993), 71.
184 Brett Williams, 'Effects-Based Operations: Theory, Application, and the Role of Airpower', in *Transformation Concepts for National Security in the 21st Century*, ed. Williamson Murray (Carlisle: Strategic Studies Institute of the US Army War College, 2002), 134.
185 The first post–Cold War Army PSO doctrine – Wider Peacekeeping was published only in 1995.
186 Andrew Vallance, interview with the author, London, 11 July 2013.
187 Mäder, *In Pursuit of Conceptual Excellence*, 120.
188 Ibid., 121.

Chapter 3

1 Extract from the unpublished (2017) autobiography of Air Chief Marshal Sir Richard Johns, CAS 1997–2000, 262–263.
2 AP 3000 (1999), Acknowledgements.
3 Ibid., Foreword.
4 Ibid.
5 Robert Owen, 'Operation Deliberate Force, 1995', in *A History of Air Warfare*, ed. John Olsen (Washington, DC: Potomac Books, 2009), 209.
6 Ibid., 210.
7 Steven Burg and Paul Shoup, *Ethnic Conflict and International Intervention: Crisis in Bosnia-Herzegovina, 1990–93* (New York: M.E. Sharpe, 2000), 63.
8 Owen, 'Operation Deliberate Force', 214.
9 Paul Szasz, 'Peacekeeping in Operation: A Conflict Study of Bosnia', *Cornell International Law Journal* 28, no. 3 (1995): 691.
10 Mark Bucknam, *Responsibility of Command: How UN and NATO Commanders Influenced Air Power over Bosnia* (AFB: Air University Press, 2003), 44.

11 Daniel Haulman, 'The United States Air Force and Bosnia, 1992–1995', *Air Power History* 60, no. 3 (Fall 2013): 25.
12 Tony Mason, 'Air Power in Peace Support Environment', in *The Dynamics of Air Power*, eds. Andrew Lambert and Arthur C. Williamson (Bracknell: HMSO, 1996), 112.
13 Bruno Simma, 'NATO, the UN and the Use of Force: Legal Aspects', *The European Journal of International Law* 10 (1999): 5.
14 Andrew Lambert, 'Synergy in Operations', in *The Dynamics of Air Power*, eds. Andrew Lambert and Arthur C. Williamson (Bracknell: HMSO, 1996), 40.
15 Ibid., 47.
16 Leighton Smith, 'NATO's IFOR in Action: Lessons from the Bosnian Peace Support Operations', *Strategic Forum*, no. 154 (January 1999): 155.
17 Lim Kok Siong, 'Airpower in Non-Conventional Operations', *Pointer* 30, no. 3 (2004), accessed 13 July 2013, http://www.mindef.gov.sg/imindef/publications/pointer/journals/2004/v30n3/features/feature4.html.
18 Andrew Vallance, interview with the author, London, 11 July 2013.
19 Robert Owen, 'The Balkans Air Campaign Study: Part 2', *Air Power Journal* 11, no. 3 (Fall 1997): 22.
20 Allen Sens, 'Living in a Renovated NATO', *Canadian Military Journal* 1, no. 4 (Winter 2000/2001): 81.
21 Chen Kertcher, 'From Cold War to a System of Peacekeeping Operations: The Discussions on Peacekeeping Operations in the UN during the 1980s up to 1992', *Journal of Contemporary History* 47, no. 3 (July 2012): 628.
22 Both were involved in preparation of Wider Peacekeeping of 1995: Mallinson was the project leader and Dobbie was the primary author.
23 Charles Dobbie, 'A Concept for Post-Cold War Peacekeeping', *Survival* 36, no. 3 (Autumn 1994): 125.
24 Phillip Wilkinson, 'Letters', *The Officer* 10, no. 3 (May/June 1998): 3.
25 Ibid., 4.
26 Richard Connaughton, 'Quo Vadis?', *The Officer* 10, no. 2 (March/April 1998): 30.
27 Connaughton, 'Quo Vadis?', 31.
28 Allan Mallinson, 'Wider Peacekeeping: An option of Difficulties', *British Army Review* 112 (April 1996): 5.
29 Ibid., 6.
30 Mäder, *In Pursuit of Conceptual Excellence*, 152.
31 Lambert, 'Synergy in Operations', 66.
32 Philip Sabin, 'Peace Support Operations: A strategic Perspective', in *The Dynamics of Air Power*, eds. Andrew Lambert and Arthur C. Williamson (Bracknell: HMSO, 1996), 110.
33 Ibid., 111.

34 Tony Mason, 'Air Power in the Peace Support Environment', in *The Dynamics of Air Power*, eds. Andrew Lambert and Arthur C. Williamson (Bracknell: HMSO, 1996), 118.
35 Ibid.
36 Andrew Lambert, 'The Reconnaissance and Surveillance Task in Peace Support Operations', in *The Dynamics of Air Power*, eds. Andrew Lambert and Arthur C. Williamson (Bracknell: HMSO, 1996), 144–145.
37 Gordon Wooley, 'Air Transport in Peace Support Operations', in *The Dynamics of Air Power*, eds. Andrew Lambert and Arthur C. Williamson (Bracknell: HMSO, 1996), 146–147.
38 Stuart Griffin, *Understanding Peacekeeping*, 2nd Edition (Cambridge: Polity Press, 2010), 203.
39 Mäder, *In Pursuit of Conceptual Excellence*, 211.
40 Rod Thornton, 'The Role of Peace Support Operations Doctrine in the British Army', *International Peacekeeping* 7, no. 2 (Summer 2000): 58.
41 AP 3000 (1999), 1.1.5–1.1.7.
42 Ibid., 1.1.7–1.1.10.
43 *Peace Support Operations* (Joint Warfare Publication 3–50) (London: MOD, 1998).
44 AP 3000 (1999), 1.1.9.
45 Ibid.
46 Ibid.
47 Tony Mason, interview with the author, Cheltenham, 19 June 2013.
48 Andrew Vallance, interview with the author, London, 11 July 2013.
49 Ibid.
50 Barry Watts, 'Doctrine, Technology and Air Warfare', in *Air Power Confronts an Unstable World*, ed. Richard Hallion (London: Brassey, 1997), 19.
51 Phil Meilinger, email exchange with the author, 29 July 2013.
52 Stephen Fought and Scott Key, 'Airpower, Jointness, and Transformation', *Air & Space Power Journal* 17, no. 4 (Winter 2003): 45.
53 Now the School of Advanced Air and Space Studies.
54 Phil Meilinger, email exchange with the author, 29 July 2013.
55 Ibid.
56 Tony Mason, interview with the author, Cheltenham, 19 June 2013.
57 Peter Gray, interview with the author, Birmingham, 18 June 2013.
58 Laurence Baxter, 'NATO and Regional Peace Support Operations', *Peacekeeping & International Relations* 25, no. 6 (November/December 1996): 7.
59 Robert Cassidy, *Peacekeeping in the Abyss: British and American Peacekeeping Doctrine and Practice after the Cold War* (Westport: Praeger, 2004), 184.
60 Steve Chisnall, 'Why Defence Reviews Do Not Deliver', *Political Quarterly* 81, no. 3 (July 2010): 420.

61 Chisnall, 'Why Defence Reviews', 421.
62 Clair Taylor, *A Brief Guide to Previous British Defence Reviews*. Standard Note SN/IA/5714 (London: House of Commons Library, 19 October 2010), 9.
63 Chris Finn, interview with the author, RAF College Cranwell, 7 November 2013.
64 Christopher Coker, 'Britain's Defence Options', *The World Today* 48, no. 4 (April 1992): 73.
65 Lawrence Freedman, *The Politics of British Defence* (Basingstoke: Macmillan, 1999), 96.
66 Ministry of Defence, *Strategic Defence Review*. Presented to Parliament by the Secretary of State for Defence (London: HMSO, July 1998), intro, 5.
67 SDR, 29.
68 AP 3000 (1999), 1.3.2.
69 SDR, 31–32.
70 Ibid., 144.
71 Robert Grattan, *Strategic Review: The Process of Strategy Formulation in Complex Organisations* (London: Routledge, 2011), 92.
72 SDR, 36.
73 Ibid., 60.
74 Ibid.
75 Colin McInnes, 'Labour's Strategic Defence Review', *International Affairs* 74, no. 4 (1998): 831.
76 *New Labour because Britain deserves better*. Labour Party Manifesto 1997, accessed 15 May 2013, http://www.labour-party.org.uk/manifestos/1997/1997-labour-manifesto.shtml.
77 Extract from the unpublished (2017) autobiography of Air Chief Marshal Sir Richard Johns, CAS 1997–2000, 262–263.
78 Ibid.
79 Phil Meilinger, email exchange with the author, 29th of July 2013.
80 Ibid.
81 Ibid.
82 AP 3000 (1999), Introduction.
83 Ibid., 1.2.2.
84 Ibid.
85 AP 3000 (1993), 13.
86 AP 3000 (1999), 1.2.13.
87 JWP 0–01 (2001), 3–5.
88 Ibid.
89 AP 3000 (1999), 1.2.13.
90 Ibid.
91 Ibid., 1.2.17.
92 Ibid.

93   Ibid., 1.3.7–1.3.10.
94   Ibid., 2.4.1–2.4.14.
95   Ibid., 2.4.1.
96   Ibid., 2.5.1.
97   Ibid.
98   Ibid., 2.5.5.
99   Ibid., 2.5.6.
100 Peter Gray, interview with the author, Birmingham, 18 June 2013.
101 AP 3000 (1999), 2.6.1.
102 Ibid., 2.6.1.
103 Ibid., 2.6.6.
104 Ibid., 2.6.9.
105 Ibid., 2.6.10.
106 Ibid., 2.7.6–2.7.17.
107 Ibid., 2.8.1.
108 Ibid., 2.4.4.
109 Ibid., 2.5.7.
110 Ibid., 2.7.15.
111 Susan Willett, *Eurofighter 2000* (London: Brassey's, 1994), 15.
112 AP 3000 (1999), 2.5.12.
113 Ibid., 1.3.10.
114 Ibid., 3.11.3.
115 Ibid., 2.6.7.

Chapter 4

1   Daddow, 'British Military Doctrine 1980–90s', 107.
2   Alistair Byford, interview with the author, Shrivenham, 11 September 2013.
3   Andrew Vallance, interview with the author, London, 11 July 2013.
4   K.S. Balshaw, 'Spending Treasure Today but Spilling Blood Tomorrow: What Are the Implications for Britain of America's Apparent Aversion to Casualties', *Defence Studies* 1, no. 1 (Spring 2001): 103.
5   Mark Smith, 'The Kosovo Conflict: U.S. Diplomacy and Western Public Opinion', *CPD Perspectives on Public Diplomacy* paper 3 (Los Angeles, CA: Figueroa Press, 2009), 5.
6   'Intervention in Syria: Britain Will Not Fight', *The Economist*, 30 August 2013, accessed 20 April 2013, http://www.economist.com/blogs/blighty/2013/08/intervention-syria.
7   David Schorr and T.K. Kerney, 'New Technologies and War-Fighting Capabilities', *Airpower Journal* 10, no. 3 (Fall 1996): 112.

8   Tony Mason, interview with the author, Cheltenham, 19 June 2013.
9   Peter Gray, interview with the author, Birmingham, 18 June 2013.
10 Colin McInnes, 'Labour's Strategic Defence Review', *International Affairs* 74, no. 4 (1998): 838.
11 Andrew Lambert and Arthur C. Williamson, eds., *The Dynamics of Air Power* (Bracknell: HMSO, 1996), foreword, iii.
12 Ibid.
13 Stuart Peach, eds., *Perspectives on Air Power* (London: HMSO, 1998).
14 Philip Towle, 'The Distinctive Characteristics of Air Power', in *The Dynamics of Air Power*, eds. A. Lambert and A.C. Williamson (Bracknell: HMSO, 1996), 3–18.
15 Philip Sabin, 'The Counter-Air Contest', in *The Dynamics of Air Power*, eds. A. Lambert and A.C. Williamson (Bracknell: HMSO, 1996), 18–39.
16 Andrew Lambert, 'Synergy in Operations', in *The Dynamics of Air Power*, eds. A. Lambert and A.C. Williamson (Bracknell: HMSO, 1996), 40–66.
17 Michael Clarke, 'Air Power, Force and Coercion', in *The Dynamics of Air Power*, eds. A. Lambert and A.C. Williamson (Bracknell: HMSO, 1996), 67–85.
18 Mike Bratby, 'Air Power and the Role of the Media', in *The Dynamics of Air Power*, eds. A. Lambert and A.C. Williamson (Bracknell: HMSO, 1996), 86–104.
19 Philip Sabin, 'Peace Support Operations – A Strategic Perspective', in *The Dynamics of Air Power*, eds. A. Lambert and A.C. Williamson (Bracknell: HMSO, 1996):, 105–111.
20 Tony Mason, 'Air Power in the Peace Support Environment', in *The Dynamics of Air Power*, eds. A. Lambert and A.C. Williamson (Bracknell: HMSO, 1996), 112–125.
21 Mike Bratby, 'Peace Support Operations – Support Requirements', in *The Dynamics of Air Power*, eds. A. Lambert and A.C. Williamson (Bracknell: HMSO, 1996), 126–132.
22 Andrew Lambert, 'The Reconnaissance and Surveillance Task in Peace Support Operations', in *The Dynamics of Air Power*, eds. A. Lambert and A.C. Williamson (Bracknell: HMSO, 1996), 133–146.
23 Gordon Woolley, 'Air Transport in Peace Support Operations', in *The Dynamics of Air Power*, eds. A. Lambert and A.C. Williamson (Bracknell: HMSO, 1996), 146–156.
24 Philip Sabin, 'The Counter-Air Mission in Peace Support Operations', in *The Dynamics of Air Power*, eds. A. Lambert and A.C. Williamson (Bracknell: HMSO, 1996), 157–172.
25 Michael Clarke, 'Air Power and Force in Peace Support Operations', in *The Dynamics of Air Power*, eds. A. Lambert and A.C. Williamson (Bracknell: HMSO, 1996), 173–185.
26 Peach, *Perspectives on Air Power*, foreword, iv.
27 Ibid., general introduction, xi.
28 Ibid., xi.

29 AP 3000 (1999), 1.1.3–1.1.4.
30 Ibid., 1.1.3.
31 Andrew Vallance, interview with the author, London, 11 July 2013.
32 Chris Finn, 'British Thinking on Air Power' – The Evolution of AP 3000,' *Air Power Review* 12, no. 1 (Spring 2009), 59.
33 AP 3000 (1991), foreword.
34 AP 3000 (1993), foreword.
35 Ibid.
36 In this context, American counterparts like Phil Meilinger and John Warden.
37 Andrew Vallance, interview with the author, London, 11 July 2013.
38 Quoted in Finn, 'British Thinking on Air Power', 60.
39 Ibid., 60–61.
40 Ibid., 61.
41 Ibid.
42 Extract from the unpublished (2017) autobiography of Air Chief Marshal Sir Richard Johns, CAS 1997–2000, 263.
43 'Vice Chief of the Defence Staff. Stuart Peach. Biography', accessed 2 April 2013, https://www.gov.uk/government/people/stuart-peach.
44 Peach, *Perspectives on Air Power*, general introduction, xi.
45 Extract from the unpublished (2017) autobiography of Air Chief Marshal Sir Richard Johns, CAS 1997–2000, 263.
46 Finn, 'British Thinking on Air Power', 61.
47 Ibid.
48 Ibid.

Chapter 5

1 *British Air and Space Power Doctrine* (AP 3000), 4th Edition. Prepared under the direction of Chief of the Air Staff (Shrivenham: Air Staff/MOD, 2009).
2 AP 3000 (2009), 5.
3 *Air and Space Warfare* (AP 3002), 2nd Edition. Prepared under the direction of Air Warfare Centre Commandant (RAF Waddington: Air Warfare Centre, 2006).
4 *A Brief History of the Royal Air Force* (AP 3003) (London: HMSO, 2005).
5 AP 3002, foreword, iv–v.
6 AP 3003, foreword, i.
7 Chris Finn, interview with the author, Cranwell, 7 November 2013.
8 Finn, 'British Thinking on Air Power', 62.
9 Chris Finn, interview with the author, Cranwell, 7 November 2013.
10 Ibid.

11 Ibid.
12 Ibid.
13 Finn, 'British Thinking on Air Power', 62.
14 Chris Finn, interview with the author, Cranwell, 7 November 2013.
15 Alexander Alderson, '"The Army Brain": A Historical Perspective on Doctrine, Development and the Challenges of Future Conflict', *The RUSI Journal* 155, no. 3 (June 2010), 14.
16 Finn, 'British Thinking on Air Power', 63.
17 Ibid.
18 Chris Finn, interview with the author, Cranwell, 7 November 2013.
19 Stuart Griffin, 'Iraq, Afghanistan and the Future of British Military Doctrine: From Counterinsurgency to Stabilization', *International Affairs* 87, no. 2 (March 2011): 323.
20 House of Commons Defence Committee, *Lessons of Kosovo*. Fourteenth Report of Session 1999–2000 (London: HMSO, 23 October 2000), para 130.
21 Mason, 'British Air Power', 57.
22 Wesley Clark, *Waging Contemporary War: Bosnia, Kosovo, and the Future of Combat* (New York: Public Affairs, 2001), 35.
23 Goldie Haun, 'A-10 FACs over Kosovo', *Air Power Review* 6, no. 1 (Spring 2003): 86.
24 Clark, *Waging Contemporary War*, 169.
25 John Lampe, 'The Lessons of Bosnia and Kosovo for Iraq', *Current History* 103, no. 671 (March 2004): 115.
26 HCDC, *Lessons of Kosovo*. Fourteenth Report of Session 1999–2000. London: HMSO, 23 October 2000, para 135.
27 Mason, 'British Air Power', 58.
28 Benjamin Lambeth, *NATO's Air War for Kosovo: A Strategic and Operational Assessment (Project Air Force Series on Operation Allied Force)* (Washington, DC: RAND, 2001), 15.
29 Mason, 'British Air Power', 57.
30 Lambeth, *NATO's Air War for Kosovo*, 12.
31 Michael Elliot and Michael Hirsh, 'Learning the Lessons of Kosovo', *Newsweek* 134, no. 24 (December 1999–February 2000): 25.
32 Lambeth, *NATO's Air War for Kosovo*, 13.
33 Peter Dye, 'The European Rapid Reaction Force: The Contribution of Aviation Logistics', *Air Power Review* 6, no. 1 (Spring 2003): 18.
34 Mason, 'British Air Power', 58.
35 Mark Oakes and Tim Youngs, Operation Enduring Freedom and the Conflict in Afghanistan: An update (House of Commons Library Research paper 01/81) 31 October 2001, 26.
36 Ibid.
37 Mason, 'British Air Power', 59.

38 HCDC, *Operations in Afghanistan*. Fourth Report of Session 2010–12 (London: HMSO, July 2011), 18.
39 Ben Clements, 'Public Opinion and Military Intervention: Afghanistan, Iraq and Libya', *Political Quarterly* 84, no. 1 (January 2013): 121.
40 Charles Haddon, *The Nimrod Review*, Report for the House of Commons (London: HMSO, 2009).
41 HCDC, *Lessons of Iraq*, Third Report of Session 2003–04, Volume 1 Report, together with formal minutes (London: HMSO, 3 March 2004), para 61.
42 Alistair Byford, interview with the author, Shrivenham, 11 September 2013.
43 *Operation TELIC – United Kingdom Military Operations in Iraq*. Report prepared by the Comptroller and Auditor General for House of Commons 60 session 2003–2004 (London: HMSO, 2003), 1.
44 HCDC, *Lessons of Iraq*, 59.
45 Ibid.
46 Benjamin Lambeth, *The Unseen War: Allied Air Power and the Takedown of Saddam Hussein* (Annapolis: Naval Institute Press, 2013), 161.
47 HCDC, *Lessons of Iraq*, 60.
48 A long-range stand-off air launch missile developed to attack infrastructure and hardened targets.
49 Lambeth, *The Unseen War*, 155.
50 Ibid., 165.
51 HCDC, *Lessons of Iraq*, 61.
52 AP 3000 (2009), 8.
53 Ibid.
54 B. Kazaryan, 'Operations, Combat Actions, and Network-Centric Warfare', *Military Thought* 19, no. 1 (2010): 85.
55 JDP 0–01 (2008), 4–11.
56 AP 3000 (2009), 28.
57 Ibid., 30.
58 Ibid., 43.
59 Ibid., 44.
60 Ibid., 45.
61 Ibid., 47.
62 Ibid., 17.
63 Ibid., 38.
64 Ibid., 47.
65 Ibid., 51.
66 Ibid., 63.
67 Ibid., 16–17.
68 Ibid., 47.
69 Ibid., 55.

70 Michael Fiszer and Jerzy Gruszczynski, 'RAF Flying into the Future', *Journal of Electronic Defence* 26, no. 8 (August 2003): 33.
71 Ministry of Defence, *The Strategic Defence Review: A New Chapter*. Presented to Parliament by the Secretary of State for Defence (London: HMSO, July 2002).
72 Ibid., 15.
73 Ministry of Defence, *Delivering Security in a Changing World. Defence White Paper*. Presented to Parliament by the Secretary of State for Defence (London: HMSO, December 2003), 3; Foreign and Commonwealth Office, *UK International Priorities: A Strategy for the FCO*. Presented to Parliament by the Secretary of State for Foreign & Commonwealth Affairs (London: HMSO, 2003), 14.
74 MOD, *Delivering Security in a Changing World*, 7.
75 Ibid., 11.
76 HCDC, *Defence White Paper 2003, Fifth Report of Session 2003–04, Volume I* (London: HMSO, 23 June 2004), 44.
77 HCDC, *The Comprehensive Approach: The Point of War Is Not Joust to Win but to Make a Better Peace*. Seventh Report of Session 2009-10 (London: HMSO, March 2010), 9.
78 *The Comprehensive Approach*, Joint Discussion Note 4/05. Promulgated as directed by the Chiefs of Staff (Shrivenham: JDCC, 2006), 1–2.
79 JDN 4/05, 1–15.
80 AP 3000 (2009), 5.
81 Ibid., 7.
82 AP 3000 (2009), 8.
83 Ibid., 14.
84 AP 3000 (1999), 1.2.1.
85 Tony Mason, interview with the author, Cheltenham, 19 June 2013.
86 AP 3000 (1999), 1.2.2.; and AP 3000 (2009), 15.
87 AP 3000 (2009), 24.
88 Ibid., 25.
89 Ibid., 25–26.
90 Ibid., 28.
91 AP 3000 (2009), 30.
92 Ibid.
93 Ibid., 32.
94 Ibid.
95 Andrew Dorman, 'Making 2+2=5: The 2010 Strategic Defence and Security Review', *Defense & Security Analysis* 27, no. 1 (March 2011): 79.
96 AP 3000 (2009), 40.
97 Ibid., 40–41.
98 Ibid., 41–42.
99 Ibid., 46.

100 Ibid., 47.
101 Ibid., 50.
102 Ibid.
103 Ibid., 54–55.
104 The current equivalent of the term is cyberspace, but, at that time, the broader term 'information environment' was used.
105 Ibid., 56.
106 Peter Gray, ed., *Air Power 21: Challenges for the New Century* (London: HMSO, 2000).
107 Mungo Melvin, 'Air Power and Expeditionary Warfare', in *Air Power 21: Challenges for the New Century*, ed. Peter Gray (London: HMSO, 2000), 153–182.
108 Finn, 'British Thinking on Air Power', 62.
109 Peter Gray, ed., *British Air Power* (London: HMSO, 2003).
110 Finn, 'British Thinking on Air Power', 62.
111 Alistair Byford, interview with the author, Shrivenham, 11 September 2013.
112 Ibid.
113 Ibid.
114 Alistair Byford, interview with the author, London, 22 June 2017.
115 Ibid.
116 Ibid.
117 Alistair Byford, interview with the author, London, 22 June 2017.
118 Chris Finn, interview with the author, RAF College Cranwell, 7 November 2013.

Chapter 6

1 DCDC, *UK Air and Space Doctrine* (Joint Doctrine Publication 0-30). Prepared under the direction of the Joint Forces Commander and Chiefs of Staff (Shrivenham: DCDC, July 2013).
2 JDP 0-30, vii.
3 Ibid., v.
4 Ibid., vi.
5 Ibid.
6 *Future Air and Space Operating Concept* (Joint Concept Note 3/12). Prepared under the direction of the Joint Force Commander and Chiefs of Staff (Shrivenham: DCDC, September 2012).
7 JDP 0-30, vii.
8 *Allied Joint Doctrine for Air and Space Operations (AJP – 3.3 (A))*. Promulgated by the Director of NATO Standardization Agency (Brussels: NATO Standardization Agency, November 2009).

9   JDP 0–30, viii.
10 Ibid.
11 HCDC, *Operations in Libya*, Ninth Report of Session 2010–12. Volume 1. Report together with formal minutes (London: HMSO, February 2012), para 96.
12 Ibid, para 102.
13 'RAF Typhoons patrol Libyan no-fly zone', last modified 22 March 2011, https://www.gov.uk/government/news/raf-typhoons-patrol-libyan-no-fly-zone.
14 HCDC, *Operations in Libya,* para 103.
15 Ibid., para 96.
16 U.S. Army Command and General Staff College, *NATO's Air War in Libya: A Template for Future American Operations* (Damascus: Penny Hill Press, 2014), 32.
17 Bruno Prommier, 'The Use of Force to Protect Civilians and Humanitarian Action: The Case of Libya and Beyond', *International Review of the Red Cross* 93, no. 884 (December 2011): 1064.
18 Steven Rose, 'Moving Forward with the Responsibility to Protect: Using Political Inertia to Protect Civilians', *Boston College International & Comparative Law Review* 37, no. 1 (Winter 2014): 223.
19 HCDC, *Operations in Libya*, para 107.
20 Ibid, para 97.
21 Ibid.
22 Christina Goulter, 'The British Experience: Operation Ellamy', in *Precision and Purpose: Airpower in the Libyan Civil War*, ed. K. Mueller (Santa Monica: RAND, 2015), 168.
23 Ibid.
24 Cabinet Office, *Securing Britain in an Age of Uncertainty: The Strategic Defence and Security Review*. Presented to Parliament by the Prime Minister (London: HMSO, October 2010), 27.
25 Ibid.
26 HCDC, *Operations in Libya*, para 108.
27 U.S. Army Command and General Staff College, *NATO's Air War in Libya,* 16.
28 Andrea Gilli, 'Procurement Lessons from the War in Libya', *RUSI Defence System* (Autumn/Winter 2012): 25.
29 Bill Sharon, *Risk Management in an Uncertain World: Strategies for Crisis Management* (London: Bloomsbury, 2012), 75.
30 Goulter, 'The British Experience: Operation Ellamy', 161.
31 Ibid., 162.
32 Rupert Smith, *The Utility of Force: The Art of War in the Modern World* (New York: Allen Lane, 2005), 18.
33 Michael John-Hopkins, 'Regulating the Conduct of Urban Warfare: Lessons from Contemporary Asymmetric Armed Conflict', *International Review of the Red Cross* 92, no. 878 (June 2010): 473.

34 Ian Black, 'Gaddafi-Controlled Media Wages Propaganda War', *The Guardian*, 17 March 2011, accessed 18 February 2014, http://www.theguardian.com/world/2011/mar/17/gaddafi-controlled-media-propaganda-war-libya.
35 JDP 0–30, 3–10.
36 Ibid., 3–13.
37 Ibid., 3–12.
38 Ibid.
39 Ibid., 2–7.
40 Ibid.
41 Ibid., 3–30.
42 Ibid., 3–31.
43 Metin Gurcan, 'Drone Warfare and Contemporary Strategy Making: Does the Tail Wag the Dog?' *Dynamics of Asymmetric Conflict* 6, no. 1–3 (October 2013): 159.
44 Samuel Issacharoff and Richard Pildes, 'Targeted Warfare: Individuating Enemy Responsibility', *New York University Law Review* 88, no. 5 (November 2013): 1525.
45 JDP 0–30, 2–9.
46 Ibid.
47 Caroline Holmqvist, 'Undoing War: War Ontologies and the Materiality of Drone War', *Millennium* 41, no. 3 (June 2013): 535–552; Paul Kahn, 'Imagining Warfare', *European Journal of International Law* 24, no. 1 (February 2013): 199–226; Samuel Moyn, 'Drones and Imagination: A Response to Paul Kahn', *European Journal of International Law* 24, no. 1 (February 2013): 227–233; Michael Boyle, 'The Costs and Consequences of Drone Warfare', *International Affairs* 89, no. 1 (January 2013): 1–29.
48 JDP 0–30, 2–8.
49 Christian Anrig, 'Allied Air Power over Libya: A Preliminary Assessment', *Air and Space Power Journal* 25, no. 4 (Winter 2011): 95.
50 JDP 0–30, 1–3.
51 Paul Cornish and Andrew Dorman, 'National Defence in the Age of Austerity', *International Affairs* 85, no. 4 (July 2009): 738.
52 Robert Wall, 'Austerity's Aftermath', *Aviation Week & Space Technology* 173, no. 4 (2011): 36.
53 JDP 0–30, 1–4.
54 Ibid., 3–14.
55 David Alberts et al., *Understanding Information Age Warfare* (Vienna: CCRP Publications, 2001), 42.
56 JDP 0–30, 3–7.
57 Ibid.
58 Ibid., 3–9.
59 Ibid., 1–8.
60 Ibid., 2–4.

61 Ibid., 3–11.
62 Ibid., 3–28.
63 Ibid., 4–9.
64 Ibid., 7–13.
65 Douglas Barrie, 'Recuperative Route', *Aviation Week & Space Technology* 171, no. 20 (2009): 36.
66 Robert Dover and Mark Phythian, 'The Politics of the Strategic Defence and Security Review: Centralisation and Cuts', *Political Quarterly* 83, no. 1 (January–March 2012): 170.
67 Cabinet Office, *Securing Britain in an Age of Uncertainty*, 17–18.
68 Ibid., 32.
69 Ibid., 25.
70 Ibid., 26.
71 Andrew Dorman, 'Providing for Defence in an Age of Austerity: Future War, Defence Cuts and the 2010 Strategic (Security and) Defence (and Security) Review', *Political Quarterly* 81, no. 3 (July 2010): 376–384; Steve Chisnall, 'Why Defence Reviews Do Not Deliver,' *Political Quarterly* 81, no. 3 (July 2010): 420–423; Paul Cornish and Andrew Dorman, 'Breaking the Mould: The United Kingdom Strategic Defence Review 2010', *International Affairs* 86, no. 2 (March 2010): 395–410; Nick Ritchie, 'Rethinking Security: A Critical Analysis of the Strategic Defence and Security Review', *International Affairs* 87, no. 2 (March 2011): 355–376; John Kiszely, 'What Does the Military Want from the Strategic Defence Review?' *Political Quarterly* 81, no. 3 (July 2010): 434–437.
72 MOD, *National Security through Technology: Technology, Equipment, and Support for UK Defence and Security*. Presented to Parliament by the Secretary of State for Defence (London: HMSO, February 2012).
73 'The Open Procurement principle is wherever possible, we (MOD) will seek to fulfill the UK's defence and security requirements through open completion in the domestic and global market' (MOD, *National Security through Technology*, 13).
74 MOD, *National Security through Technology*, 13.
75 NATO, *Active Engagement, Modern Defence*. Strategic Concept 2010, 19 November 2010, accessed 15 February 2014, http://www.nato.int/cps/en/natolive/topics_82705.htm..
76 *Developing Joint Doctrine Handbook*, 4th Edition. Prepared under the direction of the Joint Forces Commander and Chiefs of Staff (Shrivenham: DCDC, November 2013), 1–4.
77 DCDC, *Developing Joint Doctrine Handbook*, 1–7.
78 Alistair Byford, interview with the author, Shrivenham, 11 September 2013.
79 NATO, *Active Engagement, Modern Defence*.

80 NATO Standardization Agency, *Allied Joint Doctrine* (AJP - 01 (D)). Promulgated by the Director of NATO Standardization Agency (Brussels: NATO Standardization Agency, December 2010), 1–1.
81 DCDC, *Developing Joint Doctrine Handbook*, 1–4.
82 Ibid.
83 Ibid., 1–5.
84 Ibid.
85 Ibid., 1–7.
86 J1-J9 are recognized military branches: J1 – personnel; J2 – intelligence; J3 – operations; J4 – logistis; J5 – plans, J6 – communications and information technology; J7 – training; J8 – resource management; J9 – civil military cooperation.
87 DCDC, *Developing Joint Doctrine Handbook*, 1–7.
88 Alexander Wathen, 'Revised USAF Doctrine Publication: Air Force Doctrine Document 2–1.7, Airspace Control in the Combat Zone', *Air & Space Power Journal* 21, no. 1 (Spring 2007): 48.
89 *Unmanned Aircraft Systems: Terminology, Definition and Classification* (Joint Doctrinal Note 3/10). Promulgated under the direction of the Chiefs of Staff (Shrivenham: DCDC, May 2010).
90 *The UK Approach to Unmanned Aircraft Systems* (Joint Doctrinal Note 2/11). Promulgated under the direction of the Chiefs of Staff (Shrivenham: DCDC, March 2011).
91 *Future of Air and Space Operating Concept* (Joint Concept Note 3/12).
92 Chris Finn, interview with the author, Cranwell, 7 November 2013.
93 JDP 0–30, 2–6.
94 Ibid.
95 Ibid.
96 Ibid., 2–7.
97 Ibid., 3–35.
98 Ibid.
99 Ibid.
100 Lambeth, *The Unseen War*, 183.
101 Ibid., 184.
102 Iain McNicoll, 'Effects Based Air Operations: Air Command and Control and the Nature of the Emerging Battlespace', *RUSI Journal* 148, no. 3 (June 2003): 38–44.
103 JDP 0–30, 3–6.
104 Ibid., 3–20.
105 *NATO Glossary of Terms and Definitions* (AAP-06) (Brussels: NATO Standardization Agency, 2013).
106 JDP 0–30, 3–4.

107 *NATO's Future Joint Air and Space Power (NFJASP)* (Kalkar: The Joint Air Power Competence Centre, April 2008).
108 JDP 0–30, Conclusion-2.
109 DCDC, *Developing Joint Doctrine Handbook*, 2–15.
110 Ibid., 2–22.
111 JDP0–30, 1–1.
112 DCDC, *Developing Joint Doctrine Handbook*, 2–22.
113 JDP 0–30, lexicon 2.
114 Ibid., lexicon 5.
115 DCDC, *Developing Joint Doctrine Handbook*, 3–2.
116 Alistair Byford, interview with the author, Shrivenham, 11 September 2013.
117 Ibid.
118 Ibid.
119 DCDC, *Developing Joint Doctrine Handbook*, 2B-1.
120 Ibid., 2B-2.
121 Ibid.
122 Alistair Byford, interview with the author, London, 22 June 2017.
123 Ibid.
124 Alistair Byford, interview with the author, London, 22 June 2017.
125 DCDC, *Developing Joint Doctrine Handbook*, 2B-2.
126 Ibid., 2–9.
127 Ibid., 2–10.
128 Alistair Byford, interview with the author, London, 22 June 2017.
129 Ibid.
130 Alistair Byford, interview with the author, Shrivenham, 11 September 2013.
131 Ibid.
132 Ibid.

Chapter 7

1 Harald Høiback, 'The Anatomy of Doctrine and Ways to Keep It Fit', *Journal of Strategic Studies* 39, no. 2 (2016): 190.
2 Olof Krovall and Magnus Petersson, 'Doctrine and Defence Transformation in Norway and Sweden', *Journal of Strategic Studies* 39, no. 2 (2016): 280-296.
3 Ibid.
4 Ibid.
5 DCDC, *Future Air and Space Operating Concept* (Joint Concept Note 3/12). Prepared under the direction of the Joint Force Commander and Chiefs of Staff (Shrivenham: DCDC, September 2012).

6   Alistair Byford, interview with the author, London, 22 June 2017.
7   Ibid.
8   Howard Wheeldon, 'Thinking to Win – The RAF's New Leadership Strategy', accessed 26 July 2017, https://www.aerosociety.com/news/thinking-to-win-the-rafs-new-leadership-strategy/.
9   Chris Argyris and Donald Schön, *Organizational Learning II: Theory, Method, and Practice* (New York: Addison-Wesley, 1996).
10 Krovall and Petersson, 'Doctrine and Defence Transformation', 280–296.
11 Argyris and Schön, *Organizational Learning*, 22.
12 Krovall and Petersson, 'Doctrine and Defence Transformation', 284–285.
13 Ibid., 285.
14 Tony Mason, 'Innovation and the Military Mind', *Air University Review* 37, no. 2 (January–February 1986): 39–44.
15 Ibid., 41.
16 Paul Wilkins, 'Conceptualising the Conceptual Component': One Airman's Perspective,' *Air Power Review* 18, no. 1 (2015): 10–29.
17 Paul O'Neill, 'Delivering Flexibility through People: Harnessing Human Capability', *Air Power Review* 18, no. 1 (2015): 66–89.
18 Paul O'Neill, 'Developing a Flexible Royal Air Force for an Age of Uncertainty', *Air Power Review* 18, no. 1 (2015): 46–65.
19 Stephen Badsey, *The Media and International Security* (London: Routledge, 2013).
20 Dan Brown, 'Revitalising the Conceptual Component: Addressing Britain's Future Strategic Challenge', *Air Power Review* 18, no. 1 (2015): 31.
21 Alan Vick, *Proclaiming Airpower: Air Force Narratives and American Public Opinion from 1917 to 2014* (Santa Monica: RAND Corporation, 2015).
22 Ibid., xiii.
23 Ibid., xv–xvi.
24 Ibid.
25 Ibid.
26 O'Neill, 'Delivering Flexibility through People', 68.
27 Thomas Klikauer, 'What Is Managerialism?', *Critical Sociology* 41, no. 7–8 (2015): 1103–1119.
28 Quoted in Fred Kaplan, *The Insurgents: David Petraeus and the Plot to Change the American Way of War* (New York: Simon & Schuster, 2013), 6.
29 RAF, *Thinking to Win*. Innovation Strategy 2015, accessed 26 July 2017, https://www.raf.mod.uk/rafcms/mediafiles/28DBDA58_5056_A318_A8AA043B147E9F02.pdf, 3.
30 Andrew Pulford, 'Thinking to Win' (speech, London, 17 September 2015), *GovUK*, https://www.gov.uk/government/speeches/thinking-to-win.
31 Ibid.
32 Mason, 'Innovation and the Military Mind', 39.

33 Howard Wheeldon, 'Thinking to Win – The RAF's New Leadership Strategy', accessed July 26, 2017, https://www.aerosociety.com/news/thinking-to-win-the-rafs-new-leadership-strategy/.
34 Pulford, 'Thinking to Win'.
35 Sibylle Scheipers, *Heroism & The Changing Character of War: Toward Post-Heroic Warfare* (New York: Springer, 2014).
36 RAF, *Thinking to Win*, 5.
37 Details of the event https://www.aerosociety.com/events-calendar/air-power-now-and-the-future-1/.

Bibliography

Primary Sources

Interviews

Byford, Alistair. Air Commodore, Director Advanced Command and Staff course/ Assistant Commandant (Air), Shrivenham, 11 September 2013.
Byford, Alistair. Air Commodore (Retired), London, 22 June 2017.
Finn, Chris. Group Captain (Retired), RAF College Cranwell, 7 November 2013.
Gray, Peter. Air Commodore (Retired), University of Birmingham, 18 June 2013.
Mason, Tony. Air Vice-Marshal (Retired), Cheltenham Spa, 19 June 2013.
Meilinger, Phil. USAF Colonel (Retired), email exchange, 29 July 2013.
Vallance, Andrew. Air Vice-Marshall, the Ministry of Defence, London, 11 July 2013.

Official doctrine publications

A Brief History of the Royal Air Force (AP 3003). London: HMSO, 2005.
Air and Space Warfare (AP 3002), 2nd Edition. Prepared under the direction of Air Warfare Centre Commandant. RAF Waddington: Air Warfare Centre, 2006.
Allied Joint Doctrine, AJP - 01 (D). Promulgated by the Director of NATO Standardization Agency. Brussels: NATO Standardization Agency, December 2010.
Allied Joint Doctrine Development AAP-47 (A). Supplement to AAP-3(J). Promulgated by the Director of NATO Standardization Agency. Brussels: NATO Standardization Agency, September 2011.
Allied Joint Doctrine for Air and Space Operations (AJP - 3.3 (A)). Promulgated by the Director of NATO Standardization Agency. Brussels: NATO Standardization Agency, November 2009.
Allied Joint Doctrine for Counter-Air (AJP-3.3.1). Promulgated by the Director of NATO Standardization Agency. Brussels: NATO Standardization Agency, July 2010.
Allied Joint Doctrine for Land Operations (AJP-3.2). Promulgated by the Director of NATO Standardization Agency. Brussels: NATO Standardization Agency, October 2009.
British Air Power Doctrine (AP 3000), 3rd Edition. Prepared under the direction of the Chief of the Air Staff. London: TSO, 1999.

British Air and Space Power Doctrine (AP 3000), 4th Edition. Prepared under the direction of Chief of the Air Staff. Shrivenham: Air Staff/MOD, 2009.

British Defence Doctrine (Joint Warfare Publication 0-01), 2nd Edition. Prepared under the direction of the Director General Joint Doctrine and Concepts on behalf of the Chiefs of Staff. Shrivenham: JDCC/MOD, 2001.

British Defence Doctrine (Joint Doctrine Publication 0-01), 3rd Edition. Promulgated by the Chief of the Defence Staff. Shrivenham: DCDC/MOD, 2008.

British Defence Doctrine (Joint Doctrine Publication 0-01), 4th Edition. Promulgated by the Chief of the Defence Staff. Shrivenham: DCDC/MOD, 2011.

Cabinet Office, *Securing Britain in an Age of Uncertainty: The Strategic Defence and Security Review*. Presented to Parliament by the Prime Minister. London: HMSO, October 2010.

Campaign Execution (Joint Doctrine Publication 3-00), 3rd Edition. Prepared under the direction of the Chiefs of Staff. Shrivenham: DCDC, October 2009.

Campaigning (Joint Doctrine Publication 01), 2nd Edition. Promulgated as directed by the Chiefs of Staff. Shrivenham: DCDC, December 2008.

Campaign Planning (Joint Doctrine Publication 5-00), 2nd Edition. Prepared under the direction of the Joint Forces Commander and Chiefs of Staff. Shrivenham: DCDC, July 2013.

Communications and Information Systems Support to Joint Operations (Joint Doctrine Publication 6-00), 3rd Edition. Prepared under the direction of the Chiefs of Staff. Shrivenham: DCDC, January 2008.

Countering Insurgency. British Army Filed Manual Volume 1 Part 10 (Army Code 71876). Prepared under the direction of the Chief of the General Staff. London: MOD, October 2009.

Design for Military Operations – The British Military Doctrine. Prepared under the direction of the Chief of the General Staff. London: HMSO, 1989.

Developing Joint Doctrine Handbook, 4th Edition. Prepared under the direction of the Joint Forces Commander and Chiefs of Staff. Shrivenham: DCDC, November 2013.

Future of Air and Space Operating Concept (Joint Concept Note 3/12). Prepared under the direction of the Joint Force Commander and Chiefs of Staff. Shrivenham: DCDC, September 2012.

Joint Doctrine Development Process (Chairman of the Joint Chiefs of Staff Manual 5120.01). Promulgated by the Director of Joint Staff. Washington, DC: JCS/DOD, 13 January 2012.

Joint Doctrine Development System (Chairman of the Joint Chiefs of Staff Instruction 5120.02C). Promulgated by the Director of Joint Staff. Washington, DC: JCS/DOD, 13 January 2012.

Logistics for Joint Operations (Joint Doctrine Publication 4-00), 3rd Edition. Prepared under the direction of the Chiefs of Staff. Shrivenham: DCDC, April 2007.

Military Contribution to Peace Support Operations (Joint Doctrine Publication 3-50), 2nd Edition. Prepared under the direction of the Chiefs of Staff. Shrivenham: DCDC, June 2004.

NATO Glossary of Terms and Definitions (AAP-06). Brussels: NATO Standardization Agency, 2013.

NATO's Future Joint Air and Space Power (NFJASP). Kalkar: The Joint Air Power Competence Centre, April 2008.

Operations (Army Doctrine Publication). Prepared under the direction of the Chief of the General Staff. Shrivenham: DCDC, November 2010.

Operations Manual, Royal Air Force (Confidential Document 22). Prepared by Command of the Air Council for Air Ministry. London: Air Ministry, July 1922.

Operation TELIC United Kingdom Military Operations in Iraq. Report prepared by the Comptroller and Auditor General for House of Commons 60 session 2003–2004. London: HMSO, 2003.

Peace Support Operations (Joint Warfare Publication 3-50). London: MOD, 1998.

Royal Air Force Air Power Doctrine (AP 3000). Prepared under the direction of the Chief of the Air Staff. London: HMSO, 1991.

Royal Air Force Air Power Doctrine (AP 3000), 2nd Edition. Prepared under the direction of the Chief of the Air Staff. London: HMSO, 1993.

Royal Air Force War Manual. Part I – Operations (Air Publication 1300). Prepared by the direction of Command of the Air Council. London: Air Ministry, July 1928.

The Royal Air Force War Manual. Part I – Operations (Air Publication 1300), 2nd Edition. Prepared by the direction of Command of the Air Council. London: Air Ministry, February 1940.

The Royal Air Force War Manual. Part I – Operations (Air Publication 1300), 3rd Edition. Prepared by the direction of Command of the Air Council. London: Air Ministry, January 1950.

The Royal Air Force Manual. Part I – Operations (Air Publication 1300), 4th Edition. Promulgated by Command of the Air Council. London: Air Ministry, March 1957.

Security and Stabilisation: The Military Contribution (Joint Doctrine Publication 3-40), 3rd Edition. Prepared under the direction of the Chiefs of Staff. Shrivenham: DCDC, November 2009.

The Comprehensive Approach, Joint Discussion Note 4/05. Promulgated as directed by the Chiefs of Staff. Shrivenham: JDCC, 2006.

The Fundamentals of British Maritime Doctrine: BR 1806. Prepared by Command of the Defence Council. London: HMSO, 1995.

The War Aim of the Royal Air Force. CD 64. Air Staff Memorandum No. 43. S. 28279. London: the Imperial Defence College, October 1928.

UK Air and Space Doctrine (Joint Doctrine Publication 0-30). Prepared under the direction of the Joint Forces Commander and Chiefs of Staff. Shrivenham: DCDC, July 2013.

UK Defence Doctrine (Joint Doctrine Publication 0-01), 5th Edition. Promulgated by the Chiefs of Staff. Shrivenham: DCDC/MOD, 2014.

Understanding (Joint Doctrine Publication 04). Prepared under the direction of the Chiefs of Staff. Shrivenham: DCDC, December 2010.

Understanding and Intelligence Support to Joint Operations (Joint Doctrine Publication 2-00), 3rd Edition. Prepared under the direction of the Chiefs of Staff. Shrivenham: DCDC, August 2011.

Unmanned Aircraft Systems: Terminology, Definition and Classification (Joint Doctrinal Note 3/10). Promulgated under the direction of the Chiefs of Staff. Shrivenham: DCDC, May 2010.

Other official documents

Foreign and Commonwealth Office. *UK International Priorities: A Strategy for the FCO*. Presented to Parliament by the Secretary of State for Foreign & Commonwealth Affairs. London: HMSO, December 2003.

Haddon, Charles. *The Nimrod Review: An Independent Review into the Broader Issues Surrounding the Loss of the RAF Nimrod MR2 Aircraft XV230 in Afghanistan in 2006*, Report for the House of Commons. London: HMSO, 2009.

HCDC. *A New Chapter to the Strategic Defence Review*. Sixth Report of Session 2002–03, Volume I: Report. London: HMSO, 7 May 2003.

HCDC. *Defence White Paper 2003*. Fifth Report of Session 2003-04, Volume I. London: HMSO, 23 June 2004.

HCDC. *Lessons of Iraq*. Third Report of Session 2003–04. Volume 1 Report, together with formal minutes. London: HMSO, 3 March 2004.

HCDC. *Lessons of Kosovo*. Fourteenth Report of Session 1999–2000. London: HMSO, 23 October 2000.

HCDC. *Operations in Afghanistan*. Fourth Report of Session 2010–12. Volume 1 Report, together with formal minutes. London: HMSO, July 2011.

HCDC. *Operations in Libya*. Ninth Report of Session 2010–12. Volume 1 Report, together with formal minutes. London: HMSO, February 2012.

HCDC. *Preliminary Lessons of Operation Granby*. Tenths Report of Session 1990–91. London: HMSO, 1991.

HCDC. *The Comprehensive Approach: The Point of War Is Not Joust to Win but to Make a Better Peace*. Seventh Report of Session 2009–10. London: HMSO, March 2010.

HCDC. *UK Operations in Iraq*. Thirteenth Report of Session 2005–06. Report, together with formal minutes, oral and written evidence. London: HMSO, 19 July 2006.

Mark Oakes and Tim Youngs. *Operation Enduring Freedom and the Conflict in Afghanistan: An Update* (House of Commons Library Research paper 01/81). 31 October 2001, 26. Accessed 13 March 2014. http://www.parliament.uk/briefing-papers/RP01-81/operation-enduring-freedom-and-the-conflict-in-afghanistan-an-update.

Ministry of Defence. *Delivering Security in a Changing World. Defence White Paper*. Presented to Parliament by the Secretary of State for Defence. London: HMSO, December 2003.

MOD. *National Security through Technology: Technology, Equipment, and Support for UK Defence and Security*. Presented to Parliament by the Secretary of State for Defence. London: HMSO, February 2012.

MOD. *Strategic Defence Review*. Presented to Parliament by the Secretary of State for Defence. London: HMSO, July 1998.

MOD. *The Strategic Defence Review: A New Chapter*. Presented to Parliament by the Secretary of State for Defence. London: HMSO, July 2002.

NATO. *Active Engagement, Modern Defence*. Strategic Concept 2010. 19 November 2010. Accessed 15 February 2014. http://www.nato.int/cps/en/natolive/topics_82705.htm.

Pulford, Andrew. 'Thinking to Win' (speech, London, 17 September 2015), GovUK. https://www.gov.uk/government/speeches/thinking-to-win.

RAF. *Thinking to Win*. Innovation Strategy 2015. Accessed 26 July2017. https://www.raf.mod.uk/rafcms/mediafiles/28DBDA58_5056_A318_A8AA043B147E9F02.pdf.

Taylor, Clair. *A Brief Guide to Previous British Defence Reviews*. Standard Note SN/IA/5714. London: House of Commons Library, 19 October 2010.

U.S. Army Command and General Staff College. *NATO's Air War in Libya: A Template for Future American Operations*. Damascus: Penny Hill Press, 2014.

Unpublished manuscripts

Autobiography of Air Chief Marshal Sir Richard Johns, CAS 1997–2000 (2017).

Secondary Sources

Books

Alberts, David, Garstka, John, Hayes, Richard, and Signori, David. *Understanding Information Age Warfare*. Vienna: CCRP Publications, 2001.

Alderson, Alexander. 'British Doctrine'. In *Understanding Counterinsurgency Warfare: Doctrine, Operations, and Challenges*, edited by T. Rid and T. Keaney, 28–46. London: Routledge, 2010.

Argyris, Chris and Schön, Donald. *Organizational Learning II: Theory, Method, and Practice*. New York: Addison-Wesley, 1996.

Badsey, Stephen. *The Media and International Security*. London: Routledge, 2013.

Barnaby, Frank and Holdstock, Douglas, eds. *The British Nuclear Weapons Programmes, 1952–2002*. London: Frank Cass, 2005.

Biddle, Tami. 'British and American Approaches to Strategic Bombing: The Origins and Implementation in the World War II Combined Bomber Offensive'. In *Airpower: Theory and Practice*, edited by John Gooch, 91–145. London: Frank Cass, 1995.

Biddle, Tami. 'Learning in Real Time: The Development and Implementation of Air Power in the First World War'. In *Air Power History: Turning Points from Kitty Hawk to Kosovo*, edited by S. Cox and P. Gray, 3–20. Oxon: Frank Cass, 2002.

Boyne, Walter. *The Influence of Air Power upon History*. Barnsley: Pen & Sword Aviation, 2005.

Bratby, Mike. 'Air Power and the Role of the Media'. In *The Dynamics of Air Power*, edited by A. Lambert and A.C. Williamson, 86–104. Bracknell: HMSO, 1996.

Bratby, Mike. 'Peace Support Operations – Support Requirements'. In *The Dynamics of Air Power*, edited by A. Lambert and A.C. Williamson, 126–132. Bracknell: HMSO, 1996.

Brown, Andrew. *J.D. Bernal: The Sage of Science*. Oxford: Oxford University Press, 2005.

Buckley, John. *The RAF and Trade Defence 1919–1945: Constant Endeavour*. Stoke-on-Trent: Keele University Press, 1995.

Bucknam, Mark. *Responsibility of Command: How UN and NATO Commanders Influenced Airpower over Bosnia*. Maxwell AFB: Air University Press, 2003.

Burg, Steven and Shoup, Paul. *Ethnic Conflict and International Intervention: Crisis in Bosnia-Herzegovina, 1990–93*. New York: M.E. Sharpe, 2000.

Carradice, Phil. *First World War in the Air*. Stroud: Amberley Publishing, 2012.

Cassidy, Robert. *Peacekeeping in the Abyss: British and American Peacekeeping Doctrine and Practice after the Cold War*. Westport: Praeger, 2004.

Clark, Michael. 'Air Power, Force and Coercion'. In *The Dynamics of Air Power*, edited by A. Lambert and A.C. Williamson, 67–85. Bracknell: HMSO, 1996.

Clark, Michael. 'Air Power and Force in Peace Support Operations'. In *The Dynamics of Air Power*, edited by A. Lambert and A.C. Williamson, 173–185. Bracknell: HMSO, 1996.

Clark, Wesley. *Waging Contemporary War: Bosnia, Kosovo, and the Future of Combat*. New York: Public Affairs, 2001.

Clausewitz, Carl von. *On War*. Princeton, NJ: Princeton University Press, 1989.

Corum, James. 'The Luftwaffe and the Coalition Air War in Spain, 1936–1939'. In *Airpower: Theory and Practice*, edited by John Gooch, 68–91. London: Frank Cass, 1995.

Corum, James. *The Luftwaffe: Creating the Operational Air Power, 1918–1940*. Westbrooke: University Press of Kanzas, 1997.

Corum, James. 'The Luftwaffe and Lessons Learned in the Spanish Civil War'. In *Air Power History*, edited by S. Cox and P. Gray, 66–93. London: Routledge, 2002.

Cox, Sebastian. 'The Dresden Raids: Why and How'. In *Firestorm: The Bombing of Dresden 1945*, edited by Jeremy Crang and Paul Addison, 18–62. London: Pimlico, 2006.

Cox, Sebastian and Gray, Peter, eds. *Air Power History: Turning Points from Kitty Hawk to Kosovo*. Oxon: Frank Cass, 2002.

Cox, Sebastian and Ritchie, Sebastian. 'The Gulf War and UK Air Power Doctrine and Practice'. In *Air Power History: Turning Points from Kitty Hawk to Kosovo*, edited by S. Cox and P. Gray, 287–306. Oxon: Frank Cass, 2002.

Ferris, John. 'Catching the Wave: The RAF Pursues an RMA, 1918–1945'. In *The Fog of Peace and War Planning: Military and Strategic Planning under Uncertainty*, edited by Monica Toft and Imlay Talbot, 159–178. Oxon: Routledge, 2006.

Freedman, Lawrence. *The Politics of British Defence*. Basingstoke: Macmillan, 1999.

Freedman, Lawrence and Karsh, Ephraim. *The Gulf Conflict, 1990–1991: Diplomacy and War in the New World Order*. Princeton, NJ: Princeton University Press, 1993.

Goulter, Christina. 'The Royal Naval Air Service: A Very Modern Service'. In *Air Power History: Turning Points from Kitty Hawk to Kosovo*, edited by S. Cox and P. Gray, 51–65. Oxon: Frank Cass, 2002.

Goulter, Christina. 'The British Experience: Operation Ellamy'. In *Precision and Purpose: Airpower in the Libyan Civil War*, edited by Karl Mueller, 153–182. Santa Monica: RAND, 2015.

Grant, Charles. 'The Use of History in the Development of Contemporary Doctrine'. In *The Origins of Contemporary Doctrine*, edited by John Gooch, 7–17. Camberley: TSO for the Strategic and Combat Studies Institute, 1997.

Grattan, Robert. *Strategic Review: The Process of Strategy Formulation in Complex Organisations*. London: Routledge, 2011.

Gray, Colin. *Modern Strategy*. Oxford: Oxford University Press, 1999.

Gray, Colin. *The Strategy Bridge: Theory for Practice*. Oxford: Oxford University Press, 2010.

Gray, Colin. *Air Power for Strategic Effect*. Maxwell: Air University Press, 2012.

Gray, Peter. *Air Power 21: Challenges for the New Century*. London: HMSO, 2000.

Gray, Peter. *British Air Power*. London: HMSO, 2003.

Griffin, Stuart. *Understanding Peacekeeping*, 2nd Edition. Cambridge: Polity Press, 2010.

Grove, Eric. 'The Case for the RAF'. In *The Question of Security*, edited by M. Codner and M. Clarke, 211–223. London: RUSI, 2011.

Hallion, Richard, ed. *Air Power Confronts an Unstable World*. London: Brassey, 1997.

Hart, Peter. *Somme Success: The Royal Flying Corps and the Battle of the Somme 1916*. Barnsley: Pen & Sword Military, 2012.

Higham, Robin. *Unflinching Zeal: The Air Battle over France Britain, May-October 1940*. Naval Institute Press, 2012.

Hooton, Edward. *War over the Trenches: Air Power and the Western Front Campaigns 1916–1918*. Birmingham: Midland Publishing.

Hoskins, Andrew and O'Louqhlin, Ben. *War and Media*. Cambridge: Polity Press, 2010.

Howard, Michael. *War and the Liberal Conscience*. Oxford: Oxford University Press, 1981.

Jones, Reginal Victor. *Most Secret War*. London: Hamilton, 1978.

Kaplan, Fred. *The Insurgents: David Petraeus and the Plot to Change the American Way of War*. New York: Simon & Schuster, 2013.

Kiras, James. 'Terrorism and Globalisation'. In *The Globalisation of World Politics: An Introduction to International Relations*, 3rd Edition, edited by John Baylis and Steve Smith, 479–499. Oxford: Oxford University Press, 2004.

Lambert, Andrew. 'Synergy in Operations'. In *The Dynamics of Air Power*, edited by A. Lambert and A.C. Williamson, 40–66. Bracknell: HMSO, 1996.
Lambert, Andrew. 'The Reconnaissance and Surveillance Task in Peace Support Operations'. In *The Dynamics of Air Power*, edited by A. Lambert and A.C. Williamson, 133–146. Bracknell: HMSO, 1996.
Lambert, Andrew and Williamson, Arthur, eds. *The Dynamics of Air Power*. Bracknell: HMSO, 1996.
Lambeth, Benjamin. *NATO's Air War for Kosovo: A Strategic and Operational Assessment (Project Air Force Series on Operation Allied Force)*. Santa Monica: RAND, 2001.
Lambeth, Benjamin. *The Unseen War: Allied Air Power and the Takedown of Saddam Hussein*. Annapolis: Naval Institute Press, 2013.
Mäder, Markus. *In Pursuit of Conceptual Excellence. The Evolution of British Military-Strategic Doctrine in the Post-Cold War Era, 1989–2002*. New York: Peter Lang Publishing, 2004.
Mason, Tony. *The Royal Air Force Today and Tomorrow*. London: Macmillan Press, 1982.
Mason, Tony. *Air Power in the Nuclear Age*. London: Macmillan Press, 1983.
Mason, Tony. *British Air Power in 1980s*. London: Guild Publishing, 1984.
Mason, Tony. *Air Power: A Centennial Appraisal*. London: Brassey's, 1994.
Mason, Tony. 'Air Power in the Peace Support Environment'. In *The Dynamics of Air Power*, edited by A. Lambert and A.C. Williamson, 112–125. Bracknell: HMSO, 1996.
Mason, Tony. 'British Air Power'. In *Global Air Power*, edited by Andreas Olsen, 7–62. Washington, DC: Potomac Books, 2011.
Mason, Tony and Feuchtwanger, E.J., eds. *Air Power in the Next Generation*. London: Macmillan Press, 1979.
Meilinger, Philip. *The Paths of Heaven – The Evolution of Air Power*. Maxwell AFB: Air University Press, 1997.
Mockaitis, Thomas. *British Counter Insurgency in the Post Imperial Era*. Manchester: Manchester University Press, 1995.
Morrow, John. *The Great War in the Air: Military Aviation from 1909 to 192.* Washington, DC: Smithsonian Books, 1993.
Nesbit, Roy Conyers. *Eyes of the RAF: A History of Photo Reconnaissance*. Stroud: Sutton Publishing, 2003.
Olsen, John. *Strategic Air Power in Desert Storm*. Oxon: Routledge, 2003.
Olsen, John, ed. *A History of Air Warfare*. Washington, DC: Potomac Books, 2009.
Olsen, John, ed. *Global Air Power*. Washington, DC: Potomac Books, 2011.
Omissi, David. *Air Power and Colonial Control: The Royal Air Force 1919–1939*. Manchester: Manchester University Press, 1990.
O'neill, Bard. *Insurgency and Terrorism: Inside Modern Revolutionary Warfare*. Dulles: Potomac Books, 2001.
O'neill, Bard. *Insurgency and Terrorism: From Revolution to Apocalypse*. 2nd Edition. Revised. Dulles: Potomac Books, 2005.

Overy, Richard. 'Allied Bombing and the Destruction of German Cities'. In *A World at Total War: Global Conflict and the Politics of Destruction 1937-1945*, edited by R. Chickering and S. Forster, 277-295. Cambridge: Cambridge University Press, 2005.

Overy, Richard. *The Bombing War: Europe 1939-1945*. London: Allen Lane, 2013.

Owen, Robert. 'Operation Deliberate Force, 1995'. In *A History of Air Warfare*, edited by John Olsen. Washington, DC: Potomac Books, 2009.

Pape, Robert. *Bombing to Win: Air Power and Coercion in War*. Ithaca, NY: Cornell University Press, 1996.

Peach, Stuart, ed. *Perspectives on Air Power*. London: HMSO, 1998.

Peach, Stuart and Gates, David, eds. *Air Power for the New Millennium*. Lancaster: CDISS, 1999.

Posen, Barry. *The Sources of Military Doctrine: France, Britain, and Germany between the World Wars*. Ithaca, NY: Cornell University Press, 1984.

Ripley, Tim. *Air War Iraq*. Barnsley: Pen and Sword, 2004.

Ripley, Tim. *Air War Afghanistan: US and NATO Air Operations from 2001*. Barnsley: Pen and Sward, 2011.

Ripley, Tim. *British Army Aviation in Action: Kosovo to Libya*. Barnsley: Pen and Sword, 2011.

Robertson, Scot. *The Development of RAF Strategic Bombing Doctrine, 1919-1939*. Westport: Praeger, 1995.

Sabin, Philip. 'The Counter-Air Contest'. In *The Dynamics of Air Power*, edited by A. Lambert and A.C. Williamson, 18-39. Bracknell: HMSO, 1996.

Sabin, Philip. 'Peace Support Operations – A Strategic Perspective'. In *The Dynamics of Air Power*, edited by A. Lambert and A.C. Williamson, 105-111. Bracknell: HMSO, 1996.

Sabin, Philip. 'The Counter-Air Mission in Peace Support Operations'. In *The Dynamics of Air Power*, edited by A. Lambert and A.C. Williamson, 157-172. Bracknell: HMSO, 1996.

Sabin, Philip. 'The Strategic Impact of Unmanned Aerial Vehicles'. In *Air Power – UAVs: The Wider Context*, edited by Owen Barnes, 97-115. London: Ministry of Defence, 2009.

Scheipers, Sibylle. *Heroism & The Changing Character of War: Toward Post-Heroic Warfare*. New York: Springer, 2014.

Schwarzkopf, Norman and Petre, Peter. *It Does Not Take a Hero: The Autobiography of General H. Norman Schwarzkopf*. New York: Bantam Books, 1992.

Self, Robert. *British Foreign & Defence Policy since 1945: Challenges & Dilemmas in a Changing World*. Basingstoke: Palgrave Macmillan, 2010.

Sharon, Bill. *Risk Management in an Uncertain World: Strategies for Crisis Management*. London: Bloomsbury, 2012.

Shultz, Richard and Pfaltzgraff, Robert. *The Future of Air Power in the Aftermath of the Gulf War*. Maxwell AFB: Air University Press, 1992.

Smith, Rupert. *The Utility of Force: The Art of War in the Modern World*. New York: Allen Lane, 2005.
Steel, Nigel and Hart, Peter. *Tumult in the Clouds: British Experience of War in the Air, 1914–18*. London: Hodder and Stoughton, 1997.
Stoddart, Kristan. *Losing an Empire and Finding a Role: Britain, the USA, NATO and Nuclear Weapons, 1964–1970*. London: Palgrave Macmillan, 2012.
Towle, Philip. 'The Distinctive Characteristics of Air Power'. In *The Dynamics of Air Power*, edited by A. Lambert and A.C. Williamson, 3–18. Bracknell: HMSO, 1996.
Vallance, Andrew. *Air Power-Collected Essays in Doctrine*. London: HMSO, 1990.
Vallance, Andrew. *Doctrines of Air Power Strategy – and Operational Art*. London: Macmillan, 1996.
Vallance, Andrew. *The Air Weapon*. London: Macmillan, 1996.
Vick, Alan. *Proclaiming Airpower: Air Force Narratives and American Public Opinion from 1917 to 2014*. Santa Monica: RAND Corporation, 2015.
Watts, Barry. *The Foundations of US Air Doctrine – The Problem of Friction in War*. Maxwell AFB: Air University Press, 1984.
Willett, Susan. *Eurofighter 2000*. London: Brassey's, 1994.
Williamson, Murray. *Luftwaffe*. Baltimore: Nautical & Aviation Publishing Company of America, 1985.
Williamson, Murray. *Strategy for Defeat: Luftwaffe 1933–1945*. Honolulu, HI: University Press of the Pacific, 2002.
Williamson, Murray. *Transformation Concepts for National Security in the 21st Century*. Carlisle: Strategic Studies Institute of the US Army War College, 2002.
Woolley, Gordon. 'Air Transport in Peace Support Operations'. In *The Dynamics of Air Power*, edited by A. Lambert and A.C. Williamson, 146–156. Bracknell: HMSO, 1996.

Academic articles

Alderson, Alexander. 'Counter-Insurgency: Learn and Adapt? Can We Do Better? *The British Army Review*, no. 142 (Summer 2007): 16–21.
Alderson, Alexander. 'Learning, Adapting, Applying: US Counter-Insurgency Doctrine and Practice'. *The RUSI Journal* 152, no. 6 (December 2007): 12–19.
Alderson, Alexander. 'Revising the British Army's Counter-Insurgency Doctrine'. *The RUSI Journal* 152, no. 4 (August 2007): 6–11.
Alderson, Alexander. 'Iraq and Its Borders: The Role of Barriers in Counter-Insurgency'. *The RUSI Journal* 153, no. 2 (April 2008): 18–22.
Alderson, Alexander. 'The Army Brain: A Historical Perspective on Doctrine, Development and the Challenges of Future Conflict'. *The RUSI Journal* 155, no. 3 (June 2010): 10–15.
Allen, Mathew. 'British Maritime Doctrine'. *The Naval Review* 85, no. 4 (October 1997): 307–314.

Alston, M. 'A New Doctrine or the Application of Commonsense?' *The Naval Review* 87, no. 3 (July 1999): 226–229.

Ancker, Clinton and Burke Michael. 'Doctrine for Asymmetric Warfare'. *Military Review* (July–August 2003): 18–25.

Anrig, Christian. 'Allied Air Power over Libya'. *Air and Space Power Journal* (Winter 2011): 89–109.

Balshaw K.S. 'Spending Treasure Today but Spilling Blood Tomorrow: What Are the Implications for Britain of America's Apparent Aversion to Casualties'. *Defence Studies* 1, no. 1 (Spring 2001): 99–121.

Barno, David. 'Challenges in Fighting a Global Insurgency'. *Parameters* (Summer 2006): 15–29.

Barrie, Douglas. 'Recuperative Route'. *Aviation Week & Space Technology* 171, no. 20 (2009): 36–47.

Barrie, Douglas. 'Libya's Lessons: The Air Campaign'. *Survival* 54, no. 6 (December 2012): 57–65.

Baxter, Laurence. 'NATO and Regional Peace Support Operations'. *Peacekeeping & International Relations* 25, no. 6 (November/December 1996): 6–8.

Benard, Alexander. 'Lessons from Iraq and Bosnia on the Theory and Practice of No-Fly Zones'. *Journal of Strategic Studies* 27, no. 3 (September 2004): 454–478.

Bingham, Price. 'Air Power in Desert Storm and the Need for Doctrinal Change'. *Airpower Journal* 5, no. 4 (Winter 1991): 33–47.

Black, Ian. 'Gaddafi-controlled Media Wages Propaganda War'. *The Guardian*, 17 March 2011. Accessed 18 February 2014. http://www.theguardian.com/world/2011/mar/17/gaddafi-controlled-media-propaganda-war-libya.

Boyle, Michael. 'The Costs and Consequences of Drone Warfare'. *International Affairs* 89, no. 1 (January 2013): 1–29.

Brown, Dan. 'Revitalising the Conceptual Component: Addressing Britain's Future Strategic Challenge'. *Air Power Review* 18, no. 1 (2015): 30–45.

Callahan, David. 'Air Power Comes of Age'. *Technology Review* 97, no. 6 (August/September 1994): 62–71.

Cate, James. 'Development of Air Doctrine 1917–41'. *Air & Space Power Journal* 26, no. 2 (March/April 2012): 132–146.

Chin, Warren. 'British Counter-Insurgency in Afghanistan'. *Defense & Security Analysis* 23, no. 2 (June 2007): 201–225.

Chisnall, Steve. 'Why Defence Reviews Do Not Deliver'. *Political Quarterly* 81, no. 3 (July 2010): 420–423.

Clements, Ben. 'Public Opinion and Military Intervention: Afghanistan, Iraq and Libya'. *Political Quarterly* 84, no. 1 (January 2013): 119–131.

Cohen, Eliot. 'The Historical Mind and Military Strategy'. *Orbis* 49, no. 4 (Fall 2005): 575–588.

Coker, Christopher. 'Britain's Defence Options'. *The World Today* 48, no. 4 (April 1992): 72–75.

Connaughton, Richard. 'Wider Peacekeeping – How Wide of the Mark?' *British Army Review* 111 (December 1995): 57–63.

Connaughton, Richard. 'Quo Vadis?' *The Officer* 10, no. 2 (March/April 1998): 30–33.

Cornish, Paul and Dorman, Andrew. 'National Defence in the Age of Austerity'. *International Affairs* 85, no. 4 (July 2009): 733–753.

Cornish, Paul and Dorman, Andrew. 'Breaking the Mould: The United Kingdom Strategic Defence Review 2010'. *International Affairs* 86, no. 2 (March 2010): 395–410.

Corum, James. 'The Myth of Air Control: Reassessing the History'. *Aerospace Power Journal* (Winter 2000): 61–77.

Corum, James. 'Rethinking US Army Counter-Insurgency Doctrine'. *Contemporary Security Policy* 28, no. 1 (April 2007): 127–142.

Cox, Sebastian. 'The Organisation and Sources of RAF Intelligence'. *Air Intelligence Symposium: Bracknell Paper* 7 (1997): 6–13.

Daddow, Oliver. 'Facing the Future: History in the Writing of British Military Doctrine'. *Defence Studies* 2, no. 1 (Spring 2002): 157–164.

Daddow, Oliver. 'British Military Doctrine in the 1980s and 1990s'. *Defence Studies* 3, no. 3 (Autumn 2003): 103–113.

Deptula, David and Link, Charles. 'Modern Warfare: Desert Strom, Operation Iraqi Freedom and Operation Freedom'. *Air Power History* 54, no. 4 (Winter 2007): 36–45.

Dobbie, Charles. 'A Concept for Post-Cold War Peacekeeping'. *Survival* 36, no. 3 (Autumn 1994): 121–148.

Dorman, Andrew. 'Making 2+2=5: The 2010 Strategic Defence and Security Review'. *Defense & Security Analysis* 27, no. 1 (March 2011): 77–87.

Dorman, Andrew. 'Providing for Defence in an Age of Austerity: Future War, Defence Cuts and the 2010 Strategic (Security and) Defence (and Security) Review'. *Political Quarterly* 81, no. 3 (July 2010): 376–384.

Dover, Robert and Phythian, Mark. 'The Politics of the Strategic Defence and Security Review: Centralisation and Cuts'. *Political Quarterly* 83, no. 1 (January–March 2012): 163–171.

Dunlap, Charles. 'Air-Minded Considerations for Joint Counterinsurgency Doctrine'. *Air and Space Power Journal* 21, no. 4 (Winter 2007): 63–74.

Dunne, Tim and Gifkins, Jess. 'Libya and the State of Intervention'. *Australian Journal of International Affairs* 65, no. 5 (November 2011): 515–529.

Dye, Peter. 'The European Rapid Reaction Force: The Contribution of Aviation Logistics'. *Air Power Review* 6, no. 1 (Spring 2003): 11–34.

Elliot, Michael and Hirsh, Michael. 'Learning the Lessons of Kosovo'. *Newsweek* 134, no. 24 (December 1999–February 2000): 22–27.

Etzioni, Amitai. 'The Lessons of Libya'. *Review of Military Literature* 92, no. 1 (January–February 2012): 45–54.

Ferris, John. 'Fighter Defence before Fighter Command: The Evolution of Strategic Air Defence in Great Britain, 1917–1934'. *The Journal of Military History* 63 (October 1999): 845–884.

Finn, Chris. 'The Broader Implications of the Increasing Use of Precision Weapons'. *Air Power Review* 4, no. 1 (Spring 2001): 35–59.
Finn, Chris. 'Air Power in Afghanistan'. *Air Power Review* 5, no. 4 (Winter 2002): 1–16.
Finn, Chris. 'Air Aspects of Operation Iraqi Freedom'. *Air Power Review* 6, no. 4 (Spring 2003): 1–23.
Finn, Chris. 'British Thinking on Air Power – The Evolution of AP 3000'. *Air Power Review* 12, no. 1 (Spring, 2009): 56–68.
Fiszer, Michael and Gruszczynski, Jerzy. 'RAF Flying into the Future'. *Journal of Electronic Defence* 26, no. 8 (August 2003): 32–41.
Fought, Stephen and Key, Scott. 'Airpower, Jointness, and Transformation'. *Air & Space Power Journal* 17, no. 4 (Winter 2003): 40–53.
Garden, Timothy. 'Re-Inventing the Royal Air Force'. *The RUSI Journal* 141, no. 5 (October 1996): 55–57.
Gillespie, Richard. 'Insurgency and Terrorism: Inside Modern Revolutionary Warfare by B.E. O'neill. Book Review'. *The American Political Science Review* 86, no. 1 (March 1992): 278–279.
Glock, John. 'The Evolution of Air Force Targeting'. *Air & Space Power Journal* 20, no. 2 (Summer 2006): 19–25.
GoCo. 'A New Doctrine for A New Century'. *The Naval Review* 88, no. 1 (January 2000): 23–26.
Gray, Peter. 'Air Power or Aerospace Doctrine 2010?' *Air Power Review* 3, no. 2 (Summer 2000): 7–21.
Gray, Peter. 'Air Power in the Modern World'. *Air Power Review* 3, no. 3 (Autumn 2000): 1–17.
Gray, Peter. 'Air Power & Joint Doctrine: A RAF Perspective'. *Air Power Review* 3, no. 4 (Autumn 2000): 1–15.
Griffin, Stuart. 'The British Approach to "Stabilisation" Operations in Iraq'. *World Defence Systems* 9, no. 2 (March 2007): 181–185.
Griffin, Stuart. 'Iraq, Afghanistan and the Future of British Military Doctrine: From Counterinsurgency to Stabilization'. *International Affairs* 87, no. 2 (March 2011): 317–333.
Gurcan, Metin. 'Drone Warfare and Contemporary Strategy Making: Does the Tail Wag the Dog?' *Dynamics of Asymmetric Conflict* 6, no. 1–3 (October 2013): 153–167.
Hallion, Richard. 'Battlefield Air Support: A Retrospective Assessment'. *Air Power Journal* 4 (Spring 1990): 8–28.
Harvey, Claudia and Wilkinson, Mark. 'The Value of Doctrine'. *The RUSI Journal* 154, no. 6 (December 2009): 26–31.
Haulman, Daniel. 'The United States Air Force and Bosnia, 1992–1995'. *Air Power History* 60, no. 3 (Fall 2013): 24–31.
Haun, Goldie. 'A-10 FACs over Kosovo'. *Air Power Review* 6, no. 1 (Spring 2003): 79–106.
Hobkirk, Michael. 'The Heseltine Reorganisation of Defence: Kill or Cure?' *The RUSI Journal* 130, no. 1 (1985): 45–50.

Høiback, Harald. 'The Anatomy of Doctrine and Ways to Keep It Fit'. *Journal of Strategic Studies* 39, no. 2 (2016): 185–197.

Hollington, Simon. 'The Royal Navy Needs Doctrine'. *The Naval Review* 83, no. 1 (January 1995): 12–16.

Holly, I.B. 'Concepts, Doctrines and Principles – Are You Sure You Understand These Terms?' *Air University Review* (July/August 1984): 90–93.

Holmqvist, Caroline. 'Undoing War: War Ontologies and the Materiality of Drone War'. *Millennium* 41, no. 3 (June 2013): 535–552.

'Intervention in Syria: Britain Will Not Fight'. *The Economist*, 30 August 2013. Accessed 20 April 2013. http://www.economist.com/blogs/blighty/2013/08/intervention-syria.

Issacharoff, Samuel and Pildes, Richard. 'Targeted Warfare: Individuating Enemy Responsibility'. *New York University Law Review* 88, no. 5 (November 2013): 1521–1599.

Jakobsen, Peter Viggo. 'The Emerging Consensus on Grey Area Peace Operations Doctrine: Will It Last and Enhance Operational Effectiveness?' *International Peacekeeping* 7, no. 3 (Autumn 2000): 36–56.

John-Hopkins, Michael. 'Regulating the Conduct of Urban Warfare: Lessons from Contemporary Asymmetric Armed Conflict'. *International Review of the Red Cross* 92, no. 878 (June 2010): 469–493.

Jones, Reginal Victor. 'RAF Scientific Intelligence'. *Air Intelligence Symposium: Bracknell Paper* 7 (1997): 14–21.

Kahn, Paul. 'Imagining Warfare'. *European Journal of International Law* 24, no. 1 (February 2013): 199–226.

Kazaryan, B. 'Operations, Combat Actions, and Network-Centric Warfare'. *Military Thought* 19, no. 1 (2010): 82–97.

Keaney, Thomas. 'The Linkage of Air and Ground Power in the Future of Conflict'. *International Security* 22, no. 2 (Fall 1997): 147–151.

Kertcher, Chen. 'From Cold War to a System of Peacekeeping Operations: The Discussions on Peacekeeping Operations in the UN during the 1980s up to 1992'. *Journal of Contemporary History* 47, no. 3 (July 2012): 611–637.

Kilcullen, David. 'Countering Global Insurgency'. *Journal of Strategic Studies* 28, no. 4 (August 2005): 181–185.

Kiszely, John. 'What Does the Military Want from the Strategic Defence Review?' *Political Quarterly* 81, no. 3 (July 2010): 434–437.

Klikauer, Thomas. 'What Is Managerialism?' *Critical Sociology* 41, no. 7–8 (2015): 1103–1119.

Krovall, Olof and Petersson, Magnus. 'Doctrine and Defence Transformation in Norway and Sweden'. *Journal of Strategic Studies* 39, no. 2 (2016): 280–296.

Lambert, Andrew. 'The Future of Air Power'. *The RUSI Journal* 148, no. 3 (June 2003): 46–53.

Lampe, John. 'The Lessons of Bosnia and Kosovo for Iraq'. *Current History* 103, no. 671 (March 2004): 113–118.

Lidley-French, Julian. 'Fighting Europe's Wars the British Way: The European Politics of British Defence Doctrine'. *The RUSI Journal* 147, no. 2 (April 2002): 74–76.

Lim Kok, Siong. 'Airpower in Non-Conventional Operations'. *Pointer* 30, no. 3 (2004). Accessed 13 July 2013. http://www.mindef.gov.sg/imindef/publications/pointer/journals/2004/v30n3/features/feature4.html.

Lock-Pullan, Richard. 'Redefining "Strategic Effect" in British Air Power Doctrine'. *Air Power Review* 5, no. 3 (Autumn 2002): 59–69.

Lock-Pullan, Richard. 'How to Rethink War: Conceptual Innovation and Air Land Battle Doctrine'. *The Journal of Strategic Studies* 28, no. 4 (August 2005): 679–702.

Luttwak, Edward. 'Victory through Air Power'. *Commentary* 92, no. 2 (August 1991): 27–31.

Mackinlay, John. 'Is UK Doctrine Relevant to Global Insurgency?' *The RUSI Journal* 152, no. 2 (May 2007): 34–39.

Mackinlay, John and Kent, Randolph. 'A New Approach to Complex Emergencies'. *International Peacekeeping* 4, no. 4 (May/June 1997): 31–49.

Mackinlay, John and Kent, Randolph. 'Complex Emergencies Doctrine the British Are Still the Best'. *The RUSI Journal* 142, no. 2 (April 1997): 39–44.

Mahnken, Thomas. 'The British Approach to Counter-Insurgency: An American View'. *Defense & Security Analysis* 23, no. 2 (June 2007): 227–232.

Mallinson, Allan. 'Wider Peacekeeping: An option of Difficulties'. *British Army Review* 112 (April 1996): 5.

Mason, Tony. 'Innovation and the Military Mind'. *Air University Review* 37, no. 2 (January–February 1986): 39–44.

McInnes, Colin. 'Labour's Strategic Defence Review'. *International Affairs* 74, no. 4 (1998): 823–845.

McInnes, Colin. 'The British Army's New Way in Warfare: A Doctrinal Misstep?' *Defense & Security Analysis* 23, no. 2 (June 2007): 127–141.

McLaughlin, Rob. 'Naval Force and the Conduct of Peace Support Operations'. *International Peacekeeping* 9, no. 4 (Winter 2002): 105–118.

McManus, John. 'The Sword of St. Michael: The 82nd Airborne in World War II'. *Journal of Military History* 76, no. 1 (January 2012): 288–290.

McNicoll, Iain. 'Effects Based Air Operations: Air Command and Control and the Nature of the Emerging Battlespace'. *RUSI Journal* 148, no. 3 (June 2003): 38–44.

Meilinger, Philip. 'Trenchard and "morale bombing": The Evolution of Royal Air Force Doctrine before World War II'. *The Journal of Military History* 60, no. 2 (April 1996): 243–270.

Methven, Andrew. 'It Is Not High Time the Doctrine Industry Published Its Doctrine on the Limits of the Utility of Written Doctrine'. *Defence Studies* 3, no. 3 (Autumn 2003): 130–148.

Milton, Tony. 'My Job: Director General Joint Doctrine and Concepts'. *The RUSI Journal* 145, no. 2 (April 2000): 15–19.

Milton, Tony. 'British Defence Doctrine and the British Approach to Military Operations'. *The RUSI Journal* 146, no. 6 (December 2001): 41–44.

Monkman, Alister. 'Manoeuvrist Approach and Coalition Warfare'. *Air Power Review* 5, no. 2 (Summer 2002): 12–42.

Moyn, Samuel. 'Drones and Imagination: A Response to Paul Kahn'. *European Journal of International Law* 24, no. 1 (February 2013): 227–233.

O'Neill, Paul. 'Delivering Flexibility through People: Harnessing Human Capability'. *Air Power Review* 18, no. 1 (2015): 66–89.

O'Neill, Paul. 'Developing a Flexible Royal Air Force for an Age of Uncertainty'. *Air Power Review* 18, no. 1 (2015): 46–65.

Overy, Richard. 'Doctrine Not Dogma: Lessons from the Past'. *Air Power Review* 3, no. 1 (Spring 2000): 32–47.

Owen, Robert. 'The Balkans Air Campaign Study: Part 2'. *Air Power Journal* 11, no. 3 (Fall 1997): 6–27.

Parton, Neville. 'In defence of Doctrine … But Not Dogma'. *Defense & Security Analysis* 24, no. 1 (March 2008): 81–89.

Parton, Neville. 'The Development of Early RAF Doctrine'. *The Journal of Military History* 72, no. 4 (October 2008): 1155–1178.

Peach, Stuart. 'The Doctrine of Targeting for Effect'. *The RUSI Journal* 145, no. 6 (December 2000): 69–72.

Porch, Douglas. 'Writing History in the "End of History" Era – Reflections on Historians and the GWOT'. *The Journal of Military History* 70, no. 4 (October 2006): 1065–1079.

Prommier, Bruno. 'The Use of Force to Protect Civilians and Humanitarian Action: The Case of Libya and Beyond'. *International Review of the Red Cross* 93, no. 884 (December 2011): 1063–1083.

Redvers, Thomas. 'Post-Cold War Development of United Kingdom Joint Air Command and Control Capability'. *Air & Space Power Journal* 18, no. 4 (Winter 2004): 74–86.

Richards S. 'The Decisive Role of Air Power in the Pacific Campaign of WWII'. *Air Power Review* 6, no. 2 (Summer 2003): 57–74.

Ritchie, Nick. 'Rethinking Security: A Critical Analysis of the Strategic Defence and Security Review'. *International Affairs* 87, no. 2 (March 2011): 355–376.

Ritchie, Sebastian. 'Learning the Hard Way: A Comparative Perspective on Airborne Operations in the Second World War'. *Air Power Review* 14, no. 3 (Autumn/Winter 2011): 11–35.

Roberts, Adam. 'Doctrine and Reality in Afghanistan'. *Survival* 51, no. 1 (February–March 2009): 29–60.

Robertson, Scot. 'The Development of Royal Air Force Strategic Bombing Doctrine between the Wars: A Revolution in Military Affairs?' *Airpower Journal* (Spring 1998): 37–52.

Rose, Steven. 'Moving Forward with the Responsibility to Protect: Using Political Inertia to Protect Civilians'. *Boston College International & Comparative Law Review* 37, no. 1 (Winter 2014): 209–240.

Runions, Bradley. 'American and British Doctrine for Intelligence in Peace Operations'. *Peacekeeping & International Relations* 24, no. 6 (November/December 1995): 14–15.

Sabin, Philip. 'Perspectives from within the Profession'. *Air Power Review* 8, no. 4 (Winter 2005): 21–34.

Schorr, David and Kerney, T.K. 'New Technologies and War-Fighting Capabilities'. *Airpower Journal* 10, no. 3 (Fall 1996): 111–115.

Sens, Allen. 'Living in a Renovated NATO'. *Canadian Military Journal* 1, no. 4 (Winter 2000/2001): 79–86.

Simma, Bruno. 'NATO, the UN and the Use of Force: Legal Aspects'. *The European Journal of International Law* 10 (1999): 1–21.

Smith, Leighton. 'NATO's IFOR in Action: Lessons from the Bosnian Peace Support Operations'. *Strategic Forum*, no. 154 (January 1999): 153–158.

Smith, Mark. 'The Kosovo Conflict: U.S. Diplomacy and Western Public Opinion'. *CPD Perspectives on Public Diplomacy*, paper 3 (2009): 4–39.

Strickland, P. 'USAF Aerospace-Power Doctrine Decisive or Coercive?' *Air Power Review* 4, no. 1 (Spring 2001): 17–34.

Szasz, Paul. 'Peacekeeping in Operation: A Conflict Study of Bosnia'. *Cornell International Law Journal* 28, no. 3 (1995): 685–700.

Thomas, Roger. 'Doctrine and Technology: Engaged, To Be Married?' *The Naval Review* 86, no. 3 (July 1998): 217–222.

Thomas, Roger. 'Doctrine and Technology: Engaged, To Be Married? – II'. *The Naval Review* 86, no. 4 (October 1998): 339–346.

Thompson, Redvers. 'Post-Cold War Development of United Kingdom Joint Air Command and Control Capability'. *Air & Space Power Journal* 18, no. 4 (Winter 2004): 74–86.

Thornton, Rod. 'The Role of Peace Support Operations Doctrine in the British Army'. *International Peacekeeping* 7, no. 2 (Summer 2000): 41–62.

Thornton, Rod. 'A Welcome "Revolution"? The British Army and the Changes of the Strategic Defence Review'. *Defence Review* 3, no. 3 (Autumn 2003): 38–42.

Tritten, James. 'Navy Doctrine: Lessons for Today'. *The Naval Review* 84, no. 1 (January 1995): 12–19.

Tuck, Christopher. 'Northern Ireland and the British Approach to Counter-Insurgency'. *Defense & Security Analysis* 23, no. 2 (June 2007): 165–183.

Vallance, Andrew. 'Air Power Doctrine'. *Air Clues* 42, no. 5 (May 1988): 163–169.

Wall, Robert. 'Austerity's Aftermath'. *Aviation Week & Space Technology* 173, no. 4 (2011): 36.

Warden, John. 'The Enemy as a System'. *Air Power Journal*, no. 1 (Spring 1995): 40–55.

Wathen, Alexander. 'Revised USAF Doctrine Publication: Air Force Doctrine Document 2-1.7, Airspace Control in the Combat Zone'. *Air & Space Power Journal* 21, no. 1 (Spring 2007): 48–49.

Wheeldon, Howard. 'Thinking to Win – The RAF's New Leadership Strategy'. Accessed 26 July 2017. https://www.aerosociety.com/news/thinking-to-win-the-rafs-new-leadership-strategy/.

Widen, John. 'Julian Corbett and the Current British Maritime Doctrine'. *Comparative Strategy* 28, no. 2 (April–June 2009): 170–185.

Wilkins, Paul. 'Conceptualising the Conceptual Component: One Airman's Perspective'. *Air Power Review* 18, no. 1 (2015): 10–29.

Wilkinson, Phillip. 'Letters'. *The Officer* 10, no. 3 (May/June 1998): 1–3.

Wilkinson, Phillip. 'Sharpening the Weapons of Peace: The Development of a Common Military Doctrine for Peace Support Operations'. *International Peacekeeping* 7, no. 1 (Summer 2000): 63–79.

Doctoral and MPhil theses

Alderson, Alexander. 'The Validity of British Army Counterinsurgency Doctrine after the War in Iraq 2003–2009'. PhD thesis, the Cranfield University, 2009.

Parton, Neville. 'The Evolution and Impact of Royal Air Force Doctrine, 1919–1939'. PhD thesis, the University of Cambridge, 2009.

Pugh, James Neil. 'The Conceptual Origins of the Control of Air: British Military and Naval Aviation, 1911–1918'. PhD thesis, the University of Birmingham, 2013.

Vallance, Andrew. 'The Evolution of Air Power Doctrine within the RAF 1957–1987'. MPhil-thesis, the University of Cambridge, 1988.

Index

Abbott, Steve 116
academics
   choice of 175
   in doctrinal workshops 105
   in doctrine writing 146–7
   influence of 185
   involvement of 175
   role of 4, 172–5
adaptability 8
AEW. *See* Airborne Early Warning (AEW)
Afghanistan 6, 125, 127, 128, 130, 132–6, 138, 139, 144, 145, 147, 149–50, 155–8
AFMs. *See* Army Field Manuals (AFMs)
AHB. *See* Air Historical Branch (AHB)
air advocacy 6, 197
air campaigns 39, 67, 78, 80, 133, 188, 192
Air Council 40
air defence, components of 52
Air Force Constitution Act 40
Air Force Doctrine Centre Commanders (AFDC/CC) 88
air forces 186
Air Historical Branch (AHB) 128
air integration 147
air interventions 158, 201
Air Launched Anti-Radiation Missile (ALARM) 102
air mobility 143
air platforms 141
air power 133, 153–4, 201. *See also* Royal Air Force (RAF)
   advantages of 102
   attitudes towards 1
   and budgetary considerations 38
   capabilities and characteristics of 94
   characteristics of 141–2, 160–1
   in COIN environment 142
   conceptual component of 199
   conceptualization of 69, 95
   creative thinking on 49, 63
   critical thinking on 63
   cutting-edge technologies for 161
   decisiveness of 98
   definition of 126, 172
   development 50
   echnologies and unconventional use of 39
   effective implementation of 158
   'Evolving Theory' of 109
   flexibility of 157
   function of 38
   future of 200
   human aspect of 198–9
   intellectual thinking on 62–3
   intellectual vision of 183
   in joint warfare 111
   jointery-oriented discourse of 111
   multifunctional potential of 143
   offensive role of 144
   operational examples of 162
   past, present and future of 146
   in peacekeeping 83
   precision and efficiency of 131
   public perception of 193, 200
   role of 47, 70, 99–104, 109, 172
   for strategic effect 21–2
   strategic thinking on 62
   strengths of 160
   supporting roles of 161
   systematic and creative thinking on 113
   theory of 97
   use of 158
Air Power 21: Challenges for the New Century 145
air power discourse 157, 162
air power doctrine 60, 81, 200. *See also* doctrine
   authorship approaches to 119
   development of 3, 5, 77
   editions of 125
   modification of 51
   RAF 1, 37

service and history of 78
status of 167
substantial impact on 161
Air Power Publications 126
air power thinking 107
air power utility 145
air power workshops 108–9
Air Staff Manuals (ASMs) 45
air superiority 70
Airborne Early Warning (AEW) 132
aircraft, technologies of 39, 54, 101
air-land integration 148
airmindedness 129, 142, 188
AJP. *See* Allied Joint Publication (AJP)
ALARM. *See* Air Launched Anti-Radiation Missile (ALARM)
Allied doctrinal harmonization 167
Allied doctrine 164
Allied Joint Operations Doctrine (AJOD) working group 176
Allied Joint Publication (AJP) 89
Allied NATO doctrine 24
American, British, Canadian, Australian and New Zealand Armies (ABCA) programme 24
American doctrine writing apparatus 167
Anderson, Timothy 147–8
anti-doctrinal culture 115
AOO. *See* Areas of Operations (AOO)
AP 1300, first edition of 67, 115
  significance of 49
AP 1300, second edition (February 1940) 51–5
AP 1300, third edition (January 1950) 55–8
AP 1300, fourth edition of 58–60
AP 3000 1, 5, 24
  case of 184
  doctrine preparation process of 113
  replacement of 153–4
AP 3000, second edition, 1993 69–72
AP 3000, third edition of 77–8
  academic context of 108–14
  authorship of 114–20
  doctrine authors and personalities 114
  domestic politics 90–1
  external contacts 87–9
  factors of external environment 78–81
  foreign doctrines 87–90

networks (academics) 105–8
operational experience in doctrinal discourse 81–7
SDR and jointery 91–4
SDR for RAF doctrine 95–7
textual analysis of jointery and army context in 97–104
AP 3000, fourth edition of 125–6
  absence of doctrine 126–30
  internal environment 137–45
  lessons of previous operations 130–4
  reflection of operational experience in text 134–7
  role of academics 145–7
  role of authors 147–9
AP 3001: Air Power Essentials 127
AP 3002: Air Operations and *AP 3003* 127
AP 3002: Air and Space Warfare 126
AP 3003: A Brief History of the Royal Air Force 126
  doctrine authors and personalities 114
  domestic politics 90–1
  external contacts 87–9
  factors of external environment 78–81
  foreign doctrines 87–90
  networks (academics) 105–8
  operational experience in doctrinal discourse 81–7
  SDR and jointery 91–4
  SDR for RAF doctrine 95–7
  textual analysis of jointery and army context in 97–104
AP publications 126–7. *See also Specific types*
Areas of Operations (AOO) 142
Armed Forces 9, 10, 13, 18, 36, 194. *See also* Royal Air Force (RAF)
  of academic involvement 106
  characterization of 57
  cooperation with NATO 164
  internal integration of 164
  perspectives of 185
  reformation process 65
  restructuring of 163
  roles of 19
  structures and capabilities of 18
Army Doctrine Publication (ADP) Operations 23
Army Field Manuals (AFMs) 23

Index

Army-oriented approach 96
Army-oriented policymakers 100–1
ASMs. *See* Air Staff Manuals (ASMs)
asset *vs.* liability 27–9
atomic bombs 5
attack delivery, environments of 144
austerity 134, 162
authoritative doctrine 185
authors
  decision-making 5–6
  role of 5–6, 175–8
authorship 6, 114–20, 168

Bagnall, Nigel Thomas 64
BAI. *See* Battlefield Air Interdiction (BAI)
Battlefield Air Interdiction (BAI) 39
Blue Streak 59
bombing campaigns 56, 192
bombing targets, diverse implications of 52
Bosnia 80–6, 90, 91, 96, 103, 112, 116, 121, 123, 158, 205
  Operation Deliberate Force of 1995 in 72
  operational experience of 79
  PSOs in 77
  unconventional nature of 81
Boyle, Walter J. 56
Brimstone 160
Brimstone missiles 156
British Defence Forward Policy Statement 61
British doctrine hierarchy 103
British media 191
Brown, Dan 192
bureaucratic redundancy 30
Burridge, Brian 129, 133
Byford, Alistair 125, 147–9, 153, 172–5, 177, 178, 180, 184, 186, 187

Cameron, Neil 61–3, 65, 204
campaign planning 49, 120, 161
CAS. *See* Close Air Support (CAS)
cause–effect relationship 2
CD 22 41, 48
  implications of 44–7
Chamier, John Adrian 44
Chief of Air Staff 6
civilian casualties 156, 193

civil–military gap 201
Clark, Wesley 131
classification 190–1
Close Air Support (CAS) 39, 40, 43, 44, 55, 59, 67, 68, 78, 90, 95, 110, 115, 117–18, 122, 125–7, 129, 140, 145–7, 149, 151, 154, 165, 175
  Air Power Conference 146
Coalition air attacks 71
Cody, Samuel Franklin 38
Cohen, Eliot 11
COIN. *See* counterinsurgency (COIN)
Cold War strategic environment 34
collective performance 14
combat recovery 84
Command and Control Warfare (C2W) 99–100
Committee for the Scientific Survey of Air Defence (CSSAD) 54
communication technologies 55
complementarity 164–5
conceptual component 1, 187–8, 196
conceptual innovation 14
Confidential Document (CD) 1
Connaughton, Richard 82
contemporary scepticism 37–8
contemporary technologies 199
contemporary warfare 9, 157–8
Conventional Counter-Surface Force Operations 136
Corum, James 51
counterinsurgency (COIN) 30, 84
  campaigning 153–4
  doctrines 84
creative thinking
  dogma *vs.* 25–7
  problems and development of 106
culture 16
  anti-doctrinal 115
  national strategic 8, 11, 15
  organizational (*see* organizational culture)
  strategic 15, 16
  sub-service 29–30
C2W. *See* Command and Control Warfare (C2W)

Daddow, Oliver 3, 105
Dalton, Stephen 125, 140, 156

DCDC. *See* Development, Concepts and
    Doctrine Centre (DCDC)
DDefS. *See* Director of Defence Studies
    (DDefS)
Defence Academy 200
defence policy 18
    vs. military strategy 18
defensive counter-space (DCS) operations
    143
demoralization 43
Development, Concepts and Doctrine
    Centre (DCDC) 24, 129, 147–8,
    165, 200
Director of Defence Studies (DDefS) 6, 62,
    65–6, 95, 107, 110, 118, 126–7, 130,
    146, 149, 173, 175
Director of Intelligence (DI) 53
Dobbie, Charles 82
doctrinal cycle 6, 180, 181
doctrinal discourse 24, 26, 29, 52, 55, 68,
    81–6, 107, 113, 158, 171, 179, 189
doctrinal functionality, perspective of
    34–5
doctrinal instrumentalism 14–16
doctrinal jointery, horizontal level of 140
doctrine 13, 16, 36
    absence of 126–30
    adaptability 32
    authoritative *vs.* dogmatic 185
    authors and personalities 114
    authorship of 3
    British defence 13
    centralized production of 165
    changing role of 5
    characteristics of 15
    contemporary utility of 185
    debates on 25
        asset *vs.* liability 27–9
        dogma *vs.* creative thinking 25–7
        formal written *vs.* informal know-
            how 29–31
        short *vs.* long/detailed *vs.* general
            31–2
        static *vs.* dynamic 33–4
    definition of 7–9
    development of 11
    diversity of 21
    factors shaping 4
    flexibility of 119
    form and narrative of 127
    forward-looking aspect of 185
    functionality of 13, 26
    functions of 5, 9, 196
    harmonization of approaches to 129
    historical analysis of 34
    history of 5
    immediate dissemination of 201
    importance of 185
    instrumentalism and organizational
        transformation 14–15
    military audience 10–12
    in military practice 7
    purposes of 5, 7, 9, 14–15
    relationship between doctrine,
        technology and policy 18–20
    relationship between policy, strategy
        and 16–18
    roles of 5
    target audience/substitution of
        functionality 15–16
    technology and policy 18–20
    transformational function of 187
    wider audience 12–13
doctrine development 4
    American guidance on 17
    history of 72
doctrine hierarchy 20–5, 89, 137, 144, 154,
    165, 167
    functioning of 135
    levels of 140–1
doctrine writers/writing 3–5, 31, 68, 89,
    116, 162, 167, 183
    academic involvement in 107, 113
    academics in 146–7
    conceptualization of 95
    contemporary process of 6
    experiences of 103, 118
    external environment 5
    factors of 5–6, 86
    feature of 40
    gradual change in 115
    institutionalization of 104, 165
    instrumental role of 165
    internal politics 5
    logistics of 128
    process of 6, 77, 105, 171, 176
    role of 4, 5–6
    synchronization of 119
    time frame for 165–6
dogma *vs.* creative thinking 25–7

dogmatic doctrine 185
domestic political environment 4, 168
domestic politics 90–1, 104
double-loop learning 188–9
drone warfare 201
Duncan Sandys' Statement on Defence 1957 58

effective surveillance 143–4
environmental doctrine 23, 52, 126, 128, 135, 168
　joint authorship of 154
　organizational use of 183
　ownership of 144
　ways of writing 129
external contacts 87–9
external environment 5

fighting power 13–14
Finn, Chris 32, 52, 127–9
foreign doctrines 87–9
Foreign Office (FO) 12
formal doctrine 8–9
Freedman, Lawrence 91
functional doctrine 22, 167
funding 186

Gaddafi, Muammar 155, 156, 158
General 'Buzz' Moseley 129, 134
general defence policy discourse 137–40
generalization 190–1
Germany 38, 51, 54, 56, 61, 117
Ginger Group 64
global economic crisis 153
globalization 198
Goulter, Christina 157
Grant, Charles 11
Gray, Colin 10, 14–15, 18, 25–6, 28
Gray, Peter 29, 88–9, 145
Graydon, Michael 108–9, 115
Greville, P.J. 78
Grove, Eric 30, 59
Gulf War 5, 67, 68–72, 77, 79, 81, 96, 103, 117, 121, 128, 131, 133, 134, 137, 147, 170, 191, 198, 199, 204, 205

Harding, Peter 67, 115
Harkabi, Yehoshavet 28
harmonization of doctrinal publications 178

Harrier aircraft 136
Hart, Mike 147
Higgins, Thomas Charles 44–5
historical context, doctrine
　CD 22, implications of 44–7
　conceptual perspective of time 42–4
　doctrinal vacuum 1970s–1980s 60–5
　lessons of 72–5
　RAF doctrine
　　history of 65–9
　　preconditions of 37–42
historical epochs 2
Hobson, Christopher 116
Høiback, Harald 9, 10
House of Commons Defence Committee (HCDC) 139
Hudson, Mary 128
human capital 199

IFOR. *See* Implementation Force (IFOR)
Implementation Force (IFOR) 85
improvised explosive device (IED) activity 136
independent operations 44
indirect air operations 101
individual doctrine writers 3
informed decision-making 10
innovative programme 190
institutional stakeholders 10
institutionalization
　of jointery 136, 164–5, 185–6
　stages of 1–2, 4
intellectualism 63
Intelligence, Surveillance and Reconnaissance (ISR)
　practical improvement of 161–2
　for situational awareness 161
Intelligence, Surveillance, Target Acquisition and Reconnaissance (ISTAR) 132
　capabilities 163
　development and information-driven approach 135
　in Libya 156
　platform 155
　role and striking capabilities 133
　for target detection 156
interdependence 164–5
inter-institutional contacts 202
internal politics 5

International Security Assistance Force (ISAF) 132
Iraq 3, 6, 41, 69, 70, 79, 125, 128–30, 133–6, 138, 139, 145, 149–50, 155, 156
ISR. *See* Intelligence, Surveillance and Reconnaissance (ISR)
Israeli Operation Babylon 1981 158
ISTAR. *See* Intelligence, Surveillance, Target Acquisition and Reconnaissance (ISTAR)

JDC. *See* Joint Defence Centre (JDC)
JDCB. *See* Joint Doctrine and Concept Board (JDCB)
JDN. *See* Joint Doctrine Note (JDN)
JDP 0–01 136
JDP 0–30 153–5
   academics, role of 172–5
   authors, role of 175–8
   DCDC process of writing 177
   external environment/operational experience of Libya 155–7
   institutionalization of jointery 164–5
   internal factors 162–3
   NATO 165–7
   operational lessons and reflection in doctrine 157–62
   preparation process of 172
   reflection of new process in 168–72
   single-service authorship of 175
   technological dimension of 168
JOA. *See* Joint Operations Area (JOA)
Johns, Richard 79, 94, 116–17
joint approach 92
joint authorship 6, 159, 177, 183
   of environmental doctrine 154
Joint Defence Centre (JDC) 104, 119
joint doctrine 12, 164
Joint Doctrine and Concept Board (JDCB) 175
Joint Doctrine and Concepts Centre (JDCC) 125, 128
Joint Doctrine Centre 96
Joint Doctrine Note (JDN) 166–8
Joint Doctrine Publication (JDP) 22, 164
Joint Doctrine Steering Committee (JDSC) 166, 176

Joint Force Air Component Commander (JFACC) 99, 129
joint hierarchy 168
Joint Integrated Prioritised Target List (JIPTL) 98–9
Joint Operations Area (JOA) 142
Joint Rapid Deployment Forces 92
Joint Rapid Reaction Forces 92
Joint Strike Fighter aircraft 163
Joint Targeting Coordination Board (JTCB) 98–9
joint training 93
joint warfare, air power in 111
Joint Warfare Publication (JWP) 10
jointery 79
   cost-efficiency and interservice synergy of 102
   implementation of 97–8, 102, 144–5
   initial stage of 144–5
   institutionalization of 119, 128, 136, 140, 148, 167, 185–6, 203
   intensification of 139–40
   introduction of 185
   NATO 165–7
   practical implementation of 142
   presentation of 94
   principles of 93
   SDR and 95
   textual analysis of 97–9
Jones, Richard 77
JWP. *See* Joint Warfare Publication (JWP)
JWP 0–01 12

Kosovo 125, 127, 128, 130, 131–3, 135, 149, 158, 191
   bombing, media coverage of 191–2
   campaign 127, 128, 130–1

Labour Foreign Policy 91
Labour Strategic and Defence Review of 1998 77
Lambert, Andrew 80, 83, 109
Lambeth, Benjamin 133
land integration 147
leadership 14
liability, asset *vs.* 27–9
Libya 6, 153, 155–62, 170, 179, 191, 192, 207

Lincoln, George Arthur 197
linear warfare 70, 142
Long War on Terror 138

Mackay, C.J 40
Mackinlay, John 82
Mäder, Markus 64
Mallinson, Allan 82
Mason, Tony 35, 56, 61–3, 80, 90, 114, 141, 189, 190, 199
media broadcasting 158
media coverage of Kosovo bombing 191–2
media-conscious thinking 196
Meilinger, Philip 87, 88, 95
Melvin, Mungo 145
military decisions 197
military discourse 138
military doctrine
 definitions of 8
 purpose of 9
military force, conceptualization of 4
military institutions 10–11
military organizations 189, 190
military resources 18
military strategic doctrine 18
military strategy 18, 19
military thinking 12
military-political dichotomy 72
miscommunication 192
Murray, Williamson 51

Nassau Agreement for British participation in Polaris programme 58–9
national armed forces 2
national defence 134, 164
national doctrine writing 169
national military strategy 193
national strategy 10
 culture 8, 11, 15
 discourse 69–70
national-level doctrines 13
NATO. *See* North Atlantic Treaty Organization (NATO)
NATO Standardized Agency (NSA) 167
Network Enabled Capability (NEC) 126, 135
network-centric capability (NCC) 138
networks

influential elements within 3–4
 roles in doctrine writing 5–6
non-combatant casualties 156
non-governmental organizations (NGOs) 142
North Atlantic Treaty Organization (NATO) 6, 132, 164
 conceptual/doctrinal framework 169
 doctrine 13, 62, 89–90, 166
 documents 171
 flexible response strategy 61
 orientation 169, 170
 profound cooperation with 169
 references to 170
 standardization procedures 167
 Strategic Concept 166
 structure, orientation on 170
 supervision 169
 tactical doctrine 61
NSA. *See* NATO Standardized Agency (NSA)
nuclear programmes 58–9

Offensive Counter-Air (OCA) operations 99
Offensive Counter-Space (OCS) operation 143
open procurement principle 164
Operation Allied Force 130–1
Operation Babylon 1981 158
Operation Crossbow 53–4
Operation Deliberate Force of 1995 in Bosnia 72
Operation Deny Flight 79
Operation Desert Storm 80
Operation Ellamy 155–7
Operation Iraqi Freedom 128
Operation Odyssey Dawn 155, 162
Operation Unified Protector 162
operational experience 90, 145
operation-level synergy 80
organization, history of 187
organizational change, policy of 196
organizational culture 1, 8, 14, 187, 188, 200, 202
 opponents of 187
 redefining 190
 tactics-oriented thinking in 198–9
organizational development

conceptual framework for 189
  goal of 185
organizational discourse 194
organizational learning 188–9
organizational thinking 2
organizational transformation 14–15, 183, 188
organizations 190–1
Overy, Richard 33–4
Oxford Dictionary 172

parallel warfare 87, 133
Parton, Neville 27, 46, 130, 147
"pattern-of-life" intelligence 157
peace support operations (PSOs) 71, 109
  characteristics of 110
  conceptualization 83
  doctrine 81–5
  environment 79
peacebuilding process 84
Peach, Stuart W. 77, 111, 117–18
personality-driven doctrine writing 87
PGMs. See Precision-Guided Munition (PGMs)
Polaris programme 58–9
policy
  description of 17
  vs. doctrine and technology 18–20
  vs. strategy and doctrine 16–18
  technology and doctrine 18–20
policy-building 185
policymakers, secondary audience of 185
political choosing 171
political decision-making 106–7
Porch, Douglas 11
post–Cold War strategic environment 125
POWs. See prisoners of war (POWs)
Precision-Guided Munition (PGMs) 101, 160–1
  efficiency of 160–1
  precision of 133
principles of war 1, 13–14
prisoners of war (POWs) 54
PSOs. See peace support operations (PSOs)
public-oriented thinking 196
Pulford, Andrew 198

radar technology 54–5
RAF. See Royal Air Force (RAF)

RAND Corporation 193
realistic decision-making 185
reconnaissance 38
regiment-based doctrinal traditions 8
religious doctrine 7
resource allocation 4
Revolution in Military Affairs (RMA) 72
RFC. See Royal Flying Corps (RFC)
RNAS. See Royal Naval Air Service (RNAS)
Robertson, George 92
Robertson, Scot 50
ROE. See rules of engagement (ROE)
Role 3 Attack (Coerce) 158
Royal Air Force (RAF) 2, 3, 5, 67, 81–5, 101
  air power doctrine 37
  air power publications 126
  analytical history 127
  capabilities 94
  colleges, primary purpose of 184
  conceptual component of 183, 195–6
  deficiencies 132
  development and establishment of 3
  doctrine 37–44, 46, 48, 56, 63, 65–9, 95–7, 108, 130, 183, 198
  history of 1
  innovations and reformation in 63
  organizational culture of 188, 200, 202
  organizational innovations in 3
  organizational transformation 187
  perspectives 201–2
  political objectives 60
  role of doctrine in 184
  strategic culture 96
  strategic thinking 50
  substantial reshaping 60–1
  technology oriented nature of 195
  thinking 50, 86
Royal Flying Corps (RFC) 38
Royal Naval Air Service (RNAS) 38
Royal United Services Institute (RUSI) 146
rules of engagement (ROE) 79, 131, 159, 160, 192

Sabin, Philip 32, 83
SDR. See Strategic Defence Review (SDR)
SDSR. See Strategic Defence and Security Review (SDSR)

SEAD. *See* suppression of enemy air defences (SEAD)
Second Gulf War 128, 133, 170
Second World War 55, 197
semi-civilised enemy operations 49
Sentinel aircraft 156–7
single-loop learning 188–9
single-service authorship 128, 144
single-service bias 154
single-service doctrines 31, 94
single-service joint environmental doctrine 140–5
situational awareness 99
Skybolt 59
Slessor, John 45
SOF. *See* Special Operations Forces (SOF)
SOPs. *See* standard operational procedures (SOPs)
space forces 186
space power 153–4
　characteristics of 141–2
　definition of 126
Special Operations Forces (SOF) 84
stakeholders 9
　institutional 10
standard operational procedures (SOPs) 29
stealth technology, significance of 71
Stirrup, Jock 126, 127
Storm Shadow 134, 137, 156, 160
strategic attack 158
strategic bombing 42, 56–7, 100, 159
　concept of 43, 57
　dogma of 55
　dogmatic history of 68
　moral effect of 45
　sociopolitical implications of 43
　symbiosis of 44
　Trenchard's concept of 1
strategic culture 15, 16
Strategic Defence and Security Review (SDSR) 6, 143, 153, 162, 163–4
　assessment of 163
　cycle 178, 186
　general implications of 163
　prescriptions of 156
Strategic Defence Review (SDR) 1, 91–4
　implications of 95–7
　reflection of 162
　requirements 103–4

strategic discourse 134
strategic effect 133
strategic environment 9, 15, 112, 134
strategic planning, debates on 192
strategic thinking 3, 19, 52
strategy
　dimensions and components of 18
　vs. policy and doctrine 16–18
sub-service cultures 29–30
substitution of functionality 15–16
suppression of enemy air defences (SEAD) 99–100, 132
synergy 80
　principles of 93
Syria 107, 192
systematic articulation 177
systematic self-reflection 14
systematization of doctrinal cycles 6

tactical instruction 49
tactical-level manuals 23, 28–9
tactics-oriented doctrines 112
tactics-oriented thinking in organizational culture 198–9
target audience, shift of 15–16
Taylor, Neil 114–15
teaching 7–8
technology
　changes of 17
　development of 18–19
　vs. doctrine and policy 18–20
　policy and doctrine 18–20
Ten Year Rule 50
textual analysis of jointery 97–9
thematic doctrines 22–3
theory 11, 12
Thinking to Win (T2W) 199, 201
　assessment of 200
　goal of 197–8
　initiatives 183, 197–8
Thomas, Roger 19
Tomkinson, E.L. 40
Torpy, Glen 129, 133, 134
traditional modernization 164
training courses 14, 42
Trenchard, Hugh 39, 43, 47
　ideas 45
　political campaign 44
　on strategic bombing 44, 48, 58
tri-service integration 143

tri-service reviewing 130
T2W. *See* Thinking to Win (T2W)

UASs. *See* University Air Squadrons (UASs)
UAVs. *See* unmanned aerial vehicles (UAVs)
UCAV. *See* unmanned combat air vehicle (UCAV)
United Nations Protection Force (UNPROFOR) 79
United States Air Force (USAF) 87, 198, 201
   narratives 194–5
   public profile 195
   research and development programs 194
United States Marine Corps (USMC) 136
University Air Squadrons (UASs) 47
unmanned aerial vehicles (UAVs) 71
   availability of 157
   benefits of 102
   employment of 137
   justification of 160
   moral and ethical issues 160
   performance and relevance of 160
   precision and use of 158
   technologies 134
unmanned combat air vehicle (UCAV) 101

UNPROFOR. *See* United Nations Protection Force (UNPROFOR)
Urgent Operational Requirements (UOR) scheme 134
USAF. *See* United States Air Force (USAF)
USMC. *See* United States Marine Corps (USMC)

Vallance, Andrew 63, 71–2, 86, 87, 106, 114–16, 119
   primary contacts of 87
   thinking on air power 66–7
van der Veen, Martin 116
Vick, Alan 193, 194
   communication strategy 195
   principle of incorporating innovation 196–7
   USAF narrative 194–5

Walker, David 128
war campaign planning 49
warfare
   national way of 4
   principles of 10, 184
Warsaw Pact Treaty Organization 91
Wider Peace Keeping (WPK) 82–3
Wilkins, Paul 14, 200
Wilkinson, Philip 82, 84, 85
Williamson, Arthur C. 109
WPK. *See* Wider Peace Keeping (WPK)

Lightning Source UK Ltd.
Milton Keynes UK
UKHW020440310321
381291UK00003B/52